Understanding

Qualitative Research

and Ethnomethodology

Understanding Qualitative Research and Ethnomethodology

Paul ten Have

SAGE Publications

London • Thousand Oaks • New Delhi

© Paul ten Have 2004

First published 2004

 SAGE Publications Ltd
6 Bonhill Street
London EC2A 4PU

SAGE Publications Inc
2455 Teller Road
Thousand Oaks, California 91320

SAGE Publications India Pvt Ltd
B-42, Panchsheel Enclave
Post Box 4109
New Delhi 100 017

British Library Cataloguing in Publication data

A catalogue record for this book is
available from the British Library

ISBN 0 7619 6684 6
ISBN 0 7619 6685 4 (pbk)

Library of Congress Control Number: 2003105536

Typeset by M Rules
Printed and bound in Great Britain by
Athenaeum Press, Gateshead

Contents

Preface

How is qualitative social research possible? That is a question that one can try to answer in many different ways. How is it possible in principle? How is it possible in actual practice? The way in which one tries to answer such questions will depend on one's problems and interests, on one's analytical presuppositions, and on practical circumstances. In this book I offer some of my reflections on these questions by confronting more or less conventional ways of doing qualitative research with one particular qualitative tradition: ethnomethodology.

Among the many schools, perspectives and traditions within the social sciences which use or even favour qualitative research methods, ethnomethodology is a special case. It seems to stand apart from the others in presuppositions and purpose, and especially in its treatment of methods and methodology. Rather than prescribing specific research methods and stipulating an official methodology, it likes to study methods-in-use and proposes a collectivity's methodology as its central topic. Members of other 'qualitative' schools sometimes seem a bit uneasy about this strange relative, near but yet so distant. Ethnomethodologists, in turn, largely ignore what goes on among the others.

This book seeks to intervene in this rather stalemate situation by offering extensive discussions of qualitative research methods from an ethnomethodological perspective. It will use examples from both ethnomethodological studies and other kinds of qualitative research to reflect on the methodical use of interviewing, documents, ethnography, recordings, as well as general strategies for qualitative data analysis.

It should be useful as a supplementary reading in advanced courses in both ethnomethodology and qualitative research methods in sociology, anthropology, communications and professional education. Although primarily a book of reflection, it will also be a resource for methodological reconsiderations of established methods, as well as suggesting less conventional ways to collect and analyse qualitative data. It should also be useful, therefore, for the adventurous MA or PhD thesis writer, as well as the established researcher.

The book presupposes a basic familiarity with qualitative research methods and, hopefully, ethnomethodology, although it will contain summary discussions and some pointed references to help the reader to catch up with any missing pieces of background knowledge.

As far as I know, there is no other book that systematically discusses qualitative research methods from an ethnomethodological perspective. Quite a number of books, however, do treat more or less the same range of qualitative methods, including some written by David Silverman (1993, 2001), or edited by him (1997), two editions of a *Handbook of qualitative research* edited by Denzin and Lincoln (1994, 2000), a *Handbook of interview research*, edited by Gubrium and Holstein (2002) and a *Handbook of ethnography*, edited by Atkinson et al. (2001).

The text to follow can be seen as a product of a 30-year struggle of teaching and research on the topics discussed hereafter. The topics, dilemmas and examples that I treat are those I find interesting and/or important. The selections I have made are personal ones. I have become rather ambivalent about customary ways of doing qualitative research and this ambivalence was often based on considerations close to ethnomethodological concerns. Understanding what ethnomethodology is all about is not an easy matter, so what you are about to read can only be my present version of ethnomethodology – and may therefore differ from others'.

The structure of the book's argument is as follows. I start with an introductory discussion of qualitative research methods and some of the major analytic issues and concepts that I will use in subsequent chapters (1). Next, I present a selective overview of ethnomethodology, first in a theoretical mode (2), and then with a focus on the actual methods of ethnomethodological research (3). The core parts of the book will offer discussions of various styles of qualitative social research in which I will confront practices and examples of more or less conventional types of research with ethnomethodological ones. In order of appearance I will reflect on various kinds of interview-based research (4), qualitative work using natural documents (5), ethnography and field methods (6), and generalized analytic strategies, such as the 'grounded theory' approach (7). In the final chapters, I suggest ways of doing ethnomethodological research through a discussion of examples (8) and some reflections on remaining issues (9). The book was designed to be read in the order presented, but those who prefer examples over general statements might decide to skip Chapter 2 at first, and the first sections of 3, to return to those parts later.

Throughout the book, I have used bits and pieces of some previous and forthcoming publications, such as:

- 'Methodological issues in conversation analysis', *Bulletin de Méthodologie Sociologique*, 27 (June 1990): 23–51 (in Chapter 3)
- 'The notion of member is the heart of the matter: on the role of membership knowledge in ethnomethodological inquiry' [53 paragraphs]. *Forum Qualitative Sozialforschung / Forum: Qualitative Social Research* (on-line journal), 3(3): September 2002. Available at: http://www.qualitative-research.net/fqs/fqs-eng.htm (in Chapters 2, 3 and 8)
- 'Conceptualization in "grounded theory" analysis: some critical observations'. In: Jörg Blasius, Joop Hox, Edith de Leeuw, Peter Schmidt, eds. *Social science methodology in the new millennium: proceedings of the 5th international conference on logic and methodology.* Leverkusen (Germany): Verlag Leske & Budrich, 2002 (CD-ROM) (in Chapter 7)

- 'Reflections on transcription', *Cahiers de Praxématique* (forthcoming, Montpellier, France) (in Chapters 3 and 8)
- 'Teaching students observational methods: visual studies and visual analysis', *Visual Studies*, 2003 18: 29–35 (in Chapter 8)

The idea for this book emerged in email exchanges with David Silverman, but once I was at work on it, the overall concept changed in many ways. Over the years I have picked up ideas and insights from many people, too many to mention here. I have included references to their published work throughout the text, and I have been happy to meet many of them in person. Douglas Maynard read the drafts for three chapters. His comments forced me to reconsider my objectives. Harrie Mazeland read a draft for Chapter 4; the major section analysing excerpts is based on his work and co-authored by him. Special thanks to a critical and supportive anonymous reviewer and to the able and flexible staff at Sage Publications: Michael Carmichael and Zoë Elliott. The book is not dedicated to any one person in particular, but rather to the communities of researchers that I have felt at home with.

Paul ten Have

1 Qualitative Methods in Social Research

The purpose of this book is to stimulate reflection on ways of doing qualitative social research by asking the general question, 'How is qualitative social research possible?' In this chapter, I offer some basic considerations about this topic in order to prepare for the discussions in the later chapters. I will use the word *methods* in a rather loose sense, as ways of doing research, both on the level of principles, general research strategies or policies, and on the level of actual research practices. Consideration of methods is relevant 'from beginning to end', from the first intentions and ideas until the final publications and presentations. This book is about methods, but it does not offer 'a methodology'. It does not present a 'correct way of doing research', summarized in algorithms that, when followed faithfully, lead in a kind of quasi-automatic way to 'good results'. In my opinion, the only sensible way in with methods can be discussed, at least in qualitative research, is by treating them as heuristic possibilities that need to be adapted to local circumstances and project-specific purposes, if they are to be of any use.

The meaning of *social research* may seem obvious, but a few words are in order, to frame the ways in which it will be used in later discussions. I will use 'research' to refer to all kinds of knowledge production that involve the inspection of empirical evidence. 'Social research', then, collects research endeavours that focus on 'the social', that is, phenomena that are related to people living together, whether these are conceptualized as structures, processes, perspectives, procedures, experiences or whatever. Social research can be a part of many different kinds of activity, but for now I will limit my considerations to research activities within the realm of 'social science', broadly conceived. Practitioners or others involved in research without a strictly scientific purpose, like evaluation research, advocacy research or market research, will hopefully find my reflections useful, but I will deal with matters at hand mainly from a social science perspective.

What, then, is science, even if only *social science*? I think that science cannot be usefully differentiated from other inquisitive activities by claims to an exclusive relationship to some specific principles or methods. It is, rather, distinguishable as a particular way of investigative life by its general purpose and approach. Its aim, to paraphrase some notions developed by Charles Ragin (1994), is to contribute to an ongoing dialogue of ideas and evidence concerning some 'reality', in this book limited to a social reality of people living together. And its approach, I would suggest, is to take the time needed to make one's contribution a valid one. As Dick Pels (2001) has suggested, the demarcation of 'science' from other kinds of inquiry should not be seen, and treated, as a sharp 'break', but rather as a series of less sharp barriers (or barricades!) which allow practitioners of scientific inquiry to 'take their time', to think, to read and re-read, to collect data, to (re-)consider the evidence, etc. In other words, science requires some protection from the hectic nature and the haste of practical lives and interests, of politics, media attention and the market, if it is to be able to work on its mission.

Ideas and evidence in social research

In his *Constructing social research: the unity and diversity of method*, Charles Ragin (1994) has tried to catch some of the essential general properties of social research in what he calls 'a simple model of social research'. As he sees it:

> Social research, in simplest terms, involves a dialogue between ideas and evidence. Ideas help social researchers make sense of evidence, and researchers use evidence to extend, revise, and test ideas. The end result of this dialogue is a representation of social life - evidence that has been shaped and reshaped by ideas, presented along with the thinking that guided the construction of the representation. (Ragin, 1994: 55)

Because the 'distance' between abstract and general 'ideas' and concrete and specific 'evidence' tends to be a large one, his model specifies some mediating structures, called 'analytic frames' and 'images', between the two. Analytic Frames are deduced from general ideas and specified for the topic of the research, while Images are inductively constructed from the evidence, in the terms provided by an analytic framework. The researcher's core job is to construct a 'Representation of Social Life', combining analytic frames and images in a 'double fitting' process called 'retroduction' (i.e. a combination of deduction and induction).

In Figure 1.1, I 'quote' Ragin's visualization of this model.

In this schema, ideas are placed in the top left corner and evidence at the bottom. This suggests that they represent the starting points for the analysis, the 'givens', in a way. A bit to the right, we see the analytic frames below the ideas, and the images above the evidence. Arrows indicate the processes that connect these elements: from the ideas to the analytic frames a strong deduction and a weak induction in the opposite direction; similarly, there is a strong induction arrow from the evidence to the Images, and a weak deduction in the opposite direction. The general 'givens', the abstract ideas and the concrete research materials, are worked on: specified to fit the research topic. Between the analytic frames and the images, we see two arrows, one upwards and one downwards. These represent the core activity, the 'dialogue' mentioned above. Finally, more to the right, there is an arrow from the double arrows to a box labelled 'Representations of Social Life'. The results of the dialogue are to be communicated. What the figure as a whole depicts is a set

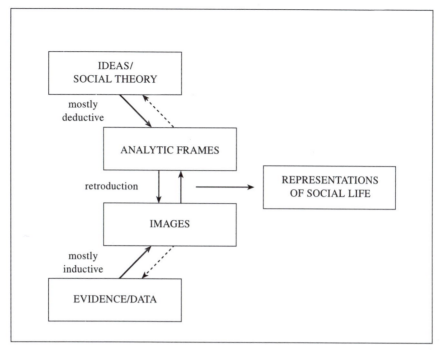

Figure 1.1   *A simple model of social research*

of dynamic relationships between the elements – arranged from the most abstract at the top, to the most concrete at the bottom; and the earlier to the left, and the later to the right – in the research process.

One can say that the various traditions in social research differ from each other in the kinds and contents of their leading ideas, in the character of the evidence used, and in the manner in which the dialogue of ideas and evidence takes form in their practices and public presentations. One major contrast would be that some stress the 'downward', deductive kind of reasoning, while others prefer to argue 'upwards', inductively. Ragin stresses, however, as visualized by his double arrows, that in actual practice there is always a two-way reasoning, a dialogue between the various levels. The model is, of course, a simplification in many ways, but it offers a useful device to organize some aspects of my discussions in this book.

Types of social research

Earlier in his book, Ragin (1994: 33 and *passim*) distinguished three major types of social research, based on their general goals and specific research strategies: qualitative, comparative and quantitative research. Qualitative research is especially used to study what he calls 'commonalities', i.e. common properties, within a relatively small number of cases of which many aspects are taken into account. 'Cases are examined intensively with techniques designed to facilitate the clarification of theoretical concepts and empirical categories.' In Ragin's version of comparative research (cf. also Ragin, 1987), the focus is on diversity and 'a moderate number of cases is studied in a comprehensive manner, though in not as much detail as in most qualitative research'. It 'most often focuses on configurations of similarities and differences across a limited number of cases'. Quantitative research, finally, investigates the covariation within large data-sets, that is, a relatively small number of features is studied across a large number of cases. So the focus is on 'variables and relationships among variables in an effort to identify general patterns of covariation'.

As a first approximation, these characterizations seem to be very useful. On the qualitative side, many would like to add some further features, preferences and assumptions. For instance, rather than trying to explore 'common' features, many qualitative researchers report their findings in terms of a typology or even a contrast. Furthermore, most qualitative research tends to be based on an 'interpretative' approach, in the sense that the meanings of events, actions and expressions is not taken as 'given' or 'self-evident', but as requiring some kind of contextual interpretation. What kind of 'contexts' have to be invoked may, of course, be a matter of preference and debate. One may look, for instance, at the surrounding text, the social setting and/or the encompassing 'culture'. Furthermore, choosing a qualitative approach suggests that the phenomena of interest are not at the moment 'countable', whether for practical and/or for theoretical reasons. And there are large differences among qualitative researchers in other respects. Some would use a 'language of variables', as quantitative researchers do, which would be an anathema to others, who prefer a less 'scientistic' and more 'humanistic' or 'holistic' approach and a language that fits that style. Most qualitative researchers prefer a relatively 'open' or 'exploratory' research strategy, starting with some 'sensitizing concepts' (Blumer, 1969) which may become more precise as the research progresses. For some this represents what they would call the preparatory phase of research, for which a qualitative approach is best fitted, later to be followed by a decisive test in a quantitative project. Others would resist such a limited job description for qualitative research, saying that exploration and testing can go on, hand in hand, within a single qualitative project, or across projects.

Qualitative versus quantitative

An obvious strategy to elaborate the core characteristics of qualitative research, then, is to contrast it with quantitative research, although this may hide internal differences. The defining feature of quantitative research, that its results can be summarized in numbers most often arranged in tables, is absent, or at least not dominant, in qualitative research. In other words, while the results of quantitative research can be presented in numerical form, those of qualitative research require verbal expressions, and often quite extensive ones at that. In the typical case, the primary material of quantitative research is also verbal, but the basic features of the design are oriented to quantification, or one might say 'numerification'. These include systematic sampling, standardization of data collection, and statistical data management techniques. The essential movement of the research is the reduction of large amounts of distributed information to numerical summaries, means, percentages, correlation coefficients, etc. As Charles Ragin (1994: 92) remarks: 'Most quantitative data techniques are *data condensers*' and 'qualitative methods, by contrast, are best understood as *data enhancers*'. The crucial feature of qualitative research, then, is to 'work up' one's research materials, to search for hidden meanings, non-obvious features, multiple interpretations, implied connotations, unheard voices. While quantitative research is focused on summary characterizations and statistical explanations, qualitative research offers complex descriptions and tries to explicate webs of meaning.

Styles of qualitative social research

While quantitative methods seem to be part of one unitary model of doing research, including standard criteria of adequacy, qualitative research offers a wide variety of methods, aims, approaches – in short, styles.

Interview studies

Without any doubt, the most popular style of doing qualitative social research, is to *interview* a number of individuals in a way that is less restrictive and standardized than the one used for quantitative research. The researcher may prepare a number of topics or even questions that are to be brought into the conversation in a more or less systematic or quasi-natural way. The respondent may be asked rather specific questions or may just be requested to talk at length on one or more themes. The encounter may be one-to-one or the researcher may organize a group discussion. There is, then, within the interview style an enormous range of variation. The crucial property, however, is that the researcher arranges sessions with the research subjects in which the latter talk about their ideas and experiences at the initiative of and for the benefit of the researcher. In that sense, the data produced in interviews have an 'experimental' quality; without the research project, they would not exist. Doing interviews has a number of obvious practical advantages. The researcher is able to collect a large amount of on-target information with a minimal investment in terms of time and social effort. One does not have to wait until a phenomenon of interest emerges naturally; one can work to have it created on the spot, so to speak. Doing an interview study is for many if not most qualitative researchers the obvious way of designing their projects. In Chapter 4 on interviewing, I will have occasion to discuss some possibly less popularly considered features of interview research, together with some less obvious possibilities.

As a classic example of an interview study, I refer to *Passage through crisis: polio victims and their families,* by Fred Davis, first published in 1963, and re-issued with a new introduction in 1991. It is mostly based on a series of interviews with the parents of children passing through the trajectory of acute paralytic poliomyelitis and its aftermath. This study, and a few others, will be discussed at some length in Chapter 4.

Using documents

A rather different style of qualitative research involves the scrutiny of documents of various kinds. One can study 'natural' documents that are produced as part of an established social practice, such as bureaucratic records, newspaper reports, cartoons, musical scores, family pictures, works of art, home videos, email messages, etc. I use the term 'document' to refer to any preservable record of text, image, sound, or a combination of these. I will focus my discussion, in Chapter 5, on natural documents, although a researcher can, of course, also produce his or her own records, or have these produced by the research subjects for the purpose of his or her project. Using natural documents will involve the researcher in some kind of consideration of the processes that have produced those documents, practices of documentation, which I will also take up in that chapter.

I will mention here just one classical study to exemplify document-based research. It was done by Norbert Elias, published in 1939 in German as *Über den Prozess der Zivilisation*, and in English in 1978 as *The civilising process*. The core piece in the first volume of this masterly work on the history of Western civilization is based on a comparative study of various manner books, as well as subsequent editions of some of these, published in Germany, France, England and Italy, from the 13th through to the 19th centuries. The changes which can be observed in these texts are taken as indications of changes in the actual behaviour of the upper and middle classes at which these books were aimed (more on this in Chapter 5).

Ethnography

A minority of qualitative researchers are committed to the close observation of the actual, 'natural' situations in which people live their lives, trying to minimize the impact of their presence on their subjects' actions. This style is known as *ethnography*. It used to be the stock-in-trade style of social and cultural anthropology. An anthropologist would live for a year with his or her tribe in order to describe crucial features of tribal life through a yearly cycle. This would involve a variety of data gathering techniques, including first of all learning the language, and then doing natural observations, asking for explanations, gathering kinship information, etc. Later, the label 'ethnography' came to be used to indicate any kind of research that involves on-site observation of, and interaction with, whatever kind of natives the researcher would like to study, such as medical personnel and patients in hospitals, drug users scoring dope, or a wide variety of people at work: police officers, sales people, software engineers, etc. Another label for this style of research work is 'participant observation', while many practitioners call it 'fieldwork'. Doing ethnography is probably the most demanding way of performing qualitative research. It takes a lot of time, the capacity to interact with a variety of people, the management of an ambiguous role, and at times real physical discomfort or even danger. But it also offers a range of very interesting possibilities and challenges. It is, in some ways, the royal way of doing qualitative research. I will discuss some major aspects of this style in Chapter 6.

A classic example of ethnography is *Street corner society: the social structure of an Italian slum*, by William Foot Whyte, researched in the late 1930s, and first published in 1943. In the second, 1955 edition of the book, an extensive 'Appendix: On the evolution of street corner society' has been added to the original report, in which the author recounts the way in which his study evolved. Enjoying the freedom of a generous fellowship, he wanted to study the lives of people inhabiting a 'slum area'. After some false starts, he was introduced to what was to become his 'key informant', as anthropologists call it, and he arranged to live in the area in order to be able to meet the local people on a daily basis. He then started to study various groups in the community, his key informant's lower-class 'gang', a 'club' of upwardly mobile men, and then more encompassing networks involving a mixture of local politics and racketeers. I will return to this exemplary ethnography in Chapter 6, in which I will also discuss some far less well known examples.

A differentiation in styles of research can, of course, be based on other aspects than the ones used above. The tripartite differentiation of interview studies, document analysis and ethnography is focused on the kinds of evidence used, but one can also differentiate in terms of topics, aims and analytic strategies. A classic anthropological ethnography, for instance, can have the format of an analytic description of a particular culture, but one can also encounter more focused 'facet-ethnographies' concentrating, for instance on economic or religious aspects of the tribal life studied. And, whatever the focus, the purpose can be limited to a descriptive characterization as such, or the researcher may attempt a comparative confrontation with a previously studied case, or even attempt to test some theoretical notions or hypotheses. In interview-based research, the purpose is often to catch aspects of the experiences and perspectives of a particular category of people, such as women, minorities or specialized workers. But interviews can also be used to study particular patterns of reasoning or talking about some topics of interest to the researcher. These and other differences will be discussed in later chapters, but two crucial issues will be introduced in the next two sections of this introductory chapter: the first concerns the status accorded to research materials as evidence and the second has to do with a research project's relation to 'theory'.

The analytic status of research materials

In his *Researching culture: qualitative method and cultural studies,* Pertti Alasuutari has made a useful distinction concerning the ways in which qualitative researchers conceive the analytic function of the evidence they collect. When questionnaires or interviews are used, these are mostly considered from what he calls 'a factist perspective' (Alasuutari, 1995: 47). This is based on 'a clear-cut division between the world "out there", on the one hand, and the claims made about it, on the other'. The research material at hand is not studied in itself, but only in so far as it can be used as evidence for happenings and conditions elsewhere: 'The characteristics of language and of the situation are only taken into account as possible noise in the channel through which information about the world is conveyed, or as distortions in the lens through which the reality is observed' (ibid.). For instance in using interview materials, the researcher is only marginally interested in the interview as a meaningful interaction or in the features of language use. He or she 'wants to find out about the actual behaviour, attitudes or real motives of the people being studied, or to detect what has happened'. When taking a factist perspective, a researcher is using research materials, such as interview responses or extracts from documents, as indirect indications of, or reports about, features of a reality *outside* those interviews or documents. So an interview response may be read as a more or less adequate report on something that happened before the interview took place (a 'testimony'), or, alternatively, as a more or less adequate representation of the respondent's underlying value orientation (an 'index'). Similarly, a document may be considered as a more or less truthful description of the scenes or patterns it reports on.

In some, mostly more recent, approaches to qualitative research, however, an alternative perspective is taken, which Alasuutari discusses as the 'specimen perspective'. Here, 'research material is not treated as either a *statement about* or a *reflection of* reality; instead, a specimen is seen as *part of* the reality being studied' (Alasuutari, 1995: 63). So, for instance, when analysing an interview, the focus may be on properties of the actual interaction, like the evasion of questions or the ways stories are told. In a related vein, a number of writers on the value and use of interview data have remarked that one can treat interview materials in principle either as a 'resource' or as a 'topic'.[1] In the first case, one uses interview statements to gain information about certain events or about the respondent, while in the second case one is interested in processes of interaction, meaning construction or descriptive practices as they are 'visible' in the interview itself.

Theoretical objects

A closely related issue concerns the theoretical conception of the phenomena which are the object of the research project's interests. Sometimes, the researcher starts his or her project with a clearly defined theoretical object – say 'identity' in one of its many meanings. In many other cases, however, the object and its theoretical features are not very clearly defined at the start but are 'allowed to emerge' in the research process. What may be problematic, however, is that quite often no clear and consistent theoretical object is defined or even implied in any phase of the project. In those cases, commonsense notions take the place of active thinking about what one is doing.

The sense of a theoretical object depends on the set of ideas in which it is embedded: a theoretical framework. Such a framework may be left implied rather than articulated, or it may be indicated, rather than explicated, by referring to a label like symbolic interactionism or ethnomethodology, or by mentioning the *locus classicus* for such a label (Blumer, 1969 and Garfinkel, 1967a, respectively). In many cases, however, there is simply no clearly defined, indicated or implicated theoretical framework: the research is 'simply' based on some current version of common sense, or what is currently accepted as self-evident. In ethnomethodological terms, common sense is used in such projects as an unexplicated resource (cf. Zimmerman & Pollner, 1971). Many popular social science concepts, such as 'culture' or 'identity', often share this fate of being left unexplicated.

Let me try to clarify what I mean when I speak of a study's 'theoretical object' or 'analytic object'. In W.F. Whyte's study, *Street corner society*, one label for its analytic object is given right in the subtitle: *the social structure of an Italian slum*. In his Introduction Whyte tells his readers that he wanted to study the daily life of real people, which is what we may call his concrete or 'material' object. But he also stresses that, contrary to the outsiders' image of slum life as chaotic, he wants to show that it is highly organized. And that aspect, 'social organization', I would call his theoretical or 'formal' object. In a later discussion (in Chapter 6) I will argue that he had a rather particular view of what constitutes 'social organization' and that this view has clearly traceable intellectual origins, which by the way he did not explicate in his main text. So we have a number of names for similar if not identical concepts: on the one hand 'theoretical', 'analytic' or 'formal' object, and, on the other hand, a theoretical or analytic framework, or perspective or focus, in which it is embedded. In other words, it is important to distinguish objects at the conceptual level, from what is actually studied materially. Material objects get their significance in a research project in terms of conceptualizations relating them to the project's formal object.

As Ragin has it:

The two main problems social scientists face as empirical researchers are the equivocal nature of the theoretical realm and the complexity of the empirical realm. As researchers our primary goal is to link the empirical and the theoretical – to use theory to make sense of evidence and to use evidence to sharpen and refine theory. The interplay helps us to produce theoretically structured descriptions of the empirical world that are both meaningful and useful. (Ragin, 1992: 224–5)

In later chapters we will see whether and/or in which ways 'the theoretical realm' and 'the empirical realm' can be usefully distinguished and/or connected, as one might also say that these realms are mutually constitutive.

Reconsidering Ragin's model

After these general overviews and characterizations of qualitative research, I propose to stand back for a moment to reconsider the ways of thinking about qualitative research that I have sketched above.

Let us take another look as Charles Ragin's 'simple model of social research' as visualized in the schema described before (pp. 2–3, above). In this two-dimensional schema we see, on theoretical axis, 'Ideas' above and 'Evidence' below. This resonates with many cultural associations in which the ideal is put high and the material low. Just think of the Marxian superstructure of ideas and the material substrate and the Freudian *Überich* or Superego contrasted with the *Es* or Id. The horizontal axis of Ragin's model suggests a time line. More to the left the two starting points, Ideas and Evidence, in the middle the subsequent elaborations in Analytic Frames and Images and the dialogue between them, which represents the actual analytic word of the researcher, and then to the right the final product of his or her work, the 'Representation of Social Life'.

Ragin's schema is suggestive in a number of ways. The Ideas up high suggest an overview of things below, a bird's eye view or a view from a mountain, at a distance. Concrete local events can be used as evidence but get their wider significance from being exemplary of notions contained in the ideas. Evidence is, at first just 'local' and 'time-bound', while Ideas have a much wider scope. A major task of research is often seen to be the ability to *generalize*, that is to offer conclusions that are valid for a larger set of phenomena, in terms of both time and place, than the original evidence. I think that what is expected of empirical social research can be summarized as, on the one hand, surmounting the 'limitations' of the localized and time-bound character of the evidence, that is general knowledge, while at the same time warranting such knowledge on the basis of such 'limited' evidence. In later chapters I will offer a fuller discussion of the various methods, tricks and rhetoric used to try to live up to these tasks, but here a few brief observations can already be presented.

Ethnographic fieldwork, as reported in Whyte's *Street corner society*, was done in one particular neighbourhood, a part of the North Side in Boston, in 1937–38. The text itself is highly descriptive, focussing on local and time-bound events and short-term developments. But now and again suggestions of a wider relevance are given. The book itself was published in 1944, again in 1955, and it can still be read today. In the Appendix, added to the 1955 edition, Whyte offers a detailed account of how he collected his evidence, which can be summarized as 'I was there, I saw what happened with my own eyes, I talked with the boys immediately afterwards or a few days later, I made notes the same evening.' But in the Preface it is already clear that his research has profited from various kinds of 'academic' input. The project was initiated as part of a four-year fellowship at Harvard and inspired by the ideas and methods of a number of Harvard professors. And after finishing the actual study, Whyte went to the University of Chicago to write the report. So the dialogue of ideas and evidence can also be seen as involving a back and forth travel between places: the academy – Harvard and Chicago – and the field – the Boston North Side. Starting off from the academy the researcher travels to the field to collect evidence which he then brings back to the academy. And, although Whyte travelled a lot between the two places, there is also in the previous generalized sentence a suggestion of a time line: academy > field > academy.

In other types of research other places may be visited or the visits may have a different character. In interview studies, researchers or their hired assistants often pay one short visit to the home or workplace of respondents, although repeated interviews are sometimes undertaken. Group interviews or 'focus groups' often take place in a laboratory setting, as do experiments of a social-psychological kind and some of Garfinkel's 'breaching experiments' discussed in Chapter 3. So within the Academy a further differentiation of places can be made, like the office, the laboratory and the seminar. And the field is also differentiated: homes, streets, bars, bowling alleys, workplaces, etc.

Why should we consider such differentiations of place at all? Because if a dialogue between ideas and evidence has to take place, there has to be a 'meeting' of one kind or another. In the discussion so far, the means to realize such a meeting has been travel. Whyte travelled between the academy/Harvard and the field/North Side. Interviewers visit homes. And focus group participants or experimental subjects are invited to come to the laboratory. But when we take a closer look at what actually happened, we see that Whyte took notes which made his evidence *transportable* from the field to his office. He did not have to rely on his memories only, but could support these with much more permanent documents.[2] Similarly, what is said in interviews, whether carried out in homes or in the laboratory, is also transformed into one or another kind of transportable object: questionnaire codes, interview notes or, nowadays most commonly, audio or video recordings. So the locally produced Evidence is first transformed into a more permanent form as documents and then transported from one place to another, as it travels with the researcher from the field or laboratory to the office. And it is only after one or another form of work-up in the office that it will be transported again to the seminar or conference, whether this place is a local or a virtual one. Seen in this light, the differences between the types of qualitative research discussed earlier – interview-based research, document analysis or ethnography – are relative. In all three kinds the study of original phenomena, events, is mediated by documents, objects in and through which ephemeral events are transformed into much more permanent 'immutable mobiles', to use a famous expression coined by Bruno Latour (1987). So documentation, I would suggest, is a basic operation that allows the dialogue of ideas and evidence to take place. And it is only through the transformation into documents that research can aspire to produce knowledge of wider relevance. But then, this always involves a loss of life.

Ragin's 'simple model' is not able to visualize all these complexities, of course. The placement of ideas and evidence to the left of the image, I noted before, suggests their status as 'givens', as unchanging elements that precede the actual analysis. While this may be a contested ideal for quantitative research, it is certainly not relevant for qualitative research, in which both ideas and evidence should be treated as 'mutable' in an analytic sense; changing in meaning as the dialogue proceeds. Qualitative research is exploratory, adventurous and its methods should therefore be used in a flexible way. The topic(s) of the research, and the questions asked about it or them, should be allowed to change as the researcher is learning what is at stake in the field under examination. Ideas and evidence should be seen, therefore, as dynamically co-constitutive, but this, of course, is hard to visualize.

Some major points

My reflections can be summarized in the following points:

- Doing research, or more generally doing scientific work *takes time*; one needs time to collect evidence, read the relevant literature, think through one's argumentation, and compose a convincing report.
- Some aspects of the process of social research can be caught using Ragin's metaphor of a *dialogue of ideas and evidence* leading to a *representation of social life*.
- Qualitative styles of social research involve the *close* study of a *limited* set of evidence, taking *many* different aspects into account; quite often this study is oriented to formulate common features or to the development of a typology.
- Based on the kinds of evidence used, three styles of qualitative research have been distinguished: the most popular one uses *interviews* to produce the required evidence, research into historical processes mostly relies on *documents*, while *ethnographers* use a variety of data-producing methods, including especially 'natural observation'.
- Considering a researcher's perspective on his or her data, such as interviews or documents, a contrast has been given, following Alasuutari, between a *factist* and a *specimen* perspective; in the first case the data are used to study a reality to which they refer, while in the second they are taken 'on their own', as interviews, documents, or whatever.
- In both perspectives, however, the researcher uses an implied or explicit conception of his or her ultimate topic, an *analytic* or *formal* object, that can be distinguished from the *material* object being studied.
- What is evident in all of these features is that research involves taking information about social life *out* of its original context to *rework* it in a

different one; in one way or another information is made to *travel* in a preservable format from one place to another, from an ephemeral state to a more permanent one.

Recommended reading

For a fuller exposition of Ragin's general approach to social research, as used in this chapter, you might read the first three chapters, pages 1–76 of:

- Ragin, Charles C. (1994) *Constructing social research: the unity and diversity of method.* Thousand Oaks, CA: Pine Forge Press

Another rather personal account of qualitative research as a part of 'cultural studies' is:

- Alasuutari, Perti (1995) *Researching culture: qualitative method and cultural studies.* London: Sage

The titles below can be inspected for useful resources on a range of qualitative approaches:

- Denzin, Norman K., Yvonna S. Lincoln, eds (2000) *Handbook of qualitative research: second edition.* Thousand Oaks: Sage
- Lofland, John, Lyn H. Lofland (1984) *Analyzing social settings: a guide to qualitative observation and analysis,* 2nd edn. Belmont, CA: Wadsworth
- Seale, Clive, David Silverman, Jay Gubrium, Giampietro Gobo, eds. (forthcoming) *Inside qualitative research: craft, practice, context.* London: Sage
- Silverman, David, ed. (1997) *Qualitative research: theory, method and practice.* London: Sage
- Silverman, David (2001) *Interpreting qualitative data: methods for analysing talk, text and interaction,* 2nd edn. London: Sage

Notes

1 Cf. Silverman (1985, 1993, 2001), Seale (1998); the contrast between use as 'resource' or 'topic' was originally developed in ethnomethodology in discussions of 'common sense' (cf. Zimmerman & Pollner, 1971; also Chapter 3, pp. 31–7).

2 When he was attacked for his study, many years later (Boelen, 1992), his defence was constructed from his re-read fieldnotes (Whyte, 1992).

2 Ethnomethodology's Perspective

> Ethnomethodology's standing task is to examine social facts, just in every and any actual case asking for each thing, what makes it accountably just what that social fact is? (Garfinkel, 2002: 251)

In this chapter I will give a general overview of ethnomethodology (EM), which will be followed in the next by a discussion of EM's 'methods', or rather its actual research practices. Stated in broad terms, ethnomethodology has, in the first place, been a new way of conceiving sociology's problems, which has led, secondly, to new ways of studying sociology's phenomena. In this chapter, the focus will be on the first of these.

What is ethnomethodology – a first sketch

As a first approximation,[1] one can say that 'ethnomethodology' is a special kind of social inquiry, dedicated to explicating the ways in which collectivity members create and maintain a sense of order and intelligibility in social life. It has emerged as a distinctive perspective and style of social research in the teachings and publications of one man, Harold Garfinkel. From a varied set of 'sources of inspiration', including on the one hand most prominently his teacher and PhD supervisor Talcott Parsons, and on other the phenomenological philosophies of Alfred Schutz, Aron Gurwitsch and Edmund Husserl, he has forged a new vision of what social inquiry could be.[2] Taking off from Parsons' impressive synthesization of various classical traditions of sociological theorizing, one can say that in ethnomethodology these have been turned on their head. For the Durkheimian strand in classical sociology, and social research more generally, the ultimate goal is to investigate 'social facts', and their determinants, where 'social facts' have the twin characteristic of being both 'external' and 'constraining' to the actions of individuals. In ethnomethodology, on the other hand – to adapt a phrase from Melvin Pollner (1974) – 'facts are treated as accomplishments', that is, they are seen as being produced in and through members' practical activities.

In other words, while classical sociology is in the business of *explaining* social facts, the effort of ethnomethodology is directed towards an *explication* of their constitution. In his *Le suicide: étude de sociologie*, Emile Durkheim tried to explain variations in suicide rates in terms of variations in kinds of social integration. An ethnomethodologist, however, might investigate the ways in which cases of sudden death get constituted as being 'suicides', or, at a different level, how statistical information about various 'rates' is used to construct a sociological explanation of suicide in terms of social 'causes'.[3] In other words, as explicated in his recent book, Garfinkel (2002) proposes a different version of a 'Durkheimian sociology', one that does not take 'social facts' as just that, as building blocks in explanatory accounts, but instead directs attention to the actual constitution of such 'social facts' and their 'factuality'.

For sociology, and social research in general, the interest in the factual status of 'social facts' is limited to technical and practical issues of getting those facts right, in a methodologically sound way, and at reasonable costs. There is, for instance, an enormous methodological literature on designing, implementing and analysing social surveys. This literature is focused on methodological choices that should guarantee a sufficient level of representativeness, validity and reliability, and on practical problems of avoiding sampling error, non-response, interviewer influences on answering behaviour, misunderstandings between interviewers and respondents, etc. For ethnomethodology, survey design and analysis, and survey interviewing, are interesting as possible topics for study as examples of accountable professional practice. The stance taken in such an investigation would not be one of 'methodological' or 'practical' interest, but rather 'disinterested' as to the purpose or the practices studied, a stance which has been called 'ethnomethodological indifference' (Garfinkel & Sacks, 1970: 345; Lynch, 1993: 141–7). In other words, ethnomethodology might be interested in studying survey-related practices as such, as exemplary ways in which the factual status of 'social facts' is being established for the practical purpose of doing a survey (Lynch, 2002).[4]

Ethnomethodology's relationship with its 'mother discipline' sociology, and by extension to all 'social science', is then rather ambiguous. Both share a deep interest in problems of social order and try to elucidate the organization of social life in all its manifestations. But their general approach is tangential one to the other. I would like to stress that this 'tangentiality' should not in the first place be seen as a difference in 'research methods', as ordinarily conceived, but, as stated above, as one of 'interests', 'problematics' or 'conception'. In other words, the fact that ethnomethodology hardly uses quantitative methods, as the dominant streams of conventional social research do, is not the point here. Rather than focussing on issues like the choice between qualitative and quantitative research, the problem is one of research purpose or the functions various methods and results are having in the argumentation of a research project. Indeed, although a substantive 'minority' of non-ethnomethodological social researchers do use qualitative research as a main or alternative style of research, this does not prevent basic differences between their various purposes and those of ethnomethodology. As I stated in the Preface, it is the basic strategy of this book to confront the research practices and logics of these qualitative colleagues with the ones available in ethnomethodology, in order to elucidate both.

The remaining sections of this chapter, as well as the next chapter, will be devoted to a more elaborate and illustrated discussion of the ethno-methodological enterprise. In the present chapter, I will expand the discussion of ethnomethodology's logic and problematic, while in the next the discussion will concern those actual research practices that can be seen as 'typical' of ethnomethodological studies. It will be inevitable to use a number of jargonistic expressions as shorthand indications of various ideas, but I do hope these will become less opaque as my discussions proceed.

A bit of history

As a full sketch of ethnomethodology's background is obviously far beyond the scope of the present book (cf. Rawls, 2002), I can only provide some rough indications of the complex intellectual network involved in its emergence (or rather invention). In the previous section, I focused on the contrast with a loosely defined Durkheimian sociology, as exemplified to a certain extent in the *oeuvre* of Garfinkel's teacher, Talcott Parsons. It should be noted, however, that there is (much) more in Parsons than 'just' a particular version of Durkheim (Garfinkel, 1967a: vii; Garfinkel, 2002). In fact, the influence of Max Weber is equally important for an adequate understanding of Parsons, and therefore of Garfinkel and ethnomethodology. A major aspect of Weber's sociology is that it is based on a specific conception of meaningful social action. This meaning needs to be 'understood' before such an action can figure in any sociological argument. 'Understanding' (*Verstehen*) in this context does not refer to some kind of intuitive empathy, but rather to a process of rational reconstruction of the sense of actions by the analyst in terms of 'ideal types'. This overall approach has been subjected to a philosophical critique by Alfred Schutz, taking his inspiration from previous philosophers like Edmund Husserl and Henri Bergson. A major point of Schutz (1972) was that the use of ideal types is not just the way in which a *verstehende* sociologist reconstructs the sense of actions, but that typification is an unavoidable aspect of everyday life, especially when people are not in direct contact with each other. Harold Garfinkel used the insights of Schutz and other phenomenological philosophers such as Aron Gurwitch, in his intellectual struggle with the Parsonian heritage, but at the same time he departed from these phenomenological ideas in important ways. In the ethnomethodological programme, the foundation for a critique of Weber or Parsons is no longer an in-depth analysis of the constitution in individual consciousness of various kinds of social knowledge. Instead, the focus is on socially shared procedures used to establish and maintain 'a sense of social structure', i.e. an intelligible and accountable local social order. What is kept from phenomenology, then, includes a stress on taken-for-granted knowledge, the strategy to 'bracket' taken-for-granted presuppositions, and a deep interest in the local constitution of practical activities in everyday life.

In contrast to both Parsons and Schutz, ethnomethodology does not make a sharp distinction between the general stance and rationality of science and everyday life. In fact, it suggests that the activities of scientists are in many ways similar to ordinary lay activities. There are two sides to this major point. On the one hand, ethnomethodology has a deep interest in and respect for the practical rationality and accountability of the most commonplace of ordinary activities. The very label of 'ethnomethodology' was coined by Garfinkel when he was involved in a study of jury deliberations and was struck by the seriousness of the 'methodology' those 'lay' deliberations displayed (Garfinkel, 1967a: 104–15; 1974). And on the other hand, ethnomethodology has studied various scientific practices to understand their grounding in local rationalities that are in many ways similar to those used in everyday life (Garfinkel et al., 1981, Lynch et al, 1983). The crux of the matter is that while Weber, Schutz and Parsons discuss idealized models of science and scientific rationality, ethnomethodology is geared to study the local accountability of *any* kind of practice. This way of making science ordinary does not mean that ethnomethodology is blind to the specifics of particular professional practices, such as doing disciplined research. On the contrary, by following professional practices in detail, ethnomethodology can do two things at the same time: show how a professional practice is embedded in quite ordinary competences, *and also* elaborate how it is special, in the sense of being part of a particular local version of a more generalized professional culture.

Harold Garfinkel's major and most influential publication, *Studies in ethnomethodology*, published in 1967, collects eight papers written over a 12–year period. In it, one can trace some aspects of his reworking of the above-named 'influences', especially that of Alfred Schutz. His then current position is most clearly expressed in the Preface and first chapter, and illustrated in the next two chapters. I will return to these sources in other sections of this book. After 1967, Garfinkel for a long time published very little: one very important paper with Harvey Sacks (1970), two papers written in collaboration with two of his former students, Eric Livingston and Michael Lynch (Garfinkel et al, 1981, Lynch et al, 1983), and a series of partly overlapping statements, published from 1988 onwards. More recently, he has published a second book, collecting a series of edited papers and introductory chapters: *Ethnomethodology's program: working out Durkheim's aphorism* (2002), with a most informative introduction by the book's editor, Anne Warfield Rawls. Garfinkel's pervasive influence has been mostly based on his 1967 book, as well as on the impact of his students, including those who studied with him after 1967. His second book documents the development of his ideas over the last 35 years and offers a number of concrete illustrations of his approach.

Early collaborators

While Harold Garfinkel was developing his specific way of doing social research, later to be called ethnomethodology, he cooperated with various other researchers who were up to more or less similar things. Best known among these were Edward Rose, Aaron Cicourel and Harvey Sacks. Rose has not published much and has had a limited influence on later developments.[5] Cicourel did publish a lot of books, of which an early one, *Method and measurement in sociology* (1964), became quite well known as a thorough critique of established sociological methods. It helped to get ethnomethodology a reputation in those days, of being first and foremost a critical movement within sociology rather than an alternative programme of social inquiry. His book, *The social organization of juvenile justice* (1968) added the theme of a critique of established institutional reporting practices, while maintaining the critical focus on the knowledge base of social science research and theory. By the mid-1970s, Cicourel had distanced himself from ethnomethodology, using an alternative label – *cognitive sociology* – for his approach. Nowadays he is no longer seen as 'a member' of ethnomethodology.

The third early collaborator mentioned above, Harvey Sacks, also gradually developed an approach of his own, now called conversation analysis (CA), but that history went rather differently. Although Sacks was the initiator of CA, he was not the only one. Emanuel Schegloff and later Gail Jefferson also contributed to its early development, and continued to develop it further after Sacks' early death in 1975. Since the mid-1970s onwards, the number of practitioners of CA has been growing and now far outnumbers those who do ethnomethodological studies in a style closer to Garfinkel's inspiration. As I have treated the general character of CA and its development quite extensively elsewhere (Ten Have, 1999a), my discussion here will be limited and mostly focused on CA's ambiguous relation to ethnomethodology. CA's early development can be traced quite well, as Harvey Sacks recorded most of his lectures between 1964 and 1972. He used to distribute copies of transcribed versions, and a large selection was edited by Gail Jefferson and published in 1992. From that collection, and Emanuel Schegloff's introductions to the two volumes, one can learn how CA as a specific focus on the local organization of talk-in-interaction emerged from a wider set of concerns raised by the detailed inspection of transcribed fragments of 'conversation'. Two major themes were present right from the beginning: the local use of commonsense knowledge organized around categories of persons, and the sequential organization of conversation. The first theme, together with a larger set of issues concerning 'mind' and 'knowledge', receded into the background,[6] while the second became the dominant one.

While Sacks and Schegloff, in their early work, mostly used data from institutional settings – calls to a suicide prevention centre, group therapy sessions and calls to a disaster centre – their analyses focused on generic features of the talk, mostly ignoring the institutional context. In later work, they tended to use data from 'ordinary conversations' – mundane and informal talk between peers. Since the late 1970s, a number of CA researchers have returned to 'institutional talk', using the generic findings of CA as a backdrop for their research into the specific properties of talk in various institutional settings such as courtrooms, medical consultations or news interviews (see Boden & Zimmerman, 1991 and Drew & Heritage, 1992 for discussions and examples).

While a lot of CA work has been based on recorded telephone conversations, audio recordings of face-to-face interactions – such as the group therapy sessions, mentioned above – were also used. A basic problem with the latter analyses was, of course, that non-vocal parts of the interactions were not recorded and were therefore not available for analysis. By using video equipment, researchers like Charles Goodwin and Christian Heath have extended CA's grasp to include visual aspects of interaction: at first aspects of bodily comportment like gaze shifts, later also actions like the manipulation of objects, the reading of screens and the typing on keyboards. This has allowed the intensive study of complicated work settings in so-called workplace studies.

At present, these *workplace studies* constitute one of the most active sub-fields of ethnomethodology, re-integrating in a way some of the more recent inspirations from Garfinkel with up-to-date findings from conversation analysis, while also providing insights into actual work practices that seem 'useful' for practitioners in such fields as computer-supported cooperative work (CSCW) and human–computer interaction (HCI).[7]

Some core notions

To round off this general introduction, I will discuss some core analytic notions that have been used in ethnomethodological studies. In order to familiarize the reader with ethnomethodology's rather special jargon, I will try to explicate some extended quotes from the literature, especially Garfinkel's early writings.

Accountability and reflexivity

In the first two pages of his Preface to the *Studies in ethnomethodology*, Garfinkel has given a very dense characterization of his programme. Here is one core passage:

> Ethnomethodological studies analyze everyday activities as members' methods for making those same activities visibly-rational-and-reportable-for-all- practical-purposes, i.e., 'accountable,' as organizations of commonplace everyday activities. The reflexivity of that phenomenon is a singular feature of practical actions, of practical circumstances, of common sense knowledge of social structures, and of practical sociological reasoning. By permitting us to locate and examine their occurrence the reflexivity of that phenomenon establishes their study. (Garfinkel, 1967a: vii)

The two core notions provided here are *accountability* and *reflexivity* and it should be noted right away that these terms have a rather special meaning in Garfinkel's hands. While 'accountability' in ordinary talk is often associated with liability, here it is closer to intelligibility or explicability, in the sense that actors are supposed to design their actions in such a way that their sense is clear right away or at least explicable on demand. People who stand in line at a service point, for example, show that they are doing just that by the way they position their bodies, but they are also able to understand and answer a question like 'Are you standing in line?' or 'Are you in the queue?'[8] So the understandability and expressibility of an activity as a sensible action is, at the same time, an essential part of that action. Garfinkel uses 'reflexivity' to focus on that 'incarnate' property, as in the following quote from the start of his explication of ethnomethodology.

> The following studies seek to treat practical activities, practical circumstances, and practical sociological reasoning as topics of empirical studies, and by paying to the most commonplace activities of daily life the attention usually accorded extraordinary events, seek to learn about them as phenomena in their own right. Their central recommendation is that the activities whereby members produce and manage settings of organized everyday affairs are identical with members' procedures for making those settings 'account-able.' The 'reflexive,' or 'incarnate' character of accounting practices and accounts makes up the crux of that recommendation. (Garfinkel, 1967a: 1)

For Garfinkel, then, *reflexivity* refers to the self-explicating property of ordinary actions. Over the last few decades, the concept of 'reflexivity', which basically just denotes an object's relation to itself, has mostly been used in the social sciences in the sense of a call to a self-conscious view of social science's activities. Such a moral-political appeal should be clearly distinguished from Garfinkel's use of the term (cf. Lynch, 2000; Macbeth, 2001).

Members' methods

As a final comment on these quotations, I would like to draw the reader's attention to the focus on *members' methods* as an indication of ethnomethodology's topic. By using such an expression, in combination with words like 'activities', Garfinkel shows that he has an interest in the dynamic properties of social life, which is procedural in character. Furthermore, in so doing he evades what seem to be the stock-in-trade analytic pair of most social science, opposing 'the individual' to 'society'. In fact, he makes it clear that he is not interested in 'the individual' and his or her intentions, strivings, norms or values. As Anne Rawls (in Garfinkel, 2002: 67) notes: 'Individuals are only dealt with as members of cohorts that populate social scenes'. It is no accident, therefore, that ethnomethodologists continuously talk about 'members', and their activities, capacities, etc. 'as members', abstracting in a way from their flesh-and-blood existence as well as their 'raw' emotions and 'inner' thoughts. The focus is, indeed, on order-producing methods, on accountability (cf. Ten Have, 2002a).

Indexicality

Over the course of his successive publications, Garfinkel has used a number of terms to denote local, time-bound and situational aspects of action.

Prominent in the early work was *indexical*, as in 'indexical expressions', or when discussed as a property: *indexicality*. Indexical expressions are, in principle, those whose sense depends on the local circumstances in which they are uttered and/or those to which they apply. Expressions like 'you' or 'yesterday' are obvious examples. But then, if you think of it, on all occasions, all expressions (and actions) are in fact indexical. Garfinkel writes about 'the unsatisfied programmatic distinction between and substitutability of objective for indexical expressions' (Garfinkel, 1967a: 4–7).

> Features of indexical expressions motivate endless methodological studies directed to their remedy. Indeed, attempts to rid the practices of a science of these nuisances lends to each science its distinctive character of preoccupation and productivity with methodological issues. . . .
>
> Nevertheless, *wherever practical actions are topics of study* the promised distinction and substitutability of objective for indexical expressions remains programmatic in every particular case and in every actual occasion in which the distinction or substitutability must be demonstrated. In every actual case without exception, conditions will be cited that a competent investigator will be required to recognize, such that in that particular case the terms of the demonstration can be relaxed and nevertheless the demonstration be counted an adequate one. (Garfinkel, 1967a: 6)

In other words, bridging the gulf between on the one hand abstract notions, as expressed in so-called objective, that is context-free expressions, and on the other hand concrete instances which are inevitably tied to local circumstances and contexts, is an endless task. This task is always cut-off before it is completely finished, that is as soon as the practical circumstances demand and allow a solution which is 'good enough' for the purpose at hand. Indexical expressions are the preferred means for such solutions and are therefore the chosen topic for ethnomethodological investigations.

> I use the term 'ethnomethodology' to refer to the investigation of the rational properties of indexical expressions and other practical actions as contingent ongoing accomplishments of organized artful practices of everyday life. (Garfinkel, 1967a: 11)

So what we have as an 'essential tension' in social life is that indexicality can never be fully 'repaired' by substituting abstract and objective, supra-situational expressions, descriptions or instructions for inevitably 'inexact' indexical expressions and acts. But, at the same time, practical actors always are able to 'get by' in one way or another. Or, to borrow from a notion that came to be used later in Garfinkel's writings (1991, 1996), the philosophical problem of the gulf between the abstract and general on the one hand and the concrete and situational on the other, can, for ethnomethodological purposes, be *respecified* as a problem that members of society solve as a matter of course in their everyday activities.

This theme surfaces again and again in the later chapters of *Studies in ethnomethodology.* Chapter 3, for instance, discusses – and demonstrates – what Garfinkel calls 'the documentary method of interpretation', which he defines in the following way:

The method consists of treating an actual appearance as 'the document of,' as 'pointing to,' as 'standing on behalf of' a presupposed underlying pattern. Not only is the underlying pattern derived from its individual documentary evidences, but the individual documentary evidences, in their turn, are interpreted on the basis of 'what is known' about the underlying pattern. Each is used to elaborate the other. (Garfinkel, 1967a: 78)

So here again we see a kind of two-layered model of social knowledge: the abstract layer of general knowledge, here 'patterns', elsewhere 'objective expressions', or in Schutz' work 'typifications', and the concrete level of actual instances, situated actions, here 'documents',[9] and elsewhere 'indexical expressions'. The always awaiting task, the 'contingent ongoing accomplishment of organized artful practices of everyday life', is to connect the two, by giving accounts, by 'hearing' what was 'meant' rather than what was 'said', etc. It is this condition that is responsible, so to speak, for the 'incarnate reflexivity' discussed before.

Later developments

A cluster of interrelated themes in Garfinkel's later work have to be mentioned here, and will re-emerge in later discussions. While some of his early writings could be read to suggest that ethnomethodology would be in the business of formulating general rules, statements, practices or procedures used in the constitution of local social orders, the later work stresses the idea that those practices etc. are too intimately tied to the occasions on which they are being used to be discussed 'independently' of them (1991, 1996, 2002). This has been especially clear in ethnomethodological studies of a range of complicated professional activities, as in studies of research laboratories (Lynch, 1985 and many other publications), mathematical proofing (Livingston, 1986) and piano improvisation (Sudnow, 1978, 2001). The general idea is that conventional studies of various specialized 'trades' miss the essential 'what' of those trades in favour of traditional sociological features like 'professionalization', 'status considerations', 'lines of communication', etc. Garfinkel has suggested that in order to be able to study the specifics – the 'quiddity' or 'just whatness' – that make up a particular trade, an investigator should develop a rather deep competence in that trade. This has been called the 'unique adequacy requirement of methods' (Garfinkel & Wieder, 1992). Still later Garfinkel dropped the term 'quiddity' or 'just whatness' in favour of 'haecceity' or 'just thisness', presumably in order to avoid suggestions of a stable 'core' that would define a particular practice. Whatever the fancy terms, the urge is still to study the rational, in the sense of reasonable, properties of indexical expressions and indexical actions (Garfinkel & Sacks, 1970). On a more general level, the mission of recent ethnomethodology has been formulated as one of *respecification* of the classic concepts of Western science and philosophy, such as 'order', 'logic', 'rationality', 'action', etc., *as* members' practices (cf. Button, 1991; Garfinkel, 1991, 1996; Lynch, 1993; Lynch &

Bogen, 1996). In other words, the grand themes of our culture are taken up in a fresh way as embodied in local, situated and intelligible practices.

As noted in my short sketch of the history of ethnomethodology, given above, while the first pages of *Studies in ethnomethodology* provide some useful summaries of Garfinkel's core notions, he did not stop there. Some of the later developments of his thinking, as well as the many 'versions' of ethnomethodology that can be discerned in the works of his students and others who took up ethnomethodological studies, will be touched upon in various later chapters of this book. For the moment, I will limit my further explication of core notions to two sets of ideas that were developed by Harvey Sacks and that have had a vast impact on many ethnomethodologists, and especially conversation analysts.

Two Sacksian notions

The first core notion from Harvey Sacks, to be taken up here, has become known as *membership categorization analysis*, while I will use the label *sequential analysis* for the second. As noted before, the intellectual development of Harvey Sacks can be followed quite closely by reading an edited selection of his transcribed lectures (Sacks, 1992), together with Emanuel Schegloff's introductions to the two volumes. In overview one can say that Sacks started his explorations of conversational materials from a wide perspective, based on extensive reading in a number of areas, while he later focused more and more on the organization of talk-in-interaction per se,[10] in terms of turn-taking procedures and sequence organization. An important theme in his earlier work was the organization of knowledge as used, relied on and displayed in actual interactions. As he noted quite early, a large part of such knowledge was organized in terms of categories of people, either in general terms (as in 'children') or in reference to the speaker (as in 'my husband'). These insights and their elaborate explication were at first based on his PhD research on calls to a *Suicide Prevention Center* (cf. Sacks, 1972a) in which callers explained their life situation and their feeling that they had *No one to turn to* (Sacks, 1967). What Sacks noted, among other things, was that people use person-categories as part of sets of categories, which he called *Membership Categorization Devices* (MCD; Sacks, 1972a, 1972b). For instance, within the MCD 'sex' or as we now say 'gender', there are two categories, 'female' and 'male', while within the MCD 'age' there is no fixed number of categories, as their use depends on situational considerations; sometimes two suffice, 'old' and 'young', but often more subtle differentiations are called for: for a newborn days or even hours, for a baby months or even weeks, and for older persons years or decades. Categories are not just named or implied, they also carry a number of different associated properties, 'category predicates', like the one that Sacks used a lot: 'category-bound activities'. So for instance, he noted that the activity 'crying' may be considered bound to the category 'baby', while the activity 'picking up (a child)' is typical of the category 'mother' (Sacks, 1972b). Other kinds of predicates might involve properties like rights and responsibilities, specialized knowledge and competencies, etc. Sacks (1972a) also made an effort to explicate 'rules of application', such as an 'economy rule' (one category is often sufficient) and a 'consistency rule' (once a category from a specific MCD is used, other categories from that device tend to be used also). When describing a medical situation, for instance, one participant may be identified as 'the physician', which is quite often enough as a practical indication, although that person might also be called 'a man', 'an adult' or 'Friso de Haan'. While many different categories may be correct, there are most often only a few that are also relevant. This relevance criterion also accounts for the consistency rule: once one person in an encounter is identified as 'the physician', others may get called 'the nurse', 'the assistant' or 'the patient'. Within the MCDs mentioned so far, we can discern a difference between those that may be used relevantly on any population, like 'gender' and 'age', while others have a more specific field of application. Furthermore, a subset of MCDs have a 'team' or 'relational' implication. Sacks used the expression 'duplicative organization' to refer to cases like 'the chair opened the meeting, the secretary read the minutes', and 'standardized relational pair' (SRP) for 'husband and wife', 'doctor and patient', etc. So *Membership Categorization Analysis* (MCA) offers a useful entrée to analysis of the social knowledge which people use, expect and rely on in doing the accountable work of living together.

These summary explications should be sufficient for the moment, to get a general idea of what is involved. In later chapters I will return to membership categorization analysis, as it was elaborated by Sacks and in a number of later publications by others (cf. note 6).

The second set of ideas from Sacks' work, sequential analysis, forms the basis of conversation analysis (CA), the most widespread form of ethnomethodology, if it can be called that, as it has gained a quasi-independent existence. The basic ideas can be summarized as follows.[11] Sacks noted that people who are talking in interaction are realizing, in and through their talk, two basic properties of 'conversation': in general one speaker talks at any given time and speaker change recurs. Together these properties rely on a system of turn-taking, as explicated in a famous paper which Sacks, with Schegloff and Jefferson, published in 1974 (cf. Sacks et al., 1978).

The fact that conversationalists take turns at talking generates a second problematic, besides turn-taking, namely that of the relations between turns. Conversations do not exist as series of independent units which each fill a turn. Sacks has devoted a large part of his work to exploring the methods people use to produce various kinds of coherence across turns. One core notion central to these explorations was that of 'adjacency pairs', two-part sequences exemplified by a question that is followed by an answer, a greeting by a return-greeting, or an invitation by either an acceptance or a rejection. This notion expresses a normative expectation which participants demonstrably use very often to produce and appreciate coherence between subsequent utterances. Other ways of connecting utterances are also used, such as formatting questions as follow-up questions, or designing talk as announcing further talk, as in telling jokes or stories. These and other kinds of connecting work contribute to the organization of sequences and CA is in important ways devoted to its analysis. It should not be hard to see that notions connected to the organization of talk can play an important role in the understanding of interviews as data-producing engines, as will be demonstrated in Chapter 4.

Conversation Analysis as ethnomethodology

I will, in these pages, in general treat conversation analysis (CA) as an example of ethnomethodology (EM). At the same time, however, I acknowledge that there is a certain ambiguity, and even ambivalence, in the CA/EM relationship. Many practitioners of CA, especially those with a non-sociological background, seem to see it as an independent (sub-)discipline, for instance as a kind of 'interactional linguistics'. In the introductory chapter to a major collection of papers in this field, Schegloff et al. offer some remarks about both the indebtedness of CA to EM as well as the differences between the two (1996a: 14–16). On the one hand, they mention 'the local determination of action and understanding' as a perspective which CA took over from ethnomethodology. However, they add, on the other, the observation that the emphasis in ethnomethodology is, in line with its phenomenological roots, on 'the uptake, interpretation and understanding of apperceivable elements of the surround, and much less on their production'. Although this remark can be read as a reproach, it could also be taken as an argument to suggest that CA has something to offer to ethnomethodology: a set of sharp instruments to bring to the fore detailed features of the production of social order. That is the line I want to take in this book, but it should not be ignored that CA, especially in its more linguistic manifestations, has been developing mostly quite apart from what was going on in ethnomethodology 'itself'.

From the ethnomethodology side, matters are different. There is now quite a number of publications in which CA is criticized from an ethnomethodological point of view. The crux of these criticisms seems to be that CA has developed into a 'normal science' in the Kuhnian sense of the term, as a relatively 'fixed' and conventionalized discipline that is after the formulation of law-like generalities (cf. Lynch, 1993; Lynch & Bogen, 1994, 1996). In a way, CA writings may be read in two alternative ways: as searching for 'rules' of a general kind, or as investigating how such 'rules' are used in particular cases. Both of these readings seem to be defensible.

For instance, when I explained some of Sacks' ideas about membership categorization and sequential organization, I was talking in general terms about members' methods, as procedural rules, recurrent patterns or generally usable devices. So in one reading, one could indeed say that MCA and CA are oriented to formulating procedural generalities. Here is a well-known quote from Sacks that may be seen in this way:

The gross aim of the work I am doing is to see how finely the details of actual, naturally occurring conversation can be subjected to analysis that will yield the technology of conversation.

The idea is to take singular sequences of conversation and tear them apart in such a way as to find rules, techniques, procedures, methods, maxims (a collection of terms that more or less relate to each other and that I use somewhat interchangeably) that can be used to generate the orderly features we find in the conversations we examine. The point is, then, to come back to the singular things we observe in a singular sequence, with some rules that handle those singular features, and also, necessarily, handle lots of other events. (Sacks, 1984b: 413)[12]

These programmatic statements by Sacks seem at odds with the stress on the local and time-bound features of phenomena that are essential to the ethnomethodological framework, as expressed in 'indexicality'. This comes close to being the core reproach from the ethnomethodological side. When it is said that ethnomethodology and conversation analysis are ultimately different enterprises; this quote might be used to support such a claim.

Others however, might say that one should not take some of the expressions used by Sacks, such as 'technology', 'generate' or elsewhere 'machine' and 'machinery', too literally. Such 'mechanical' terms should be seen as loose metaphors rather than theoretically serious base concepts. And furthermore, later contributors to the CA enterprise use such expressions only rarely. They may have had their function in the early phase of constructing a new approach, to break the hold of existing paradigms.

One can also, moreover, read this and similar quotes as being in accordance with the ethnomethodological programme in the following way. The 'rules, techniques, procedures, methods, maxims' that Sacks talked about would refer to normative rules which conversationalists use and rely on. They are technical formulations of orientations that are observable in members' conduct. In other words, the generality of the rules etc. is not so much a construction made by the analyst to gloss observed patterns of conduct, as a feature of observed members' orientations themselves. For instance the ways in which conversationalists react to a 'missing answer' display their general orientation that questions should be answered in a way that fits the question. 'You did not answer my question' is a sensible complaint because members orient to the supposed generality of the relevant rule. In other words, the generality is the observable phenomenon, and an analyst's formulation of it as an adjacency pair obligation is no more than a technical formulation of such an oriented-to rule. What is studied in CA, then, is not rules as such but rules as used by members in interaction.

This reading does not deny that CA studies tend to show a stronger orientation to an investigation of quite commonly occurring phenomena, while more radical forms of ethnomethodology are prone to focus on the particulars of specific times, places or forms of life. We will encounter these differences and similarities again and again in the next chapters.

Some major points

Let me note here, to finish off this chapter, some of the major characteristics of ethnomethodology in contrast to most other branches of social science inquiry:

- The focus in ethnomethodological studies is always on *procedural* aspects of members' situated practices, not on overall causes, conditions or effects of those practices.
- Key terms like *account, accountability* and *reflexivity* should be read in the sense they have acquired within the ethnomethodological framework, as indicating essential features of commonsense practices.
- Ethnomethodological studies are *not* interested in anything that 'goes on in the mind' or 'internal processes', 'intentions', 'emotions' and other so-called psychological phenomena; what are studied are *overt activities*, what is 'scenic' (that is directly observable) to participants, and their intelligibility and organization.
- For ethnomethodology, *generalities* such as rules or norms are members' resources for the production and understanding of social order in its local particularities, rather than analytic instruments (although on this point CA and EM seem to differ).

Recommended reading

Garfinkel's own publications, although quite hard to read for the uninitiated, are essential for gaining a deeper understanding of what ethnomethodology is all about.

- Garfinkel, Harold (1967) *Studies in ethnomethodology.* Englewood Cliffs, NJ: Prentice-Hall

From his first book, you might choose the programmatic parts, such as the preface, pages vii–ix and Chapter 1, pages 1–34, or the relatively concrete case studies, such as the one reported in Chapter 5, on 'the managed achievement of sex status' by a transsexual, pages 116–85.

From that basis, you might proceed to his more recent programmatic writings, such as:

- Garfinkel, Harold (1991) 'Respecification: evidence for locally produced, naturally accountable phenomena of order*, logic, reason, meaning, method, etc. in and as of the essential haecceity of immortal ordinary society (I) an announcement of studies'. In: Graham Button, ed. *Ethnomethodology and the human sciences.* Cambridge: Cambridge University Press: 10–19
- Garfinkel, Harold, D.Lawrence Wieder (1992) 'Two incommensurable, asymmetrically alternate technologies of social analysis'. In: Graham Watson, Robert M. Seiler, eds. *Text in context: studies in ethnomethodology.* Newbury Park, etc.: Sage: 175–206

- Garfinkel, Harold (1996) 'An overview of ethnomethodology's program', *Social Psychology Quarterly* 59: 5–21

See also his second book:

- Garfinkel, Harold (2002) *Ethnomethodology's program: working out Durkheim's aphorism*, edited and introduced by Anne Rawls. Lanham, MD: Rowman & Littlefield

Here, the introduction by the editor, Anne Warfield Rawls (pp. 1–64) gives a lot of background information, clear characterizations and an overview of the book's content. Then there is a short 'Author's introduction' (pp. 65–76), and an 'Author's acknowledgments' section which offers some academic autobiographical details as well. The rest of the book is organized in two parts, the first mostly programmatic and expository, the second dealing with a range of more concrete situations and studies: teaching in lecture format, 'formatted queues' and a report of a demonstration of Galileo's. Reading the second book is also hard but instructive work.

In comparison, two empirical papers published together with his former students, Eric Livingston and Michael Lynch, are much more accessible, but still very instructive. They both deal with the work of scientists:

- Garfinkel, Harold, Michael Lynch, Eric Livingston (1981) 'The work of a discovering science construed with materials from the optically discovered pulsar', *Philosophy of the Social Sciences*, 11: 131–58
- Lynch, Michael, Eric Livingston, Harold Garfinkel, (1983) 'Temporal order in laboratory life'. In: Karin D. Knorr-Cetina, Michael Mulkay, eds. *Science observed: perspectives on the social study of science*. London: Sage: 205–38

Among the many introductory discussions of ethnomethodology, I have specifically selected:

- Heritage, John (1984) *Garfinkel and ethnomethodology*. Cambridge: Polity Press

This is especially strong in explicating Garfinkel's 1960s achievements in terms of his struggles with Parsons and phenomenology, while it also has a chapter on conversation analysis.

- Sharrock, Wes, Bob. Anderson (1986) *The ethnomethodologists*. Chichester: Ellis Horwood

Although this book covers more or less the same ground as Heritage's mentioned above, its tone is rather different – let's say argumentative rather than expository.

- Lynch, Michael (1993) *Scientific practice and ordinary action: ethnomethodology and social studies of science*. New York: Cambridge University Press

Although this book is not written as an 'introduction' to ethno-methodology, but as a confrontation of various current approaches to studies of 'science', some chapters can be read as either introductory or as critical discussions: Chapter 1 (pp. 1–38) offers a concise exposition of core notions in ethnomethodology, Chapter 6 (pp. 203–64) is a rather critical discussion of conversation analysis, while Chapter 7 (pp. 265–308) treats recent conceptual developments in ethnomethodology.

Harvey Sacks' transcribed and edited lectures are a goldmine for ethnomethodological and conversation-analytic ideas. Schegloff's introductions offer an extensive overview of the development of his overall approach.

- Sacks, Harvey (1992) *Lectures on conversation*, 2 vols. Edited by Gail Jefferson with introduction by Emanuel A. Schegloff. Oxford: Basil Blackwell

There is, as far as I know, only one book which focuses specifically on Harvey Sacks:

- Silverman, David (1998) *Harvey Sacks: social science and conversation analysis*. Oxford: Policy Press

Notes

1 My characterization of ethnomethodology is a personal and selective one, constructed for the rather specific purposes of this book. Among the many other sources, I would specifically suggest that you consult Heritage (1984a) for a broad scholarly overview, Sharrock & Anderson (1986) for a concise and sharp discussion of basic issues, Button (1991) for ethnomethodological ways of treating some of the classic themes of the human sciences, and Lynch (1993) for some pointed and polemical discussions confronting ethnomethodology and the sociology of scientific knowledge.

2 See Rawls (2002: 9–17) for a very informative sketch of Garfinkel's personal and intellectual biography.

3 Garfinkel (1967a: 11–18; 1967b), see also Atkinson (1978) for some early efforts in these directions.

4 Cf. Benson & Hughes (1991) for an ethnomethodological consideration of survey research logic, and Houtkoop-Steenstra (1995, 2000), Maynard (1996), Maynard et al. (2002), Maynard & Schaeffer (1997, 2000) and Suchman & Jordan (1990) for studies of survey interviewing.

5 Cf. Carlin (1999) and Slack (2000) for more information on Rose.

6 It has, however, been revived in recent years under the label of membership categorization analysis (MCA); cf. among other sources Jayyusi (1984), Hester & Eglin (1997), as well as my discussion later in this chapter.

7 See Button (1993), Heath & Luff (2000), Luff et al. (2000), Suchman (1987) and a large number of other publications by these authors.

8 Cf. Livingston (1987: 4–6, 13–15, 81–3) and Garfinkel (2002: 245–61).

9 It should be noted that the word 'documents' is used here in an abstract sense, as any concrete 'thing' that can be used as evidence for a 'pattern'. This usage, and the expression 'documentary method of interpretation', should not be confused

with 'documents' as a particular type of research material, as introduced in Chapter 1, and discussed more fully in Chapter 5.

10 The expression talk-in-interaction was coined in the 1980s by E.A. Schegloff as a substitute for the confusing 'conversation' with its suggestion of informal talk.

11 My explications of CA-notions will be rather limited here as I have published much more extensive discussions elsewhere (Ten Have, 1999a).

12 From one or more lectures given in 1970.

3   Ethnomethodology's Methods

[Ethnomethodological] studies seek to treat practical activities, practical circumstances, and practical sociological reasoning as topics of empirical studies, and by paying to the most commonplace activities of daily life the attention usually accorded extraordinary events, seek to learn about them as phenomena in their own right. (Garfinkel, 1967a: 1)

In this chapter, I will present a general discussion of the ways in which ethnomethodological research is carried out. In the social science community at large, EM is probably best known for Garfinkel's early 'breaching experiments', and for the use of recordings and transcripts in conversation analysis, but other research strategies, at times using one or the other of these two as elements within a larger approach, should also be considered. Garfinkel's breaching experiments and CA's use of recordings and transcripts provide an interesting contrast in that the first can be seen as 'provoking' the phenomena of interest, while the latter is based on a careful avoidance of 'researcher-provoked data' (Silverman, 2001: 159). This theme of researcher provocation versus natural occurrence will be this chapter's main thread as regards the quality of data, but of course, data quality can only sensibly be discussed within the framework of an overall approach to research, in terms of a research project's analytic purpose. After a general discussion of the ways in which ethnomethodology has struggled with such problems, I will present fuller discussions of the two most typical strategies of ethnomethodological research, breaching experiments and the use of tapes and transcripts, and conclude with some overall reflections.

Ethnomethodology and common sense procedures

Since ethnomethodology has an interest in the procedural study of common sense as it is used in actual practices, it is faced with a peculiar methodological problem. This may be glossed as 'the problem of the invisibility of common sense'. Members have a practical rather than a theoretical interest in their constitutive work. Therefore, they take common sense and its constitutive practices for granted, unless some sorts of 'trouble' make attention necessary. So an early strategy of Garfinkel was to 'breach' expectations in order to generate this kind of trouble (Garfinkel, 1963, 1964,1967a: 35–75). For ethnomethodology, commonsense practices are the topic of study, but those practices are also, unavoidably, used as a resource for any study one may try to undertake. Without the use of commonsense, its object of study would be simply unavailable, because it is constituted by the application of commonsense methods, such as 'the documentary method of interpretation' (cf. Chapter 2, pp. 21–2; Garfinkel, 1967a: 76–103). So the problem for ethnomethodology is how commonsense practices and commonsense knowledge can lose their status as an unexamined 'resource', in order to become a 'topic' for analysis (cf. Zimmerman & Pollner, 1971). They characterize the situation in sociology at large as follows:

> In contrast to the perennial argument that sociology belabors the obvious, we propose that sociology has yet to treat the obvious as a phenomenon. We argue that the world of everyday life, while furnishing sociology with its favored topics of inquiry, is seldom a topic in its own right. Instead, the familiar, common-sense world, shared by the sociologist and his subjects alike, is employed as an unexplicated resource for contemporary sociological investigations.
>
> Sociological inquiry is addressed to phenomena recognized and described in common-sense ways (by reliance on the unanalyzed properties of natural language), while at the same time such common-sense recognitions and descriptions are pressed into service as fundamentally unquestioned resources for analyzing the phenomena thus made available for study. Thus, contemporary sociology is characterized by a confounding of topic and resource. (Zimmerman & Pollner, 1971: 80–1)

To remedy this 'confusion', they offer the following:

> We propose to suspend conventional interest in the topics of members' practical investigations and urge the placing of exclusive emphasis on inquiry into practical investigations themselves, lay or professional. The topic then would consist not in the social order as ordinarily conceived, but rather in the ways in which members assemble particular scenes so as to provide for one another evidence of a social order as-ordinarily-conceived. (Zimmerman & Pollner, 1971: 83)

Formulated in this way, it is a double-faced problem: on the one hand a problem of minimizing the unexamined use of commonsense, and on the other that of maximizing its examinability. This double-sided problem seems to be in principle unsolvable, one is bound to lose either the resource or the topic. So what one has to do is to find practical solutions, which are unavoidably compromises. I will presently suggest a typology of the solutions that have been tried in ethnomethodology so far.

Four strategies

The first strategy is especially prominent in Garfinkel's early work (1967a). This strategy consists of the close study of sense-making activities in situations where they are especially prominent. Such situations are those in which sharp discrepancies, between on the one hand existing expectations and/or competencies, and on the other practical behavioural and/or interpretive tasks, necessitate extraordinary sense-making efforts by members. Such situations may occur naturally – as in the case of a 'transsexual' studied by Garfinkel (1967a: 116–85) – or they may be created on purpose – as in the 'breaching' experiments, mentioned before.

In order to escape some of the practical and ethical problems generated by such experiments, a second strategy was developed. In this researchers study their own sense-making work by putting themselves in some kind of extra-ordinary situation. This may be a situation where routine sense-making procedures are bound to fail, or where one has to master a difficult and unknown task, or where one is instructed by a setting's members to see the world in a way that is natural for them but not for oneself. Mehan & Wood (1975) use the expression 'becoming the phenomenon', while Schwartz & Jacobs (1979) recommend strategies of becoming the Stranger or the Novice. Out of many possible examples I would like to mention David Sudnow's (1978, 2001) study of becoming a jazz piano player, and Lawrence Wieder's (1974a and b) study of his being instructed in the use of 'the Convict Code' as a general interpretive and explanatory device in a half-way house for paroled addicts.[1] A special case of a (partly) 'procedural self-study' is available in a book by Albert Robillard, *Meaning of a disability: the lived experience of paralysis,* (1999), in which he describes his experiences as a disabled person suffering from the ASL disease (amyotrophic lateral sclerosis, causing severe paralysis).

The third strategy is the one that most resembles traditional ethnographic fieldwork. It consists of closely observing situated activities in their natural settings and discussing them with the seasoned practitioners, in order to study the competences involved in the routine performance of these activities. To further this close study, or to be able to study these activities after the fact, recording equipment may be used, but quite often researchers using this strategy rely on traditional note-taking in order to produce their data. Examples of this kind of study can be found in Garfinkel's (1967a) work on juries and coroners, Zimmerman's (1969) study of case-workers in a welfare agency, and Lynch's (1985) research on laboratory scientists.

The fourth strategy involves the study of ordinary practices by first mechanically recording some of their 'products', by the use of audio or video equipment, as is the standard practice in CA. These recordings are then transcribed in a way that limits the use of commonsense procedures to hearing what is being said and noting how it has been said. The transcriptions are used to locate some 'orderly products'. It is the analyst's task, then, to formulate one or more 'devices' which may have been used to produce that 'product' and phenomena like it (cf. Sacks, 1984a). I will discuss various aspects of these procedures in a later section of this chapter (pp. 41–52).

In actual practice, these strategies tend to be combined in various ways. In examples of the first three types, a tendency exists to use literal quotes from what was said by the research subjects, as in Garfinkel's (1967a) reports of his 'experiments', while in more recent studies recordings and transcripts tend to be used, as in Garfinkel et al. (1981) and Lynch (1985). So a technical aspect of the fourth strategy is often adopted in the first three. Wieder's study, here cited as exemplifying the second strategy, can also be seen as an example of the third, as his analysis of his own learning of and being instructed in 'seeing' the world of the half-way house in terms of 'the code' is embedded in general ethnographic descriptions. There is a major difference, however, between the first three strategies – ethnomethodological studies in the stricter sense – and the fourth – CA, at least in its 'pure' form. In the first set, specific circumstances are created or sought out, where sense-making activities are more prominent and consequently easier studied. In this way ethnomethodology displays a strategic preference for the extra-ordinary.[2] In contrast to this, pure CA tends to focus on the utterly mundane, the ordinary chit-chat of everyday life. While in ethnomethodology the 'visibility problem' is – in part – solved by the creation or selection of 'strange' environments, in CA this 'estranging' task is performed by the recording machine and the transcription process. In more recent years, however, CA-type analyses are increasingly embedded in and inspired by more ethnographically informed understandings, especially in so-called 'workplace studies' focused on technologically complex environments.[3]

The general idea behind the use of these strategies is thus to evade as far as possible the unthinking and unnoticed use of commonsense that seems to be inherent in empirical research practices in sociology. The ethnomethodological critique of these practices comes down to the objection that in so doing one studies idealized and de-contextualized 'reconstructions' of social life, made by the research subjects and/or the researcher, instead of that life in its own situated particulars.[4] So ethnographers may be said to study their own field notes as an unexamined resource for their study of a community's life. Or researchers using interviews study the responses they have recorded as an unexamined resource for their study of 'underlying' opinions and unobserved activities. In both cases, the situated 'production' of those materials is not given systematic attention in its own right. The theoretical objects of such studies tend to be either individuals or collectivities. In contrast to such a 'methodological individualism' or 'collectivism', ethnomethodology and CA prefer a position that is closer to what Karin Knorr-Cetina (1981, 1988) has called 'methodological situationalism.'[5]

Common sense as inevitable resource

The above critique concerning researchers' reliance on commonsense can also be turned against ethnomethodology and CA themselves. Although the 'unthinking' use of commonsense may be minimized, it cannot be eliminated completely, but this fact is not too often acknowledged. I will now discuss three cases where ethnomethodological writers have discussed this problem quite frankly. The first of these is Don Zimmerman's Preface to Wieder's (1974a) half-way house study.

Zimmerman points to the general, sensible and unavoidable use of what he calls 'idealizations' in the natural and social sciences as well as in everyday life. Idealizations are selective, abstract and logically coherent constructions that are used to collect phenomena in terms of selected features judged to be relevant from a specific, for instance theoretical, point of view. Although he acknowledges the success of this procedure in the natural sciences, he sees certain drawbacks in its use in the social sciences: 'a necessary consequence is the suppression of whole classes of data'. He specifically objects to uses that ignore the fact that idealization is itself a feature of the social life studied, both as a natural part of 'scientific theorizing', 'as well as within the domain of everyday life – in the form of common-sense typifications'.

> The phenomena of interest, then, are what Schutz (1962) refers to as second-order phenomena, namely members' idealizations of their own and others' behavior . . . Social reality consists of the common-sense, practical activity of everyday 'idealizations' of the social world and activities within it. . . . For ethnomethodologists, idealizations (or rational constructions) of the social world must be recognized as also having the features of being 'done from within the world' and being 'part and parcel of that world', i.e., what Garfinkel (1967) calls 'reflexive features'. (Zimmerman in Wieder, 1974a: 22–3)

So idealizations are always and unavoidably used, in ordinary life as well as in the sciences. The point is to recognize this and to take it into account in one's own idealizing practices. How this is to be done is less clear, however. My second case throws some light on this from a CA-inspired perspective. In a critique of 'speech act theory' as proposed by J.L. Austin, Roy Turner formulates a position which I will quote in full, because it is so carefully drafted.

> As a solution to the vexed problem of the relation between the shared cultural knowledge (members' knowledge) that the sociologist possesses and the analytic apparatus that it is his responsibility to produce, I propose the following:
> A. The sociologist inevitably trades on his members' knowledge in recognizing the activities that participants to interaction are engaged in; for example, it is by virtue of my status as a competent member that I can recurrently locate in my transcripts instances of 'the same' activity. This is not to claim that members are infallible or that there is perfect agreement in recognizing any and every instance; it is only to claim that no resolution of problematic cases can be effected by resorting to procedures that are supposedly uncontaminated by members' knowledge. (Arbitrary resolutions, made for the sake of easing the problems of 'coding', are of course no resolution at all for the present enterprise.)
> B. The sociologist, having made his first-level decision on the basis of members' knowledge, must then pose as problematic how utterances come off as recognizable unit activities. This requires the sociologist to explicate the resources he shares with the participants in making sense of utterances in a stretch of talk. At every step of the way, inevitably, the sociologist will continue to employ his socialized competence, while continuing to make explicit what these resources are and how he employs them. I see no alternative to these procedures, except to pay no explicit attention to one's socialized knowledge while continuing to use it as an indispensable aid. In short, sociological discoveries are ineluctably discoveries from within the society. (Turner, 1971: 177)

What Turner suggests is that ethnomethodological research is done in two phases. In the first the researcher uses his own membership knowledge to understand his materials, while in the second he analyses this understanding from a procedural perspective.[6] The four strategy-types, discussed above, differ in the way in which they produce their materials. But always the study of these materials can be seen as organized into these two phases of membership understanding and procedural analysis. In Wieder's (1974a) book on a half-way house, for instance, the first part is largely devoted to an ethnographic study of the setting from which the concept of a convict code emerges, while the second deals with the ways in which this code is used as a daily interpretive and explanatory device.

My third case of ethnomethodologists discussing their reliance on commonsense is taken from the book by Michael Lynch and David Bogen *The spectacle of history: speech, text, and memory at the Iran-Contra hearings* (1996), which is the study of the ways in which the parties to these hearings struggle to have their version of 'what happened' recorded as the facts of the case.

In the Introduction they write that their aim is to describe 'the production of history', and not to 'deconstruct' it. In fact, a major phenomenon in those hearings was the pervasiveness of 'deconstruction' as a practical activity, as each party tried to undermine the accounts provided by the other. Therefore, the activity of 'deconstruction' is not part of their own methodological agenda, but is instead what they call 'a perspicuous feature of the struggle' they are dealing with. They concede that they will have to use 'commonsense', although they do not use that particular expression when they write:

> We shall assume an ability to describe and exhibit recognizable features of the video text we have chosen to examine. In this effort we shall inevitably engage in constructive (i.e., productive) practices, such as using the video text as a proxy for the live performances of interrogators and witnesses, and selectively using written transcripts to exhibit recurrent discursive actions. (Lynch & Bogen, 1996: 14)

In other words, they rely on their own ordinary members' competences as any (informed) viewer/hearer of the tapes would, and they concede that their own use of tapes and documents inevitably also involves 'constructive' work, which might be criticized as such by others.

Furthermore, they explicitly refuse to follow the common practice in the social sciences of formulating a pre-given set of methodological procedures as grounds for the selection and interpretation of their data. Instead they trust that their methods are self-evident from their text and they add that these are 'are organized around, and take many of their initiatives from, the complexity and circumstances of the case at hand'. So again, they present their own, ethnomethodological work on the data as 'ordinary' and intelligible to 'any member'. And then they construct a contrast between this ordinary way of knowing and what is presented as ideal in conventional social science.

> Although it is fashionable to attribute latent epistemologies to a text or practice being analyzed, ethnomethodology's approach to practical action and practical reasoning is more in line with the Aristotelian concept of 'phronesis.' Unlike episteme – the geometrical method of deducing proofs from axioms – phronesis takes its departure from the conventional recognizability of a perspicuous case. The

presumption is that a community of readers will grasp enough of the details in question, with no need to justify such understanding on ultimate grounds, so that relevant maxims and precedents can be brought to bear on the case and extended to others like it. The failure of such a method to live up to the universal standards of procedure and proof associated with Euclidean geometry carries no necessary stigma. Indeed, it can be argued that science and mathematics do not fully exemplify episteme, and that at the moment of their production all inquiries involve an effort to come to terms with relevant circumstances. (Lynch & Bogen, 1996: 15)

In effect, then, the authors offer a contrast between 'ordinary' understanding practices and 'formal' idealizations concerning proper ways of knowing, that are ascribed to mathematics and the sciences, although they suggest that even inquiries that fall under the latter auspices in actual fact also require 'ordinary' practices of understanding (cf. for further elaborations and illustrations: Livingston, 1986, 1999; Lynch, 1985, 1993). So, rather than claiming adherence to a set of formal principles, they, as ethnomethodologists, refer to their co-membership of a 'community of readers' as a good enough basis for the intelligibility of their research materials as well as their own elaborations of those materials.

Ethnomethodology makes a topic of cases under inquiry in law, medicine, science, and daily life. This does not necessarily place the ethnomethodologist at a metaphysical or epistemological advantage *vis-à-vis* the practical actions studied, since any analysis of such actions is itself responsible for coming to terms with the circumstantially specific and immanently recognizable features of the case before it. (Lynch & Bogen, 1996: 15)

They are not after some sort of 'deeper' understanding of what happened and they do not try to replace one or another theory of meaning with their own. And neither are they trying to evaluate the truth value of one or another version of 'what happened'.

In view of the fact that so much social-scientific, literary, and philosophical effort has been devoted to getting to the bottom of discourse, our aim of sticking to the surface of the text may strike some readers as curious. It is our view, however, that any deeper readings would have to ignore the complexity and texture of the surface events, and thus they would fail to explicate how an order of activities is achieved as a contingent, moment-by-moment production. (Lynch & Bogen, 1996: 16)

What should again be evident in these remarks is that ethnomethodology takes a very special position *vis-à-vis* commonsense knowledge and ways of knowing, as constituting an unavoidably used resource, as well as the topic of inquiry. We can note, moreover, two important consequences of this position. The first is that in the 'first phase' of their inquiries, ethnomethodologists' reliance on commonsense methods of knowing puts them in the relation of cultural colleagues *vis-à-vis* their readers, and therefore they do not need any special warrants for their claim to understand their materials. The second consequence, however, connected to the second phase of inquiry, necessitates that they take a distance *vis-à-vis* the differential interests and disputes of commonsense life. So in the case of the study by Lynch and Bogen, they are not in a position to take issue with the disputes they study, but instead they study the ways in which these differences are 'produced' in the circumstances in which they occur. The label used to point to this particular kind of distantiation is 'ethnomethodological indifference', which I will discuss in the last chapter. But now I will proceed to a treatment of the (in-)famous 'breaching experiments' and, as a contrast, ethnomethodology's and especially CA's, reliance on electro-mechanical recordings.

Garfinkel's breaching experiments

The aspect of Garfinkel's work that was most surprising to outsiders was his use of experimental demonstrations in which covert expectations were 'breached'. Of course people were familiar with a range of experimental set-ups in social psychology, which often involved quite elaborate deceptions, but these were based on a strictly defined cause-and-effect model and used elaborate 'controls' and quantitative methods to produce reliable results. In contrast to these, the design of Garfinkel's experiments was 'loose' and their effects were not discussed in terms of causes and effects. Furthermore, only some of them were done in a laboratory setting, while many were 'field experiments' given as assignments to his students. And while Garfinkel used the terms 'experiment' and 'experimenter' in his reports, he also stressed their special character as follows:

> A word of reservation. Despite their procedural emphasis, my studies are not properly speaking experimental. They are demonstrations designed, in Herbert Spiegelberg's phrase, as 'aids to a sluggish imagination.' I have found that they produce reflections through which the strangeness of an obstinately familiar world can be detected. (Garfinkel, 1967a: 38)

So in terms of their function, these arrangements might be called 'pedagogical demonstrations', and as such they are part of a larger collection of often ingenious, surprising and at times humorous instructions. The ultimate 'target' of these demonstrations was always the 'incompleteness' of efforts at literal description of, or pointed instructions for, real-worldly events. Because of this 'incompleteness', such descriptions and instructions always and inevitably involve further 'work' when used in everyday situations. In the first chapter of the *Studies*, for example, Garfinkel reports on a study of coding practices (18–24). Two graduate students had to code the contents of clinic folders in terms of a coding sheet designed as part of a study of selection criteria and patient careers. It soon became clear that the coders, in order to code the folder contents to their satisfaction as adequate descriptions of what happened in the clinic, constantly used informal knowledge of clinic procedures. In other words, the instructions contained in the coding sheets were always insufficient to do the coding. Coders had to rely on additional reasoning which Garfinkel glosses as '*ad hoc* considerations', including '"et cetera," "unless;" "let it pass," and "factum valet" (i.e., an action that is otherwise prohibited by a rule is counted correct once it is done)' (20–1).

Garfinkel's student assignments often had a similar overall target. He asked his students, for instance, to write up at the left of a sheet of paper a conversation in which they had participated, adding in a separate column to the right 'what they and their partners understood that they were talking about' (38). He quotes one example and discusses it at some length in two different chapters (24–31, 38–42).

> Students filled out the left side of the sheet quickly and easily, but found the right side incomparably more difficult. When the assignment was made, many asked how much I wanted them to write. As I progressively imposed accuracy, clarity, and distinctness, the task became increasingly laborious. Finally, when I required that they assume I would know what they had actually talked about only from reading literally what they wrote literally, they gave up with the complaint that the task was impossible. (Garfinkel, 1967a: 26)

Both parties to a conversation used and relied on a presupposedly common body of knowledge to 'hear' what was said as making sense, using the progression of successively produced items as 'documents' to be elaborated in a process of discovering what was meant, as an underlying 'pattern' (cf. 'The documentary method', discussed in the previous chapter, p. 21). Garfinkel concludes that:

> The anticipation that persons will understand, the occasionality of expressions, the specific vagueness of references, the retrospective-prospective sense of a present occurrence, waiting for something later in order to see what was meant before, are sanctioned properties of common discourse. (Garfinkel, 1967a: 41)

Many of the breaching experiments can be seen as further elaborations of this theme of the 'incompleteness' of literal descriptions and instructions, and the unavoidable use of *ad hoc* considerations relying on available informal knowledge. For instance: 'Students were instructed to engage an acquaintance or a friend in an ordinary conversation and, without indicating that what the experimenter was asking was in any way unusual, to insist that the person clarify the sense of his commonplace remarks' (1967a: 42).

Here's one of the examples quoted by Garfinkel:

> The subject was telling the experimenter, a member of the subject's car pool, about having had a flat tire while going to work the previous day.
> (S) I had a flat tire.
> (E) What do you mean, you had a flat tire?
> She appeared momentarily stunned. Then she answered in a hostile way: 'What do you mean, "What do you mean?" A flat tire is a flat tire. That is what I meant. Nothing special. What a crazy question!' (Garfinkel, 1967a: 42)

In another experiment students were asked to look at familiar scenes *as if* these were not familiar at all. They had to spend 'from fifteen minutes to an hour in their homes viewing its activities while assuming that they were boarders in the household', while not acting out that assumption (p. 45).

Garfinkel remarks that the students 'behaviorized' their descriptions of the household scenes observed. They omitted their knowledge of personal histories, relationships and motives, as in: 'A short, stout man entered the house, kissed me on the cheek and asked, 'How was school?' . . . He walked into the kitchen, kissed the younger of the two women, and said hello to the other.' (One could say that such descriptions seem like a parody of 'doing science'.) The students were surprised about the 'personal' ways in which family members treated each other, and also about bad table manners and lack of politeness. Quite often they reported that taking the boarder attitude brought about an impression of 'quarrelling, bickering, and hostile motivations' that was not the 'true' picture of their family.[7]

In a subsequent assignment, the students were asked not only to take a boarder's perspective for themselves, but also to act on it. As Garfinkel reports:

> the scenes exploded with the bewilderment and anger of family members. . . . In [most] cases family members were stupefied. They vigorously sought to make the strange actions intelligible and to restore the situation to normal appearances. Reports were filled with accounts of astonishment, bewilderment, shock, anxiety, embarrassment, and anger, and with charges by various family members that the student was mean, inconsiderate, selfish, nasty, or impolite. Family members demanded explanations. What's the matter? What's gotten into you? Did you get fired? Are you sick? What are you being so superior about? Why are you mad? Are you out of your mind or are you just stupid? . . .
>
> Explanations were sought in previous, understandable motives of the student: the student was 'working too hard' in school; the student was 'ill'; there had been 'another fight' with a fiancee. When offered explanations by family members went unacknowledged, there followed withdrawal by the offended member, attempted isolation of the culprit, retaliation, and denunciation. (Garfinkel, 1967a: 47–8)

In general the results of these and other breaching experiments can be summarized as follows: when the 'seen but unnoticed' assumptions, on which the perception of 'a world known in common and taken for granted' is based, are somehow contradicted, members first try to ward off the danger involved by various ways of alternative sense-making, but if this does not solve the issue, they display often quite strong affects of shock, bewilderment and anger.

As I said, most of these demonstrations were field experiments with student experimenters, but a few were done in a laboratory setting with similar results. In one set-up subjects were instructed to ask questions about some personal problem in yes/no format and – after they received an answer – record their comments and interpretations, before asking another question. In fact the choice of an answer as 'yes' or 'no' was based on a table of random numbers. The subjects did not know this and were most of the time able to hear the 'yes' or 'no' as a sensible answer to their question. Garfinkel used this experiment as a demonstration of 'the documentary method of interpretation', treating it not so much as a specific 'method' of 'interpretative sociology', but rather as one used unavoidably in everyday life as well as in all kinds of sociological inquiry (Garfinkel, 1967a: 76–103; cf. also previous discussions on pp. 21–2).

Taken as a whole, Garfinkel's 'breaching experiments' were explicative devices or pedagogical tricks clarifying and demonstrating conceptual issues, rather than research projects as ordinarily perceived. In later periods he has continued to use these and similar devices. He has, for example, asked people to do normally simple tasks, like filling a cup with water, while wearing 'inverting lenses', which produce an upside-down view of the world (Garfinkel, 2002: 207–12). He has also continued to refer to what might be called 'natural breaches', as for instance provided by people with various kinds of sight impairment (2002: 212–16). One student reported that she avoided a particular coffee machine because people waiting to use it did no form a neat queue but just crowded around the machine, while still being able to know who was 'next' without saying anything. The problem she had with this set-up was that, because she lacked peripheral vision (seeing things from 'the corner of your eye'), she could not adequately join this ordering game. In other words, her inability in this situation made the others' unacknowledged abilities discernible in contrast. What is remarkable in these later 'breach' observations is that they 'open our eyes' to tacit skills of a visual, pre-verbal kind, of bodily enactment, rather than the more verbally oriented previous ones.

But Garfinkel's experiments and demonstrations have not become stock-in-trade ways of doing ethnomethodological studies, although in some respects they have influenced the ways in which ethnomethodologists choose research settings and approaches, for instance by investigating settings or experiences in which sense-making was, for some 'natural' reason, especially acute.

Recordings and transcripts

As noted before, many if not most studies that belong to the family of ethnomethodology and conversation analysis use recordings of actual, mostly 'natural' interaction as their major, and in CA often only, data source. I will concentrate in this section on the ways in which this is done in CA, as this is the most obvious and standardized way in which recordings are used. And I will especially discuss how recordings are transformed into CA 'data' by transcribing tapes using a set of conventions originally devised by Gail Jefferson.[8]

A couple of quotes from Harvey Sacks' lectures and from an introductory essay for a collection of CA papers, may help to further clarify the intimate relationship between CA's purposes and its methodological practices.

> When I started to do research in sociology I figured that sociology could not be an actual science unless it was able to handle the details of actual events, handle them formally, and in the first instance be informative about them in the direct ways in which primitive sciences tend to be informative – that is, that anyone else can go and see whether what was said is so. And that is a tremendous control on seeing whether one is learning anything. . . .

I started to work with tape-recorded conversations. Such materials had a single virtue, that I could replay them. I could transcribe them somewhat and study them extendedly – however long it might take. The tape-recorded materials constituted a 'good enough' record of what happened. Other things, to be sure, happened, but at least what was on the tape had happened. It was not from any large interest in language or from some theoretical formulation of what should be studied that I started with tape-recorded conversations, but simply because I could get my hands on it and I could study it again and again, and also, consequentially, because others could look at what I had studied and make of it what they could, if, for example, they wanted to be able to disagree with me. (Sacks, 1984a: 26)[9]

So, for Sacks, working with tape-recorded conversations had a kind of exemplary value in making the details of actual human action available for close scrutiny and formal analysis. As already indicated in the previous chapter, that meant for him being able to formulate 'rules, techniques, procedures, methods, maxims' that would 'provide for' the observed details (cf. p. 26). He also quite often used the word 'machinery' to point to his ultimate analytic object, as in the following:

Thus is it not any particular conversation, as an object, that we are primarily interested in. Our aim is to get into a position to transform, in an almost literal, physical sense, our view of 'what happened,' from a matter of a particular interaction done by particular people, to a matter of interactions as products of a machinery. We are trying to find the machinery. In order to do so we have to get access to its products. At this point, it is conversation that provides us such access. (Sacks, 1984a: 26–7)[10]

It should be noted that this metaphor of 'machinery', i.e. a set of rules, that produces conversation has been more or less dropped from the CA vocabulary. What is still important, however, is that an analytic understanding of the 'technology of conversation' that interactants are using requires *access* to a detailed record of 'what happened', i.e. what was done and how. It is this detailed access that recordings provide.

In the quote below, Heritage and Atkinson spell out some further virtues of CA's reliance on recorded data.

(T)he use of recorded data serves as a control on the limitations and fallibilities of intuition and recollection; it exposes the observer to a wide range of interactional materials and circumstances and also provides some guarantee that analytic conclusions will not arise as artifacts of intuitive idiosyncrasy, selective attention or recollection or experimental design. The availability of a taped record enables *repeated* and *detailed* examination of particular events in interaction and hence greatly enhances the range and precision of the observations that can be made. The use of such materials has the additional advantage of providing hearers and, to a lesser extent, readers of research reports with *direct* access to the data about which analytic claims are being made, thereby making them available for public scrutiny in a way that further minimizes the influence of individual preconception. (Heritage & Atkinson, 1984: 4)

Recording, then, provide researchers with a transportable object that can be studied again and again, and put on display for others. It is only in this way that one can get access to the details of turn-taking and sequencing practices, which are of major interest in CA studies.

As noted in the first quote in this section, one virtue of using recordings is that one can produce a transcription of what is being said. In principle, a transcription is a 'translation' of the oral language used in the interaction, as heard and understood by the transcriber, into the written version of that language. In a typical CA transcription the written rendering of the spoken discourse is modified to a certain extent to simulate the way in which the utterances were actually produced, while a variety of symbols are added to the text as indications of still more production details. The conventions for this kind of transcription, fitted to CA's evolving interests, were devised by Gail Jefferson, in close cooperation with Harvey Sacks and Emanuel Schegloff. It is generally felt that transcriptions should be seen as a practical compromise between various desirabilities and possibilities. They never catch all the relevant details of the recording and should not, in principle, be treated as 'the data', but only as a selective rendering of the data (cf. Heritage & Atkinson, 1984:12). The activity of transcription constitutes a particular phase in the process of doing conversation analysis, as depicted in the following sequential schema:[11]

> Original (inter-)action → *recording* → (audio/video-)record → *transcription* → transcript → (action) *understanding* → procedural *analysis* → analytical argument

In this schema, the *italicized processes* are selectively reductive *vis-à-vis* the preceding states/products. One may consider the specific properties of these selective reductions, which can be seen as 'losing' features of the preceding state and/or as focusing on (and foregrounding) features of specific interest. When 'looking forward' the processes may be seen as instrumental in gaining a sharper focus on the phenomena of interest, which were already present in the preceding state. 'Looking backwards', however, you will have to admit that you cannot reconstitute the earlier state from the later rendering, because features that may have been essential in constituting the earlier state in its full richness are no longer available in the later rendering. This is another version of the asymmetrical properties of the action–account pair, as often noted by Harold Garfinkel (cf. Garfinkel & Wieder, 1992).

The purpose of the first two processes, i.e. *recording* and *transcription*, is to produce a non-perishable, transportable and manageable representation – an 'immutable mobile,' as Bruno Latour (1987: 228) calls it – to assist in the later processes of *understanding* and *analysis*.

Gail Jefferson starts her 1985 essay on the transcription and analysis of laughter as follows:

> I take it that when we talk about transcription we are talking about one way to pay attention to recordings of actually occurring events. While those of us who spend a lot of time making transcripts may be doing our best to get it right, what that might mean is utterly obscure and unstable. It depends a great deal on what we are paying attention to. It seems to me, then, that the issue is not transcription per se, but what it is we might want to transcribe, that is, attend to. (Jefferson, 1985: 25)

In other words, the inevitable reduction, simplification and idealization which are the effect of these processes, have to be considered in terms of the specific analytic interests that are brought to bear on the original events. Before discussing the cost of the inevitable losses which the two processes of *recording* and *transcription* bring about, one has to clarify which aspects, properties or features of the original will have to be analysed and explicated. In short, one has to be clear about one's analytic object.

In her 1985 essay on the transcription and analysis of laughter, Jefferson contrasts, referring to everyday occasions, the treatment *in* subsequent talk *of* previous talk and of previous laughter: while talk may be quoted (and perhaps even mimicked), laughter does not seem to be 'quotable' to the same extent. Similarly, in transcripts, laughter used to be *described* rather than *transcribed*. It may be useful to elaborate this contrast a bit, exploring the rendering of problems in another area of practical activity, field biology.

Bird song depictions in field guides

Consider what the writers of field guides for bird watchers do when they discuss bird songs as a property of a species.

KLEINE KAREKIET [Reed Warbler]

. . . Geluid: een laag *tsjur*, een scherp, alarmerend *skurr* (als dat van Rietzanger) en een zwak tikkend geluid. Aangehouden zang lijkt op die van Rietzanger, maar is meer herhalend en maatvast: *tsjirruk-tsjirruk, djek, djek, tirri-tirri-tirri*, vermengd met vloeiende en nabootsende geluiden. Zingt overdag en 'snachts.

[Voice: a low *tsjur*, a sharp, alarming *skurr* (like that of the sedge warbler) and a weak ticking sound. Prolonged song similar to that of the sedge warbler, but more repetitive and steady: *tsjirruk-tsjirruk, djek, djek, tirri-tirri-tirri*, mixed with flowing and imitative sounds. Sings in daytime and at night.] (Peterson et al., 1984)

Kleine Karekiet

GELUID Roep een kort, onopvallend *tsje,* soms iets harder, bijna smakkend *tsjk.* Bij opwinding een langgerekt, schor *sjrieh,* een vet, rollend *sjrrre* en een tweelettergrepig *trr-rr.* Zang 'babbelend' in laag tempo, bestaand uit nerveuze, 2–4 keer herhaalde noten (onomatopoëtisch), af en toe onderbroken door imitaties of fluittonen, *trett trett trett TIRri TIRri truu truu TIe tre tre wi-wuu-wu tre tre truu truu TIRri TIRri. . . .* Tempo af en toe hoger, maar nooit met crescendo van Rietzanger.

[SOUND Call a short, unremarkable *tsje,* at times a bit louder, almost smacking *tsjk.* In excitement a long-drawn, hoarse *sjrieh,* a fat, rolling *sjrrre* and a two-syllable *trr-rr.* Song 'babbling' at a slow tempo, consisting of nervous, 2–4 time repeated notes (onomatopoetic), now and then interrupted by imitations or whistlings, *trett trett trett TIRri TIRri truu truu TIe tre tre wi-wuu-wu tre tre truu truu TIRri TIRri. . . .* Tempo now and then higher, but never in crescendo like the sedge warbler.] (Mullarney et al., 2000)

Note in these examples a mixture of *descriptions* and some efforts at *transcription*, with for the same species rather different results! The purpose of the *trans*criptions is, of course, to compensate for the limited success of *des*criptions for the purpose at hand: making actually heard calls and songs identifiable as produced by specific species of birds. The language of humans is of limited use in providing a recognizable image of calls and songs produced by birds. In the same vein, laughter by humans seems to be difficult to 'picture' as well, as we will see next.

Transcription versus description

Returning to Jefferson's essay, I quote two different versions of transcripts by her of the same recording:

(7) (GTS:1:1:14, 1965)
Ken: And he came home and decided he was gonna play with
    his orchids from then on in.
Roger: With his <u>what?</u>
Louise: heh heh heh beh
Ken: With his orchids.   [He has an orchid-
Roger: [Oh heh hehheh
Louise: ((through bubbling laughter)) Playing with his organ yeah
    I thought the same thing!
Ken: No he's got a great big [glass house-
Roger: [I can see him playing with his
    organ hehh hhhh

                                        (Jefferson, 1985: 28)

(GTS:1:2:33:r2, 1977)

Ken: An'e came <u>h</u>ome'n decided'e wz gonna play with iz o:rchids.
    from then on i:n.
Roger: With iz <u>what</u>?
Louise: mh hih <u>h</u>ih [huh
Ken: [With iz <u>o</u>rchids.=
Ken: Ee [z got an <u>o</u>rch[id-
Roger: [Oh:.   [<u>h</u>ehh[h a h 'he:h] '<u>h</u>eh
Louise: [<u>h</u>eh huh '<u>hh</u>] PLAYN(h)W(h)IZ 0(h)R'N
    ya:h <u>I</u> [thought the [same
Roger: [<u>u</u>h::   ['<u>h</u>unhh 'hh 'hh
Ken: [Cz eez gotta great big [gla:ss house]=
Roger: [I c'n s(h)ee
Ken: =[(
Roger: =[im pl(h)ay with iz o(h)r(h)g'(h)n 'uh

                                        (Jefferson, 1985: 29)

The crux of Jefferson's argument is that the later transcription allows one to analyse the interaction taking place in greater depth, because it provides details of timing and interaction that are not available in the first rendering. In the case at hand, she suggests, it does not seem to be an accident that the girl laughs through the obscenity, producing it in a suggestive but not well-articulated manner, while continuing afterwards in an undisturbed voice. Extending her argument, one can suggest that the standard orthography rendering of spoken interaction, i.e. in the language of writing, is a poor means to picture the hearably functioning details of that interaction.

When CA researchers start working on a transcription task, they are faced with a number of choices. Any actually produced transcription is analysable as a practical but always ambivalent solution to inescapable dilemmas in transcription routines.

- The use of standard orthography, with more or less adaptations to display some of the properties of the actual speech production: 'words-as-spoken' versus 'sounds-as-uttered'.
- The use of mechanical timing devices for pauses, versus a reliance on informal procedures like counting syllables in muttered words, as an unavoidable subjective 'measure' that may take into account pace relativity.
- Decisions regarding formatting issues, for example line breaks to signal 'describable actions' versus a more continuous rendering.

I have discussed these and other practical issues of doing transcriptions elsewhere (Ten Have, 1999a: 75–97; cf. also Psathas & Anderson, 1990). For now, I will just illustrate some of the issues raised so far on the basis of an extract from my own research.

Illustration

The excerpt given below has been taken from a transcript of a recording of a medical consultation made in the Netherlands in the late 1970s. A mother consults along with her daughter. She has described her daughter's complaints in lay terms and then the physician has asked the girl to show him her tongue. After some more descriptions from the mother and one question/answer exchange with the daughter, the physician provides a preliminary diagnosis as follows:

Extract 3.1
54 A: 'hh nou we zullen es kijken,
54 A: 'hh well we will take a look
55 A: d't kan eh (0.5) ↑eenvoudig (0.9) 'te zijn=
55 A: it can uh (0.5) simply (0.9) be
56 A: =>dat ze (bevoorbeeld) wat tekort aan bloed heeft.<
56 A: that she has for instance a little blood shortage
57 A: ze is [↑negen ↓jaar,
57 A: she is [nine years
58 M: [(°ja heb ik ook al°)
58 M: [(°yes I have also already°)
59 A: 'hhh de leeftijden ↑één jaar ↑vier jaar ↑negen,
59 A: 'hhh the ages one year four years and nine
60 A: ja tien elf >zo'n beetje rond-tie tijd,=
60 A: yes ten eleven araound that time

```
61 A: =als ze een beetje< ↑uit gaan schieten.
61 A: when they begin to grow
62 A: 'hhh dat zijn >tijden waarop kinderen vaak=
62 A: 'hhh those are times when children often
63 A: =een beetje ↑bloedarmoede [hebben.
63 A: have a little blood sh[ortage
64 M:                                    [(jjjh) twee jaar >ge↑leden=
64 M:                       [ (jjjh) two years back
65 M: =heeft ze 't ↑ook gehad,=
65 M: she also had that
66 M: =toen ↑ook in september,=
66 M: also in September then
67 M: =toen waren we bij de ↑schoolarts,=
67 M: when we visited the school doctor
68 M: =en toen had ze ↑ook bloed[armoede.<
68 M: =and she also had a blood [shortage then
69 A:        [↓hmm
69 A:        [↓hmm
70 (1.6)
71 A: >'k wee- niet of het wat ↑is=
71 A: I don't know whether it's something
72 A: =maar we kunnen ('t) even (↓prikken).<
72 A: but we can just prick
73 (1.4)
```

As a reader of this transcript, you take on a kind of virtual overhearer's perspective. What you see is a rendering of speaker A talking in lines 54–7, then a short and incomplete contribution by speaker M, partly overlapping A's talk (58), A's continuation in lines 59–63, and just before he is finished, M taking up again, continuing for a few lines (64–68), and just before she finishes, a short 'hmm' from A, then a pause, and finally A starting to talk again (71 and following).

Using the contextual information I provided, you know that A is a physician and M the mother of a young patient. From line 54 onwards, the physician 'has the floor', which he uses to announce a further action (54) and a preliminary diagnosis (56). In line 58 the mother mutters something which I have rendered as '°ja heb ik ook al°', and translated as '°yes I have also already°'. This utterance is obviously not complete, but it can be plausibly expanded into 'ja heb ik ook gedacht', yes I've been thinking of that also already. The doctor does not hearably/visibly react to this muttering; he may not have heard it or he may have chosen to ignore it. In any case, he continues his explanation (57, 59–63), suggesting that the diagnosis may fit into an age-related pattern. Something similar to the earlier muttering happens in line 64, but this time the mother gets the floor, to refer to an earlier experience with a equivalent complaint, which was diagnosed by another doctor. The physician reacts to this in a minimal fashion '↓hmm' (69), then there's a pause, after which he initiates a new phase in the encounter (71).

In such an overall hearer's/reader's description, it is hard to avoid action ascriptions. The overall theme in the account just given is one of turn-taking (Sacks et al., 1978). And it is in terms of turn-taking that most of the CA-specific details in the transcription gain their significance. It is in these terms that one can speak of having the floor, producing a secondary speaker remark, keeping the floor, changing speakership, etc. The turn that A takes in lines 55–6 can be heard as complete, both in terms of propositional content, and of intonation: line 55 is produced hesitantly, while 56 is faster and it ends with a downward, final intonation. Therefore, the mother may have taken his announcement as finished, although in fact it isn't. As she starts her comment a bit slowly, the physician can continue talking. She solves the overlap problem by falling silent before she is finished, although she was able to produce a word or two in the clear. The physician seems to 'accept' her overlap solution by producing a hearable inbreath before he continues his explanation. And again, the transcriptional details provide us with the materials to understand the next speakership change in lines 63/64. We can analyse the explanation's semantic structure to propose that it is possibly complete at that point, while the intonation contour, with a stress on the pre-final key term, and the downward ending of the last one, 'confirms' such an analysis. The mother, however, does not even wait for this final word and produces a semantically empty pre-start item, before she makes another remark, relatively fast and without pauses.

What I have just given can be characterized as a technically informed effort at an 'action understanding' of this small episode. It is technically informed in that I use the CA transcription conventions to point to particular kinds of production details which 'invite' an understanding of the interaction in terms of turn-taking or 'floor management'. What I have done, then, is to use some theoretical and methodological 'tricks of the trade' of CA to elucidate the episode as a negotiation of turns-at-talk. We see the physician keeping the floor for some time and the mother 'watching' him, looking for a usable opening to insert her comments in. Further analyses, for example using ideas from that other Sacksian tradition of membership categorization analysis (cf. the explanation in the previous chapter on pp. 23–4), could be added to it. In MCA terms we can say that we see/hear the physician announcing a diagnosis and the mother inserting her comments of recognition of it as 'another case of what I thought it would be'; that is, the physician is doing his category-bound job, while the mother offers a display of her lay understandings.

Whether we use CA or MCA or both, we start with an overhearer's perspective and then try to use the information we are able to get to reconstruct the participants' perspectives as enacted in the 'overheard' interaction. What we as analysts do, then, is try to convince our readers of the plausibility of this action understanding and the analysis that is based on it, referring to the utterances' properties *foregrounded* by our transcript's details.

In my exemplary analysis, above, I have not used all of the transcript details. In other words, my analysis has not 'exhausted' my transcript. For instance, the intonational information given might be used as grounds for a further analysis of the internal organization of the various turns-at-talk. In the extract's first turn, the part given in line 54 is produced in ordinary pace, the next one in line 55 is 'slower' or 'hesitant' with an 'uh' and two small turn-internal pauses, while the last part on line 56 is 'latched' to the previous part and produced more quickly. One might suggest that there is a certain parallelism here between these production details and the semantic message of these three parts: the first an unproblematic announcement of an upcoming examination, the second an indication of the hypothetical quality of the diagnosis, and the third the actual 'possible diagnosis', with an inserted 'for instance' and the quick pace stressing its 'dismissible' character. Next, the low volume of the mother's unfinished inserted remark may be related to both its quality as an insertion in overlap with the physician's turn, and its semi-private, 'lay' character. When we look at the rhythm of the next two utterances, first by the physician (59–63) and second by the mother (64–8), we can see how they stress the essential and/or enumerative elements in their contributions. The mother's turn, for instance, can be analysed as a three-part list (Jefferson, 1990), with the core elements in lines 65, 66 and 68, and an explanatory insertion in line 67. This structure is punctuated, so to speak, by the three times stressed *also*'s in the core parts. Together with their latched production and continuous intonation, these features make this into a 'strong', hard to interrupt (or ignore) package.

The analytic suggestions given in this section could be elaborated further in various ways. One could discuss comparative instances to substantiate the various claims as to the functional significance of the features discussed. Or one could use these observations as contributions to an analysis of the local accomplishment of, or negotiations about, institutional relationships (Ten Have, 2001a). In the present context, however, the purpose was to offer a restricted demonstration of the analytic fruitfulness of using the Jefferson conventions as a kind of perceptual and thereby analytic shopping list.

Transcription reconsidered

Before I conclude this treatment of transcription,[12] I would like to return for a moment to the earlier digression concerning the description and transcription of bird songs and calls. The examples I quoted and discussed were taken from a particular pragmatic context: field guides to be used by lay or professional ornithologists as an aid in the identification of species of birds.[13] Such usage is based on the assumption of identifiable 'species', i.e. sets of birds that are willing and able to mate and produce fertile offspring. Species, then, are the theoretical objects to which the usage of field guides is oriented. The pragmatics of bird species identification by songs and calls abstracts from individual and local, or as one might say 'cultural' intra-species variations in order to focus on the differential identification of the species. 'A species' is always and inevitably a momentarily 'fixed' construction, a 'violent' cutting-up of the immense variability of life. The proliferation of 'sub-species' in recent field guides as well as phenomena of bastardization attests to the relative arbitrariness of species distinctions.[14]

This analysis can be used to refocus on the pragmatic context of CA transcription. It may be suggested that the theoretical object which is the target of a CA transcription is the set of core devices that has been so far identified in the corpus of CA inquiries. The Jeffersonian transcript conventions represent the accumulated wisdom of the first generation of CA researchers as to the kinds of phenomena that would be good candidates for a CA type of analysis. Individual and local specifics of the recorded sound production are, of course, to be noted to a much greater extent than is done in field guides. But still, making the core phenomena of CA interests – such as the organization of turn-taking, sequencing, repair, etc. – visible is a major function of a CA transcription's selectivity.

However, although this overall orientation to CA's core phenomena seems to be the guiding principle of CA transcription work, two related but distinct abilities are required to bring off useful transcriptions. These are the ability:

- to recognize words; and
- to clearly hear sounds.

The first requires knowledge of a language's vocabulary embedded in the ability to understand spoken language in terms of its written analogue. In that sense transcription is really 'textualization': translating oral language into written language. This phase of hearing what was said involves a kind of applied member's work, in which the transcriber relies on his or her 'ordinary' or 'vulgar' competence as a member of a particular linguistic community.

The second requires the ability to distance oneself to a certain extent from the 'official' language, to hear the sounds as actually spoken. This would seem to be the 'real' transcription, which can be used either to modify the textual version, or to be rendered as such. In this phase, then, the transcriber has to pay a specifically focused and 'constrained' attention to a range of details, as specified in the Jeffersonian conventions, treated as an analytic shopping list. Actual transcription can be seen as a compromise between the two, balancing realist rendering and analytic utility, while still hoping to preserve a certain readability.

Earlier I used Bruno Latour's concept of an 'immutable mobile' to characterize the functions of tapes and transcripts, but of course transcripts are not 'immutable' in a strict sense. One can use different versions of a transcript for different purposes, while the two versions of the laughter sequence transcribed by Jefferson, that I quoted before (p. 45), demonstrate the fact that a transcript can be ameliorated by adding more details. The transcript by myself, which I quoted as an illustration, is a temporarily 'finished' product of a long period of successive ameliorations.[15]

A transcript, then, is no more than a practically useful rendering of a recording of an actual interactional event. What is left of the original is limited to what can be heard and/or seen on the tape. The process of transcription reduces most of the actually hearable sounds to recognizable words in the standardized written version of the language used on the tape, while also allowing the addition to this reduced version of a number of symbols that evoke those aspects of the hearable sounds that have in the CA tradition acquired the status of potential interactional relevance, and thereby theoretical interest. Furthermore, a transcript may serve – when given with a playing of the audio or video record – to *instruct* an audience as to what is there to be heard on the tape. In fact, when working on the transcript, the researcher may become only gradually aware of what there is to be heard.[16] The relationship between this after-the-fact constitution of the sense of an event, and the lived order of that event, is a problematic one. There are no final solutions to sense-making.

Reflecting on ethnomethodology's methods

It was suggested in this chapter that ethnomethodology has some essential methodological problems. The catch-phrase I used was 'the invisibility of commonsense'. The so-called breaching experiments can be seen as efforts to make the workings of commonsense visible and therefore amenable to reflection. At the time these pedagogical demonstrations were devised and enacted, Garfinkel used the concept of 'background expectancies' to elucidate the effects of the breaches. The underlying rationale of the experiments seems to have been that, because the expectancies to be breached are so pervasive, any breach could teach us how members would react in general. One may wonder how this suggestion of generality relates to the stress on local sense-making, which is evident for instance in the remarks on indexicality, as discussed in the previous chapter. One way to deal with this issue is to suggest that, at that time, Garfinkel's overall perspective was still rather close to the philosophy of the natural attitude, as developed by Schutz, which is made explicit in the papers in which the experiments were reported (cf. Garfinkel, 1967a: 35–8, 55–6, 68, 76). But a more substantial argument is that ethnomethodology is interested in the way in which members themselves deal with issues of generality and occasionality, with how in any particular situation generally shared notions and presuppositions can be used to make sense of whatever happens in the scene-at-hand. It is that ordinarily invisible 'work' that is the focus of the breaching experiments. In later phases of the development of the ethnomethodological perspective, ethnomethodological studies were done differently, although Garfinkel continued to use variants of breaching experiments as eye openers for his students (cf. Garfinkel, 2002).

When we turn to the second methodological style discussed in this chapter, the use of *recordings and transcriptions*, as exemplified most clearly in CA, the issues are partly different. Recordings and transcripts are used to document original events in order to produce *immutable mobiles*. The activity of this documenting proceeds in two phases. The first, making the recording, is in general treated as an unproblematic rendering, a 'reproduction', although some technical limitations are recognized. The second, transcription, is, on the other hand, considered an 'artful practice', a 'representation', even a 'construction', which is therefore often officially denied the status of 'data'.[17]

The rationale for working with tapes and transcripts can be summarized as follows. Because tapes can be played again and again, and transcribed with great care, one can gain *access* to details of the organization of verbal interaction that would not otherwise be available. While such details are hard to observe and even harder to remember, one needs repeated replays to capture them. It could be objected that when these details are too difficult to perceive naturally, it seems unlikely that they are relevant for the organization of interaction. The many studies done by conversation analysts have demonstrated, however, that such details *do* in fact play a role in the moment-by-moment fine-tuning which conversationalists practise, even if they may not be able to remember and explicate what they are doing. The Jeffersonian transcription conventions serve as a guide to perception for the analyst, who needs to notice these details before they can be noted. Furthermore, tapes and especially transcripts can be used to share this access to detail, as a check on subjective perception, and as a way to demonstrate the empirical grounds for one's analytic results. In other words, tapes and transcripts have both heuristic and confirmatory functions.

There are, roughly speaking, two ways in which CA studies get done, as *single case* analyses or as *collection studies*. In the first, one piece of data, often an extended fragment, is analysed in detail, while in the second, a larger set of extracts is used to develop a point to be made, with a series of standard cases, different variants, seemingly contrary cases, etc. (cf. Ten Have, 1999a). In the first style, the focus is on one localized and time-bound occasion of interaction, which may be used to display how a particular device is used, but often involves a variety of phenomena in combination. In collection studies, on the other hand, the analyst most often focuses on one particular topic, as on the change-of-state token 'oh' in Heritage (1984b), which is examined in a variety of sequential environments, different types of usage, etc. One can say, therefore, that while the first style still allows phenomena to be located in actually lived situations, the second abstracts from these – except in terms of a local sequential environment – in order to study some general patterns of usage. These and other methodological issues will surface again in the following chapters.

After having examined some methodological aspects of ethnomethodology, in the next chapters we will turn to a contrastive consideration of methods, as used in more conventional qualitative research and in ethnomethodology. First interviews, then documents, and finally ethnography.

Some major points

- It was argued that ethnomethodology has a peculiar methodological problem, because its phenomena of interest, sense-making practices, are

- *hard to notice* in ordinary situations, because they are constitutive of those very situations;
- *unavoidably used* in any research practice itself.
- The research practices common in ethnomethodology can be considered as variant solutions to this problem. Four strategies were discussed:
  (1) *breaching experiments*: creating artificial situations in which members have to do extra sense-making work in order to repair missing or contradicted background expectancies;
  (2) researchers *studying their own* sense-making practices by putting themselves in an extraordinary situation, such as trying to master a difficult task;
  (3) using *field methods* to study natural situations in which sense-making is rather acute for the local participants;
  (4) *recording and transcribing* more or less ordinary activities, in order to study their constitutive methods at some ease.
- As the use of sense-making is inevitable, even for ethnomethodologists, what can be done is to distinguish two phases in the research process:
  (1) understanding the activities under study, using ordinary members' sense-making practices;
  (2) analysing the methods used in the first phase as one's research topic.
- The two strategies discussed in detail in this chapter are evidently not just solutions to a problem, they also generate problems of their own and are necessarily of limited use:
  - breaching experiments were mainly used in instruction, to sensitize students to ethnomethodology's phenomena;
  - recordings, and especially transcripts, are useful to create fixed data extracted from the stream of life; as such they are as 'artificial' as the experiments; they allow, however, the focused study of particular kinds of phenomena which are hard to catch in ordinary observation.
- What remains is a tension between life and science, between the particular and the general.

Recommended reading

For the 'breaching experiments', see Chapters 2 and 3 in Garfinkel's 1967 book (pp. 35–75 and 67–103, respectively); the latter discusses the 'yes/no' experiments (page 40 above):

- Garfinkel, Harold (1967) *Studies in ethnomethodology.* Englewood Cliffs, NJ: Prentice-Hall

For general introductions to the methods and general approach used in conversation analysis, see:

- Have, Paul ten (1999a) *Doing conversation analysis: a practical guide.* London, etc.: Sage

- Hutchby, Ian, Robin Wooffitt (1998) *Conversation analysis: principles, practices and applications*. Cambridge: Polity Press
- Psathas, George (1995) *Conversation analysis: the study of Talk-in-Interaction*. Thousand Oaks, CA: Sage (Qualitative Research Methods 35)

On transcription, read for an overview and instruction:

- Psathas, George, Tim Anderson (1990) 'The "practices" of transcription in conversation analysis', *Semiotica*, 78: 75–99

And for an exemplary consideration:

- Jefferson, Gail (1985) 'An exercise in the transcription and analysis of laughter'. In: Teun A. van Dijk, ed. *Handbook of discourse analysis*, Vol. 3. London: Academic Press: 25–34

Critical discussions of CA's transcription practices can be found in:

- Ashmore, Malcolm, Darren Reed (2000) 'Innocence and nostalgia in conversation analysis: the dynamic relations of tape and transcript', *Forum Qualitative Sozialforschung / Forum: Qualitative Social Research*, 1 (3). Available at: http://qualitative-research.net/fqs-texte/3–00/3–00ashmorereed-e.htm
- Bogen, David (1999) 'The organization of talk', in *Order without rules: critical theory and the logic of conversation,* New York: SUNY Press: 83–120, at 90–3

Notes

1 This study is discussed at greater length in Chapter 6, pp. 124–6.
2 This seems less so for the third type. There is a tendency, though, to select settings in which fact-production is a major task, as in the examples quoted earlier.
3 See note 7 in the previous chapter.
4 For that reason those analyses are often called 'constructive' (Garfinkel & Sacks, 1970); note that in his recent book (2002), Garfinkel uses the label Formal Analysis, rather than 'constructive analysis'.
5 She has formulated this position in terms of the then-current micro/macro and agency/structure debates: 'I shall call methodological situationalism the principle which demands that descriptively adequate accounts of large-scale social phenomena be grounded in statements about actual social behaviour in concrete situations' (1988: 22).
6 A similar model for ethnomethodological research has been developed by Ilja Maso (1984). I used the pair understanding/analysis earlier in my explication of CA's practice (Ten Have, 1999a).
7 This finding is remarkably similar to remarks repeatedly made by Labov & Fanshel (1977) to the effect that what they call microanalysis 'magnifies the aggressive mechanisms of conversation and effectively cancels the work of mitigating devices' (p. 352). They report the following incident. 'One student submitted to us a half-hour tape recording of a dinner party with two couples present, including her and her husband. According to her recollection, there

would be nothing in this conversation that would prevent it from being used as an example for analysis in a seminar. After two hours' discussion, she was horrified at the aggressive mechanisms revealed, and she insisted that all copies be withdrawn immediately and destroyed.' (p. 353).

8   For a more extensive and practical discussion, see Ten Have (1999a): 46–98; and on transcription also: Psathas & Anderson (1990); an explanation of the intended meaning of the various symbols is given in the Appendix at p. 183–4.

9   From a lecture given in the fall of 1967.

10   Lecture 1, winter 1970.

11   This schema was partly inspired by Ashmore & Reed (2000), which I have discussed elsewhere (Ten Have, forthcoming).

12   I have taken issue with some critical treatments of transcription practices in Ten Have (forthcoming).

13   For an incisive analysis of the visual identification of bird species using field guides see Law & Lynch (1988).

14   The topic of recognizing bird species by their song will be taken up again in Chapter 8, pp. 154–6.

15   Here is an earlier version of the transcript used in the Illustration section:

A 'hh nou we zullen es kijken d't ka̲n eh (.) e̲envoudig (.) 'te zijn dat ze wat tekort aan blo̲ed heeft ze is ne̲gen jaar   'hhh de le̲eftijden é̲en jaar vi̲er jaar en ne̲gen
P   (ja heb ik ook al)
A ja ti̲en e̲lf zo'n beetje ro̲nd-tie tijd als ze een beetje ui̲t gaan schieten 'hhh-dat zijn ti̲jden waarop kinderen vaak een beetje blo̲edarmoede hebben
P   (jjjh) twee jaar gele̲den heeft ze 't o̲ok gehad toen o̲ok in september toen waren we bij de scho̲olarts en toen had ze o̲ok bloedarmoede
A hmm (..) 'k wee' niet of het wat i̲s maar we kunnen even (prikken)

16   David Goode (1994:150–62) provides some telling illustrations of these sense-making, sense-changing and sense-instruction possibilities; some of these will be taken up in Chapter 6.

17   Cf. p. 43 above, Heritage & Atkinson (1984: 12), Psathas & Anderson (1990), Hutchby & Wooffitt (1998: 74).

4   Interviews

Following the lead of Ragin (1994), as discussed in Chapter 1, we can say that a major problem of social research is to collect evidence that can be used – in a dialogue with ideas – as an empirical basis for the construction of a representation of social life that is adequate and relevant. Methods of data collection can therefore be discussed in terms of their fitness for the part they have to play in this game we call qualitative social research. For the discussion in this book, I have grouped data collection methods in a few broad classes such as interviews, documents and field methods. The choice of any of these can be assumed to be based on a variety of considerations, including for example: assumptions about (aspects of) the social realms to be examined, specific theoretical, practical and/or empirical interests, conditions such as available means, practical arguments about efficiency and access, and others. In this and the next two chapters, I will discuss three classes of data collection methods as solutions to problems of social research. Quite often, I will contrast ethnomethodologists' preferences and uses with those more common among qualitative researchers. This contrast is not primarily meant to convince other researchers to follow ethnomethodological examples, but rather to stimulate reflections on methods, or, if you like, as provocations for reconsiderations of methodological habits.

For most social researchers, interviewing people is the obvious, if not to say 'natural', way to collect data. For ethnomethodologists, this is not the case. This does not mean, of course, that ethnomethodologists never talk to people or listen to what they have to say, but rather that they tend to avoid formal research interviews as their major data source. When they do study interviews, these are taken as a *topic* rather than as a *resource*, that is, interviews may be studied as objects in themselves, to see how they are produced, but rarely in order to collect information on phenomena 'outside' the interview context. This is one aspect of ethnomethodology's 'situationalism', discussed previously (cf. p. 34), and it is compatible with a 'specimen perspective', rather than a 'factist' one (cf. p. 8). I will, therefore, focus the discussion in this chapter on aspects of interviews and interview methods as topics: how interviews are organized as interactional events, and how they are used in analyses and research reports.

The interview society

It has been suggested that we live in an 'interview society', in which what is revealed in public interviews provides a cultural model for how one could or even should experience one's life.[1] In fact, a cursory overview of current social practices shows that interview-like forms of talk-in-interaction are an extremely pervasive way of doing a large variety of information-producing jobs. Young children interview each other as part of their educational training. Tests and examinations follow an interview format. Suspects and witnesses are interrogated in police stations and during court sessions. Applicants are questioned about their abilities in order to judge their eligibility for a particular job. Patients are interviewed by doctors and therapists, either as a preparation for treatment or as part of the treatment itself. Politicians spend part of their professional time subjecting themselves to questioning by journalists in news interviews and during press conferences. Celebrities are interviewed by mass media workers about their careers, love life and innermost feelings. During news broadcasts 'hosts' interview reporters in the field. And indeed, researchers of various kinds interview their subjects in order to gather data on them, elicit expressions of their views and experiences, or to gain information about past events.

A number of themes emerge from this overview. Interviewees are treated as (potentially) able to provide certain items of information to which they are supposed to have privileged access. In various ways they may be held responsible for what they have to say. Furthermore, interviewers present themselves as having a right to get this information, but at the same time they may suggest that they are not to be held responsible for the implications of their questions. Actual interviews can be analysed as arenas in which these abilities, responsibilities and rights are negotiated. In examinations, pupils are judged on the basis of their demonstrated ability to answer certain questions correctly. During police interrogations and court sessions, answers to questions are judged in terms of their plausibility in light of otherwise available information, and as materials to evaluate someone's possible guilt. For politicians, it is the acceptability and efficacy of their proposed or actual policies that is at issue, while their interviewers try to seduce them to reveal information or make quotable statements that have value as 'news' on the media market. In job interviews, applicants may not just be asked to provide information about themselves, their past achievements and future plans, but they may also be invited to demonstrate their abilities in impromptu role play. And even patients are held accountable for being 'good patients', taking care of themselves, following treatment instructions and asking for medical attention neither too early nor too late. In sum, interviews are often deeply *moral* events with important implications and consequences for the interviewee, while interviewers do interviews as part of their standard professional routines. So, while interviewers tend to ask their questions in a neutral manner, taking an aloof, professional stance, interviewees are at stake in a much more personal way.

The issue that we face, therefore, in looking at research interviews, is whether and in which ways similarly morally loaded negotiations are to be expected in those cases as well. It might very well be that interviewees at times feel that they are being 'interrogated', that they have to account for their actions and saying as responsible persons, or that they seem to be requesting support for their views and actions. In any case, research interviewers tend to take for granted that they somehow have the 'right' to ask the questions they ask, although usually they will formulate their requests in very polite ways, accepting any answer they may get. In other words, the fact that interview-like formats are used so pervasively and in such a variety of institutional contexts, may burden the research interview with associations and felt implications that are at odds with the research interviewer's intentions and purposes.

The interview format

Whatever the institutional setting and its related official purpose, the interview format tends to be based on an asymmetrical distribution of interactional jobs. The interviewer is to produce utterances that can be taken as 'questions', although their actual format may be not be question-like. Furthermore, he or she will often also respond to whatever the other party has produced, before posing the next question. The interviewee's job, on the other hand, is limited to giving answers to the questions. Anything said after a 'question' has to relate in some way to the themes or terms of the preceding utterance. Questions, then, project frames into which the answers have to be fitted, while the questioner can come back after the answer to evaluate that fit. In so doing, interviews can basically be seen as consisting of a series of question/answer sequences, in which a third position can be used optionally.[2]

As these terms suggest, I will often, especially in this section, rely on conversation-analytic notions and methods to discuss the actual production of (research) interviews.[3] The remarks refer, in the first place, to one-to-one qualitative interviews, which I will discuss in the present section, referring to a few extracts from three qualitative research interviews. In the next section, I will also mention some features of variations on this basic format, in terms of alternative elicitation techniques and number of participants. The present section is based on research by Harrie Mazeland, and written in close cooperation with him.[4]

Turn-by-turn interviews

Let us first take a look at a transcript from the start of one audio-recorded face-to-face interview:

Extract 4.1 (<u>LC1/Mazeland</u>)

1	IR:	OK↓EE:
		okay
2		(.)
3	IR:	je ↑HEET: <u>John°nie</u>
		your name is Johnny
4		0,4
5	IE:	<u>Johnnie</u> ↑ja-
		Johnny yes

```
6    IR:·   hhh hoe ↓oud ben ↑je?
            how old are you?
7           0,3
8    IE:    >zeventien.
            seventeen
9           0,4
10   IR:    ze:ventien.=
            seventeen
11   IR:    =·hh heb je broe:rs en zus↑(j)e
            do you have brothers and sister(s)
12          (.)
13   IE:    ja=één zus↑je
            yes one sister
14          0,6
15   IR:    ↓eh:m (.) is die °jonger of Ouder?
            umm is she younger or older?
16          0,3
17   IE:    °jonger dan ↑mij
            younger than me
18          0,9
19   IR:    >gaat die ook naar< scho↑o:l?
            does she also go to school?
20          0,4
21   IE:    prima.
            great
22          (.)
23   IE:    ja jha:ha dus= ((lachend))
            yes y(h)e(h)es apparently ((laughing))
24   IR:    =J↑a: H:e:Hh: ((lachend))
            yes hey ((laughing))
25          0,3
27   IR:    wat voor scho↑ol?
            what kind of school?
28          0,4
29   IE:    e::h effe kijke ze zit op de:: (°na)
            uh let me think she's at the
30   IE:    lagere school zit ze nog, vijfde klas.
            elementary school still fifth grade
31          0,4
32   IR:    °vijfde klas lagere school.
            fifth grade elementary school
33          (.)
```

[continues with questions about the respondent's father]

It should be obvious that the purpose during this episode is to gather 'basic facts' about the respondent, so it represents the interview format in a rather basic form, as a regular alternation of questions, answers and reactions to those answers. The extract contains six question/answer sequences (starting at lines 3, 6, 11, 15, 19, and 27).

The first 'question' is produced as a statement, which recognizably refers to previously gained knowledge: *your name is Johnny* (line 3).[5] The answer is a repeat and a *yes* (5), both confirming the already available knowledge. There is no post-answer uptake in this sequence, which corresponds to the researcher-given character of the information that is the topic of the sequence. What this exchange accomplishes is that what previously was known in a practical relational sense, is now reaffirmed in the context of the research interview. It may be that the interviewer has written it down on a sheet of paper, and it is in any case recorded on the tape and therefore preserved as research data – even if only as a bureaucratic identification of the interview. In this fashion, the epistemological status of the talk is changing, from momentary chit-chat to preserved research information.

Contrary to the information-confirming character of the opening sequence, the question in the next sequence is seeking new information from the recipient. It is marked by an interrogative term (*how*), a subject/verb inversion and a rising intonation at the end: *how old are you?* (6), and gets a prompt one-word answer: *seventeen* (8). This is acknowledged by repeating it: *seventeen* (10). This specific reception device regularly occurs in an environment characterized by short, factual questions which get minimal answers, as is prominent in this extract. What it does is, firstly, interactionally to register the fact stated in the answer as from now on shared mutual knowledge, which can be used as background for subsequent elaborations, and secondly, to fix it as research datum, possibly written down or in any case recorded on tape, as noted for the previous sequence.

The sequence starting on line 11 is the first of a series of four connected sequences dealing with the respondent's sibling(s). The first question, *do you have brothers and sister(s)* (11), gets a confirming *yes*-answer, followed by a number and gender specification: *one sister* (13). In this way, the range of sibling possibilities is limited to one gendered case. The subsequent question is contingent upon the information provided in the preceding answer: *umm is she younger or older?*(15).[6] Instead of using a categorical descriptor to refer to the person that was introduced in it – like *your sister*, for instance – the questioner accomplishes referential continuity by the use of the locally subsequent reference form *'she'* (Dutch *die*, literally *'that one'*; cf. Schegloff, 1996b: 450 ff.). The interviewee's sister is being dealt with as an interactionally available, already identified, given identity about whom further inquiries can be made. The answer is again short and clear: *younger than me* (17) and is followed by yet another question concerning the same referent: *does she also go to school?* (19). Although this question is shaped as an offer of a candidate answer[7] that can be confirmed simply by a *yes* or *no*, it gets *great* instead (21). This seems to be an answer to a question that has not been asked, something like **how is she doing at school?**. However, before the interviewer reacts to it in the next turn, the interviewee corrects himself by providing a better-fitting answer. He does so in a laughing manner: : *yes y(h)e(h)es apparently* (23), which is taken up by the equally laughing: *yes hey*

(24) in the interviewer's reaction. So the puzzle of the unfitting answer is solved immediately by the interviewee himself, and interactionally recognized as such by the laughing mode in which the participants deal with it. In the final sequence of this series, the interviewer asks about the type of school that the sister attends: *what kind of school?* (27). The answer, *uh let me think she's at the elementary school still fifth grade* (29–30), starts with a display of some needed mental activity before the answer can be given, followed by the requested information (school type), plus an additional item (grade) which was not included in the question. So what we see in this sequence is that the respondent takes some liberty with the agenda set by the question, anticipating a possible next question, which has not actually been asked, but which makes the requested answer inferable. The answer is received by a 'summarizing repetition', that is a summary consisting of the purely informative items: *fifth grade elementary school* (32). This way of 'fixing' the answer again stresses the factual character of this phase of the interview, after which the interviewer moves to the next question series concerning another aspect of the interviewee's 'background'.

Note first that various question formats are used in this series of questions and that there seems to be some regularity in the order in which these formats are used. The interviewer first asks one or more questions that already offer a candidate answer to the addressee (cf. lines 3 & 19). This kind of question not only shows what the questioner already knows or assumes, but already guides the addressee to respond in a preferably confirmatory manner. A confirming answer may provide the interactional basis for a more open type of questioning (cf. lines 6 & 27). In this latter type of question, the core part of the questioning utterance consists of a category-indicating question word together with a category-specifying descriptor (*how old* in line 6, *what kind of school* in line 27). The utterance may also contain a locally subsequent reference form that relates the category to its domain (*you* in line 6) and a verb phrase specifying the relation between this referent and the questioned category (*are* in line 6).

In spite of these differences, however, all of these questions are very similar with respect to the kind of answering information that is elicited by them. They provide for very short answers in which precise, factual information is given. Although the answerer may elaborate upon the answer by anticipating a contingent follow-up question, the continuation itself too is never oriented to as a basis for telling more.[8]

The conciseness of answers like the ones above is not just a consequence of the type of information that is provided in them, it is also modelled by the way the interviewer asks questions. In terms of ordinary interview practices, factually oriented episodes, such as the one from which extract 4.1 was quoted, are quite common at the *start* of qualitative interviews. They may even be marked as such, as in extract 4.2 below (lines 5 and 7):

Extract 4.2 [IS1/Mazeland]

```
 5   IR:    ik wou eh eerst 'n paar e↑:h
            I would uh first ( like to know) a few uh
 6          0,3
 7   IR:    achtergrond gegevens ehhuhuh van jhou whete,
            background data uhuhuh from you
 9          0,6
10   IR:    ↓nou jou naam is< > [voornaam achternaam]
            well your name is [first name last name]
11   IE:    [ja↑:h
            yes
12   IR:    hhhh
13          (.)
14   IR:    en jouw geboorteda°↑tum
            and your birth date
```

[continues]

In such episodes, the respondent is treated as a 'conventional knower', as someone who has access to a collection of demographic facts which are conventionally ordered in collections of categories or associated predicates, like one's name and birth date, one's family members and some basic information about them. Because of the conventionality of the circumstances in which these descriptors can be relevantly used, the interviewer only has to indicate the category or the type of predicate to get the required information as a matter of course. Starting an interview in this manner not only provides the interviewer with the requested information, but also establishes the interview relationship as one of requester and provider of personal information. And it establishes a particular, factually oriented, interactional format.

Extracts 4.1 and 4.2 provide examples of one particular type of interview organization, which is characterized by a turn-by-turn allocation of speakership. Harrie Mazeland (1992, also Mazeland & Ten Have, 1996) has coined the expression *turn-by-turn interviews* (TBT-interviews) as a shorthand for this type. TBT-interviews mainly consist of an alternation of relatively short speaking turns, such as questions, answers and acknowledgement tokens or similar objects.

Discourse Unit interviews

Such TBT-interviews can be contrasted with interviews which are organized rather differently, as illustrated in the next extract.

Extract 4.3 [QW/jq; Mazeland]

```
12   IR:    u begon al even te vertelle, e:h
            you started already a bit to tell uh
13          (.)
```

14	IR:	wat °voor <u>KLACHT</u>e u <u>had</u> h\O(e,`)?
		what kind of complaints you had huh
15		(.)
16	IE:	ja:h,=
		yes
17	IR:	=MAAR, (0,5) °dat
		but that
18	IR:	we: <u>heb</u>be 't nog niet uitvoe:rig:e:h <u>o</u>ver ge<u>had</u>,
		we did not discuss it extensively
19	IR: ·	hh maar:, kunt u me daar wat <u>meer</u> v('r) v::-er<u>te</u>lle,
		but can you tell me some more about that
20	IR:	want <u>is</u> dat ook waar <u>u</u> die <u>medi</u>cijne voor ge<u>had</u> he[bt?
		because is that also what you had that medication for
21	IE:	[ja:.=
		yes
22	IR:	=ja.
		yes
23	IE:	°inderdaad.=
		indeed
24	IR:	NOU (eh) wil ik- eh,
		well I want uh
25	IR:	't kan me niet <u>sche</u>le hoe <u>dok</u>ters dat <u>noe</u>me,
		I don't care what doctors call that
26	IR:	·hh maar: e:h ik wil wel graag <u>we</u>:te,
		but uh I would like to know
27	IR: ·	h nou: hoe<u>lang</u> u dat nou <u>hebt</u>,=
		well how long you have that
28	IR:	=e::h <u>wan</u>neer u dat voor 't <u>eerst</u> hebt ge<u>had</u>
		uh when did you get that for the first time
29	IR: ·	hh <u>en</u>: (.) ho(e-)
		and how-
30	IR:	<u>wat</u> voor <u>klach</u>te precies
		what kind of complaints exactly
31	IR:	in uw <u>eige</u> woo:rde:,
		in your own words
32		0,9
33	IE:	NOU: 't be<u>gon</u> met-,
		well it started with

[continues with a long story about the complaints, the search for help, treatments, etc.]

At the start of this extract, the interviewer refers to complaints which the interviewee apparently had already voiced before she switched on the tape recorder (#12–14). She mentions that this previous discussion was not very extensive (#17–18), making it clear that she would prefer to have such an extensive coverage now (#19), implicitly referring to her research interest in medication (#20). Then she starts a rather lengthy invitation to tell a story about these matters (#24–31). Note first that she sums up a whole list of questions (#27–9). She wants to know how long the informant has suffered from the complaint, when it started, and how he would describe the complaints. After none of each of these questions, however, does she provide the opportunity to answer them separately. This kind of *multiple-question series* appears to work as a device for inviting a longer telling. The interviewer's questions are not treated as questions that should be answered successively and independently. Rather, the interviewee treats them as demarcations and characterizations of some kind of *answering space*. The interviewer instructs her recipient about the kind of things she would like to hear about and is interested in. She invites her interlocutor to elaborate them along the lines and directions that are targeted in the questions. Note further that the interviewer does not just explain her interests positively, in terms of the kinds of things she would like to know, as she interrupts herself soon after she has started (#24) in order to state what she is *not* interested in, i.e. medical jargon, *what doctors call that* (#25). In introducing the topic in this manner, she invites the informant to tell his story at some length, while this invitation is embedded in encouragement to do so from his own perspective, first negatively (#25), then positively *in your own words* (#31). Following that, the informant starts a long story, noting that he picks it up at the beginning (#33).

In this interview, the requested information does not involve the filling in of conventional information slots about the respondent, but the telling of a personal story, in the teller's own words. Because there is no conventional, or even theoretical schema available for such a telling, it wouldn't make sense to try to have it broken up into limited portions by asking separate questions. Therefore, the fine control of the telling is left to the informant himself. This interview is not organized, then, in terms of relatively short question/answer sequences, but as a succession of multi-turn units like the one produced by the interviewer in extract 4.3 (#24–31), and the informant's story which I haven't quoted here. In such Discourse Units or DU's (Houtkoop & Mazeland, 1985), one party is the *primary speaker,* while the other limits him- or herself to minimal responses and other short supportive contributions as a *recipient*. Mazeland has called interviews in which the interaction is mainly organized in terms of such discourse units *DU interviews* (Mazeland, 1992; Mazeland & Ten Have, 1996). The implication of this kind of organization is that the informant is the *expert* on the topic at hand, while the interviewer is just an interested listener. These remarks, and the contrast between TBT and DU interview formats more generally, suggest that forms of interactional organization constitute schemes of knowledge distribution, which may have various moral implications.

In DU interviews, the interviewer provides the informant with a set of overall and specific instructions as to how he is to tell his story and what should be included in it. During the interviewer's DU production, the recipient limits his contributions to short confirmations at the relevant points (at #16, #21, #23). And when her DU is obviously finished, he takes off to start his own, responsive DU. So while in the DU format the interviewee is treated as the expert on his own experiences, and is therefore given a free hand to tell his story, he is, at the same time, provided with a wish list concerning the story's overall character.

Mixed formats

It should be noted that within one particular interview both formats, TBT and DU, as well as various intermediate formats can be used, with corresponding knowledge presuppositions. As I indicated above in my discussion of extracts 4.1 and 4.2, TBT formats seem particularly useful for gathering itemized informations that serve as starting points or backgrounds to exchanges later in the encounter. Extract 4.4, below, illustrates this, as it is taken from a later part of the same interview as extract 4.1.

Extract 4.4 [(LC1/Mazeland)

NOTE: in this part of the interview, three different types of school are discussed: elementary school (ages 6–12), MAVO, which offers a less advanced type of general education (ages 12–16), and LTS, for basic technical training (also ages 12–16); going from MAVO to LTS was generally considered a degradation. The interviewee is at present at an LTS.

```
213  IR:   ben ↑je:- toen na: de lagere school meteen naar
           did you then after elementary school immediately
214  IR:   deze school gega↑an
           go to this school
215        0,5
216  IE:   ↓ne↑e:
           no
217        0,3
218  IE:   >e[erst >naar de ma↓vo:
           first to the MAVO
219  IR:       [ni↑e:
               no
220        0,4
221  IR:   ↑j[ah!
           yes
222  IE:       [>en >toen naar de:eh () >el tee es:
               and then to the LTS
223        2,1
224  IR:   hoe eh- () >wilde je ze↑lf naar deze scho↑ol
           how uh was it your own idea to change to this school
225        0,4
226  IR:   (·mt) hoe's dat gega↓an.=van die mavo↓:[=(0)
           how did that happen at the MAVO
227  IE:                                          [=NOU↓:
                                                   well
228  IE:   >ik zat (ech-) >ik ging eerst naar de mavo to↑e:
           I was (real-) I went first to the MAVO
229        0,3
```

230 IR: waarom ging je naar de ↓ma°↑vo
             why did you go to the MAVO
231   (.)
232 IE: NOU ('k-) dan HEI je <u>mee</u>r aan 't di<u>pl</u>oma hè
             well (I-) then you get more from your diploma right

[continues]

What we see in this extract is that the interviewer halts (#224)at the
information that is provided in the expansion of the preceding answer (#222).
She questions her interlocutor's previous answer in such a way that he is
invited to elaborate upon the events that are mentioned in it. Note that again
this is accomplished by a series of questions: *how uh was it your own idea to
change this school? . . . how did that happen at the MAVO?* (#224–6). This time,
the interviewer is not asking a series of clearly different questions, however.
Rather, the second question is designed as a more general paraphrase of the
first one (cf. Bergmann, 1981). But quite similarly to the discourse unit answer
that was invited by the multiple-question series in extract 4.3, the respondent
clearly prepares for launching a longer story. He projects the telling of a longer
exposé, both by beginning to talk about a chronologically ordered series of
events in his opening move (*I went first to the MAVO*, #228), and by prefacing
it with the particle *nou* ('well'), which is quite regularly used in setting up the
space for a longer explication. Note, by the way, the similarity of the manner
in which the delivery of a larger unit is projected in each of these two cases,
both with respect to the use of *nou*, and in the way the beginning of a longer
story is presented (#32):

Extract 4.3 – detail [QW/jq; Mazeland]

29 IR: hh <u>en</u>: (.) ho(e-)
            and how-
30 IR: <u>wat</u> voor <u>klacht</u>e precies
            what kind of complaints exactly
31 IR: in uw <u>eig</u>e woo:rde:,
            in your own words
32   0,9
33 IE: NOU: >t be<u>gon</u> met-,
            well it started with

So DU answers may also develop from a TBT episode in the interview. In
general terms, TBT and DU episodes differ not only in the overall
organization of speakership, but also in the specific means used to produce
such an organization. Especially, the use of a multiple-question series may be
oriented to as a device for opening up a wider and flexible answering space.

Questions and answers

Questions are forward-looking conversational objects: they set the agenda for
the next interactional slot. But as we have seen in the examples discussed

above, they are often also constructed in a way that connects them to what went before, as an obvious item in a conventional list (as in extracts 4.1 and 4.2) or more prominently by using tying devices such as pro-terms[9] and repeats of keywords, which indicates their locally contingent character (cf. especially 4.3 and 4.4). In this way, many questions in these interviews are formatted so as to display a responsive aspect. Before discussing this further, I will make a few remarks about the interviewee's work: providing answers.

Questions are, in CA perspective, first pair parts in an adjacency pair, which establish an 'obligation', on the part of the recipient, to produce a fitting second pair part, as soon as the first pair part is obviously finished (see Schegloff & Sacks, 1973: 295–6; also Ten Have, 1999a: 20). The concept of 'obligation' should here be understood in terms of a locally established expectation, which, when not fulfilled, creates an accountable absence. The party who is under the obligation to produce the second pair part will be held responsible for its absence and will often produce an account for it or, lacking that, others may use the absence as grounds for making various kinds of inferences ('he didn't hear me', 'maybe she is angry at me'). Quite often, a first pair part not only establishes a general obligation, like providing an answer, but also may suggest a 'direction' or 'value' for that second part. It is also possible that a more general 'preference' is operative on a particular type of first pair part, such as an acceptance following an invitation. In the conversation analytic tradition terms like (dis)preference refer to conventional expectations which are demonstrated in the format chosen, with preferred responses being immediate and short, while dispreferred ones are often delayed, hedged, preceded by formal positives, and/or accounted for in a more or less elaborate manner (cf. Heritage, 1984a: 265–80).

Let us now consider some properties of answers. Returning to our previous examples in extracts 4.1–4.4, I will present some more or less obvious observations in summary form. Questions that are formatted as statements (with or without inversion) get a confirmation or a denial. Confirmations are the 'preferred' alternative and are done with a yes-answer and/or a repeat of the keyword (as in 4.1 #5). These answers are mostly given without much delay. We could say that they conform to a preference for immediate delivery, once the question is hearably complete. Denials are 'dispreferred' and get a more elaborate answer, as in 4.4 #216–22: first a *no* and then an explication. Questions that inquire into rather conventional facts get short answers that follow the questions' instructions (4.1 #8), and at times information related to the main item is added to it, as in 4.1 #29–30: not only the school type but also the grade, what may be called an answer expansion.

For reasons of space, I have not quoted the full DU answers in the episodes from which extracts 4.3 and 4.4 were taken, but I will summarize what was produced on those occasions. In extract 4.3, we encountered a rather complex questioning DU, which contained a number of points to be covered and instructions about the kind and extent of the requested story. In the quote below, I will again present the last lines of this questioning DU, and the first few of the answering DU:

Extract 4.3 – extended [QW/jq; Mazeland]

28 IR: =e::h <u>wan</u>neer u dat voor 't <u>eerst</u> hebt ge<u>had</u>
           uh when did you get that for the first time
29 IR: ·hh <u>en</u>: (.) ho(e-)
           and how-
30 IR: <u>wat</u> voor <u>klachte</u> precies
           what kind of complaints exactly
31 IR: in uw <u>eige</u> woo:rde:,
           in your own words
32 0,9
33 IE: ↓NOU:< >'t be<u>gon</u> ↑met-
           well it started with
34 0,6
35 IE: 'n <u>knel</u>lende pijn:, in:- in me <u>ku</u>↑it
           a squeezing pain in- in my calf

We can see here that the answering DU takes off rather precisely from the last few elements of the questioning DU. As requested in #28, the informant starts his story with his first experience of his complaints (in #33, 35), which he tries to describe in detail (cf. #30) and in his own words (cf. #31). After this start, the informant tells his story in a rather extensive fashion, talking about his complaints, especially the pain, detailing his efforts to contact his GP, the doctor's diagnosis, and how his pains developed in relation to the medication he received. In short, he works hard to do his assigned job according to the specifications in the questioning DU.

Supportive actions

In this detailed telling, the interviewee is supported very actively by the interviewer. This is done in a number of ways: by producing 'acknowledgement tokens' (mostly *yes*), summarizing 'formulations' and supportive questions. Formulations offer a summarizing interpretation of the locally relevant tenor of the information just provided, and as such offer a demonstration of (a particular) understanding of the information produced so far (cf. Garfinkel & Sacks, 1970; Heritage & Watson, 1979; Heritage, 1985). They may focus on the *gist* of what went before, or they may spell out an *implication* of it; they may foreground some aspects or features, while leaving out others, and so redirect the conversation in particular ways. By being formatted as statements, formulations tend to have confirmations as their 'preferred' next utterances. Some kinds of contingent questions can work in a similar fashion.

In the next extract, from the same interview as extract 4.3, we can observe some of the ways in which such 'supportive' moves are placed and formulated, and with what kinds of effect. We have first a question in #111 and then a formulation in #120–21.

Extract 4.5 [QW/jq; Mazeland

106 IE: >*jah die- >toen dat- werd die:< >pijn in de kuit
     yes that- then that- became that pain in the calf
107 IE: die werd:< >hevig↑er
     became more severe
108   2,0
109 IE: ·hhh:
110   1,9
111 IR: >en >dan [>voelde >u >'t in >uw₁ >↑hak of ↓zo:=
     and then did you feel it in your heel or so
112 IE: [*eh:::::*
113 IR: [=↑dat u::eh:=
     that you uh
114 IE: [º*e::::*
115 IE: =N:EE!
     NO!
116   0,3
117 IE: ↓nee=
     no
118 IR: =ºne[e?
     no?
119 IE: [nee. in de kuit voornamelijk.=
     no mostly in the calf
120 IR: =>maar >de PIJN >aan >de KUIT werd heviger,
     but the pain in the calf became more intense
121 IR: en daardoor [kon u niet <goed º<lo:↑pe
     and therefore you could not walk very well
122 IE: [*e::h*
123   (.)
124 IR[10]: º↑jah::=
     yes
125 IE: =NOU↓:< >ik kon nog wel lo:↑pe=
     WELL I could still walk
126 IE: =dat is juist 't vreem↑de,

    that is so strange

The question in #111 is uttered after a pause, an inbreath, and another pause following a description by the informant of the pain becoming more severe (#106–7). Such pauses after a possible complete statement evidently work as an invitation to react. The reaction this time takes the form of a question suggesting a different location of the pain, the *heel* instead of the *calf*, while ignoring the aggravation of it that has just been mentioned. This suggestion is first strongly denied with the threefold *no* (#115, #117, #119)), followed by a hedged (*mostly*) reaffirmation of the location in the calf (#119). Then the interviewer comes in immediately with a formulation of the earlier (#106–7) mentioned aggravation (#120), which she had ignored a moment before (#111). This formulation can also be seen as a 'resumption proposal' (Mazeland & Huiskes, 2001), redirecting the interviewee to continue talking about the formulated theme of aggravation. She continues with another formulation, this time of an inferred implication of the informant's report: *and therefore you could not walk very well* (#121). The informant, however, has to deny this again (#125), adding that this was remarkably *strange* (#126). It was only in a later phase that he could no longer walk (not quoted here).

So what we see in the episode quoted in 4.5 is that, apart from producing acknowledgements and similar rather neutral objects, a DU recipient can also participate as a more active secondary speaker in a DU production. Voicing supportive questions and offering formulations of the gist and/or implications of what has been said may refocus the ongoing telling, may stimulate clarifications or work to correct possible misunderstandings. It may also, of course, disturb the flow of the story. In any case, secondary speaker actions demonstrate that any telling-in-interaction must be seen as a collaborative production, based on turn-by-turn negotiations, even during a more extended discourse unit.

To conclude

Taken together, these extracts not only provide illustrations of the overall variation in interview structure, but also show some of the detailed means that participants may use to construct questions, answers and reactions. Let me summarize some major points that have emerged in the foregoing discussions. What we have seen is that both participants – the interviewer and the interviewee – take great care to fit their contributions to what went before. The interviewer, of course, has the main initiative, but most of the time she either connects subsequent questions to previously provided answers, or she marks such answers as complete. The interviewee, on the other hand, carefully fits his answers to the instructions contained in the questions, occasionally adding further details to the main answer. There were moments when the subtle flow of mutually fitting contributions was disturbed in one way or another. There was a puzzling answer that was immediately repaired by the interviewee (4.1: #19–24) and a formulation from the interviewer that the interviewee had to mark as incorrect (4.5: #121–6). In answering questions about his schooling, the interviewee had to report a less flattering career switch (4.4: #216 etc.), which seems to have led to some disfluencies in the interviewer's questioning, and afterwards to quite extensive accounting work from the interviewee (not quoted above). These observations suggest that the *moral* standing of both participants is continuously at stake. As conversational participants, they unceasingly watch and manage their own and their partner's standing as a careful and sensitive interactant. In terms of an interview's content, it is the interviewee's life that is topicalized. Therefore, it is the quality of his management of that life that is inevitably on the interview agenda. For the interviewee, this leads to more or less 'visible' accounting work, and for the interviewer to 'protective face-work' (Goffman, 1967).

Variations on the classic interview format

Until now, I have limited my discussions of interviews to the canonical dyadic interview format: one interviewer posing verbal questions to one interviewee. Over the years, researchers have developed a number of variations on this format. In this section, I will mention some of these, including variations in the number of participants and in the ways in which interviewees are stimulated to talk.

Multiple interviewees

Probably the most common departure from the canonical format occurs when more than one person is being interviewed. Sometimes the presence of another person was not foreseen by the interviewer, as was probably the case in the interview from which extracts 4.3 and 4.5 were taken. Here the wife of the informant was present and at times added a comment or a correction, but her husband continued to be the main storyteller. One could, of course, also arrange to interview a couple together, for instance about their common experiences or their relationship. In so doing, a different class of phenomena would become observable: their co-telling a story, the ways in which they deal with disagreements, etc. An increasingly popular format is the group interview or 'focus group' (Gibbs, 1997). In a group interview, a number of people are interviewed at the same time, but basically the format used is the canonical one: questions, answers and reaction, probably with a tendency to use DU-like forms. In a focus group, however, it is the interaction between the participants that is the basic data-source. In this set-up, a number of people, who may know each other or not, but who are often co-members of some social category, are invited for a session to discuss one or more themes of interest to the researcher(s). A moderator (sometimes two) is present to introduce the theme(s), stimulate the discussion and keep the participants on track. This format is used especially to get information on the perspectives of a group or category on certain topics, as well as possible variations among their members. In all these multi-informant settings, what may get talked about depends on various kinds of group process, rather than 'only' on the interviewer/interviewee interaction. So one may get leader/follower effects, either pre-existing or emerging on the spot. Some participants will talk a lot, others much less, etc. Whatever happens, it should be taken into account when using that material as data.

Alternative elicitation techniques

Another kind of variation comes into play when the canonical questioning is replaced by or supported with a different 'elicitation technique'. One such a technique has been called 'photo elicitation'. In this set-up, respondents are asked to talk about a series of photographs, either provided by the researcher or shot by themselves. They may be asked to describe the picture, talk about the background of who is in it, about the (personal) histories involved, or just talk about any associations the photograph may raise. This technique has been used in urban research, to have people talk about their neighbourhood, and in studies of the history of everyday life, out-of-date technologies, etc. (cf. Harper, 1994: 410; 2000: 725–7).

A related technique involves confronting people with a film or video, and either inviting them to comment freely on what they see and hear, or to answer specific questions. A particular application is to show people a video of their own activity and ask them to stop the tape any moment they want to talk about what they did, a so-called play-back session. Some researchers using this technique seem to work on the explicit or implied assumption that 'people themselves know best what they are doing and why'. From an ethnomethodological, or more broadly a situationalist perspective, it may be argued that what is said in the play-back session needs to be understood primarily in the context of that particular situation, rather than as a context-free and detached comment on the primary situation that is being shown. In other words, the talk in the play-back session should be seen as demonstrating accounting practices, recipient-designed for the researcher.[11]

The object to be commented on can also be a document. The researcher may, for instance provide the respondent with a written description of one or more 'standard cases' and ask him or her for comments. In studies of case-based decision-making one can ask a case-worker to read the case and reach a decision on it while 'thinking aloud'. In this way one might try to get a better understanding of the ordinarily silent process, while at the same time getting displays of variations in decision-making styles among colleagues. This strategy has been used by Henk van de Bunt in his study of the work of public prosecutors (1986, 1987). Or one might write one or more stories and ask respondents for comments. Such 'vignettes' (Barter & Renold, 1999) are often used with 'difficult' respondents like children, or in exploring sensitive topics.

Finally, the document to be discussed can also be provided by the informants themselves. A well-known technique is to ask people to keep a diary of their activities for a specified period, and then interview them afterwards on the basis of their diary notes. Zimmerman and Wieder used what they called the diary/diary-interview method to study Californian hippies' daily activities in the late 1960s (1977a, 1977b). Marianne van Elteren-Jansen (2003) has used a similar approach to study everyday medical care provided by mothers for their young children. In both cases the method was used to gain access to scattered activities that would be hard to observe, while trying to avoid the vagueness of abstract questioning and stimulating accurate recall. Just the same, one will get 'selected' information and recipient-designed accounts.

Reconsidering interviews as data

In the preceding sections, I first discussed the interview as an established social format in societies that have been characterized as an 'interview society', and afterwards I noted and tried to demonstrate some interactional aspects of that format as applied in qualitative research projects. There is an enormous literature on how to do and use interviews in qualitative research, which, over the last 20 years or so, has become increasingly critical of established practices and conceptions. This is not the place to present an overview of this literature and these recent developments (cf. Fontana & Frey, 2000 for a useful effort), but I will treat a few selected themes from it. I start by recalling some of the issues I introduced in Chapter 1 of this book.

Taking off from Charles Ragin's (1994) model of social research, we can say that interviews are one way of producing evidence, to be elaborated in terms of a chosen set of ideas, in order to start a 'dialogue' between the two that should result in an interesting representation of social life (cf. pp. 1–3). A crucial function of the chosen set of ideas is to specify what I have called the 'theoretical object(s)' of the research project at hand (pp. 8–10). In other words, the issue is how a researcher would define, in analytic terms, what he or she is looking for. Returning now to the theme of the present chapter, the question is how interview materials can be used to serve as evidence in the study of various types of theoretical objects. As a primary framework for this discussion, I want to recall the distinction, also discussed in Chapter 1, made by Pertti Alasuutari (1995) between what he has called a *factist* perspective and a *specimen* perspective (cf. p. 8). Using a factist perspective on data means that materials such as interview expressions are treated as statements about or reflections of an external reality, while in the specimen perspective they are seen as part of the reality under study. Therefore, in a factist perspective, the crucial methodological issue is the quality of representation within the data of the external reality that is the intended object of study. Did the respondents give a truthful report on their life circumstances? Did they express themselves in an authentic fashion? In other words, in a factist perspective the problem is that informants may be lying or present themselves as different from how they 'really are'. In the specimen perspective, on the other hand, ways of presenting oneself can be studied as such, as phenomena, and lying, hiding or 'confabulations' may be a part of the reality being studied, without invalidating the data as evidence.

In these terms, most qualitative research based on interview data seems to use a factist perspective. It tends to treat answers provided by interviewees either as factual information about the respondent's situation and history, or as expressions of his or her experiences and perspectives. This would, for instance, probably be correct for the projects from which the earlier quoted extracts were derived. Such a factist usage implies that the interviewee possesses information which the interviewer lacks, especially information about the interviewee's conditions, experiences and perspectives. Questions are used to specify the kind of information that is being requested, while answers will be heard as efforts to provide that information; that is information relevant for the research project, and fitting in the current interactional context. The *yes*-responses that so frequently accompany or follow answers seem to function mostly as indications of the relevance and fitness of the answer, rather than as 'agreements'. Interviewers in qualitative research are rarely in a position to judge the veracity of answers, because most of the time they don't have access to independent information; they can only evaluate their plausibility. Therefore, it is not surprising that the factual correctness or authentic expressivity of an interviewee's answers is rarely contested, at least not within the confines of the interview itself (Mazeland, 1992). Such contesting will probably be avoided in order not to undermine the willingness of the interviewee to collaborate in the interview.

Using qualitative interviews in a factist perspective, then, implies a basic problem of veracity and authenticity that cannot be easily solved. The most common solution (apart from just ignoring it) seems to be to 'trust' the interviewee, and to try to promote truthful and honest reporting and expression by showing oneself to be nice, accepting and neutral. This is not an easy task, of course, and its success cannot be definitely assessed. The literature contains many suggestions on how to achieve 'good rapport' as it is mostly called. In the transcripts quoted before, it can be seen that it is especially during and after answering that interviewers seem to work to achieve this, with frequent *yes*-responses, repeats, formulations and supportive questions.

What also can be seen, however, is that even when interviewers do their utmost to be nice and understanding, accepting whatever the respondent has to say, the basic interview format is unavoidably asymmetrical. It is the interviewer who leads, who sets the agenda, and who acts as the ultimate judge of an answer's acceptability. The interviewee, on the other hand, is supposed to provide various kinds of personal information – not getting anything similar back from the other party. In that sense, then, the interview relationship lacks conversational reciprocity and is ultimately hierarchical, with the interviewer taking the upper position. This is one reason why many qualitative researchers have searched for alternative formats. These include more reciprocal exchanges of experiences and viewpoints, collective formats such as focus groups, and also efforts to change the ways in which interview materials are used and reported. Many of these initiatives have been inspired by anti-paternalist, anti-racist and/or anti-colonialist considerations. The canonical interview format is seen as instrumental in, or at least part of, oppressive regimes, not only because of the format itself, but also because of its individualizing and 'otherization' effects (Madriz, 2000). As such, this kind of critique, and the search for alternatives that it has motivated, is part of a larger movement to reconsider research practices in moral and political, rather than 'just' cognitive and scientific terms. These tendencies seem to be especially prominent among qualitative researchers in the United States, in connection with trends like post-structuralism, post-modernism and cultural studies generally.[12]

Interviews and ethnomethodology

I started this chapter by noting the relative absence of interviewing as a research activity in ethnomethodology, in contrast to its popularity in other kinds of qualitative research. One could cite a variety of reasons for this remarkable difference. I will concentrate my discussion on a fundamental feature of various research traditions: the key terms of their problematic. Most kinds of qualitative social research are basically interested in 'people' – individuals, categories and collectivities of persons, their characteristics, values, orientations, motivations, experiences, relations, etc. etc. Whatever the theoretical terms used, most of them ultimately refer to (the properties of) people. Therefore, studying people is an obvious way to proceed in most kinds of social research. One could, of course, study people by observing them, and this is indeed often done, as I will discuss in Chapter 6. But even when people are observed, researchers tend to do a lot of 'interviewing': they want to hear why people do things the way they do, how they see their life situations and the larger worlds in which these are embedded. The major interest is in what people think, feel, experience, etc., and they are supposed to a certain extent to be able to formulate what is 'on their mind'. The interest in studying 'people' tends to be narrowed to studying their 'minds', and the major way to study 'minds' is to study what people have to say. Rather than listening to what people have to say while they are busy living their ordinary lives, it is often much more efficient to invite them to a special talking session and ask them about what is of specific interest in the research project at hand, hence to question them using one or another interview format.

For ethnomethodology, the interest is *not* in people as such, but in people as *members*, as competent practitioners, because ultimately ethnomethodology is interested in order-producing *practices*, and this interest can be further narrowed to *procedures* of order production (cf. Chapters 2 and 3, also Ten Have, 2002a). Furthermore, these practices are seen as specifically local and situated. Although order-producing practices may have general features, their ultimate effect is considered to depend on their context-sensitivity. Because of these rather specific aspects of ethnomethodology's interests, interviews are of limited usefulness. The 'reality' to be studied in ethnomethodology is a local accomplishment of members' practices. One can, of course, ask people to answer questions or tell stories in an interview context, but what is then made available for study is 'answering questions' or 'telling stories'. This can be done, and it has been done, as my previous references to Harrie Mazeland's work have demonstrated. In that case, interview excerpts are used in a specimen perspective, as examples of research interview interaction, and mainly analysed in terms of sequential organization. But research interviews constitute and display a rather restricted slice of human life, so we still have the issue of how what happens inside the interview context is related, or can be related, to 'interview-external' forms of life. Carolyn Baker (1997) has used MCA rather than CA to analyse interview talk, as a kind of demonstration of members' use of person categories. She concludes her essay as follows:

> The artful production of plausible versions using recognizable membership categorization devices is a profoundly important form of cultural competence. What we hear and attend to in these interview accounts are members' methods for putting together a world that is recognizably familiar, orderly and moral. (Baker, 1997: 143)

What this seems to suggest is that the interviews studied provide useful specimens of members' methods for creating an intelligible social world. The suggestion seems to be that the methods as used here are not too dissimilar from those used on other, 'natural' occasions. Similar suggestions have been made by other researchers, as we will see.

Taking up the challenge to interviews

As I mentioned before, criticism of qualitative interviewing has led some researchers to experiment and promote different, less asymmetrical interview formats, while others have challenged qualitative research's dominant reliance on interview data as such. A major theme in these criticisms is that interview expressions are local collaborative 'constructions', rather than purely individual expressions of 'mind'. Some authors have taken up such challenges as an impetus to reconsider the sense of interview expressions, without abandoning interviews as data-gathering instruments. What they seem to be doing is taking interviews as demonstrations of, and occasions for, the use of accounting practices that can be analysed as such in a specimen perspective.

Jody Miller and Barry Glassner (1997), for instance, formulate a response to Silverman's (1993) critique of interviews. They want to 'identify a position that is outside of [an] objectivist-constructivist continuum yet takes seriously the goals and critiques of researchers at both of its poles' (p. 99). For them, what they call an 'in-depth interview' offers an occasion for interviewees to work at a continuous process of maintaining a meaningful social world. They tell various kinds of 'stories' directed at the interviewer, and at what they think will be done with the interview materials. Some of these stories will be fashioned after existing cultural stereotypes, but others may well be told to resist conventional images of the research subjects. The stories are taken as examples, then, of ways in which interviewees construct their social world, and therefore of the (sub-)cultural resources that they have available for these kinds of activities.

James Holstein and Jaber Gubrium (1997, cf. also 1995) have in a parallel fashion formulated their conception of the sense of qualitative interviewing in reaction to Silverman's treatment of the topic. While rejecting traditional conceptions of the interview as a way that ignores the active and collaborative construction of meaning in interviews, they propose what they call 'active interviewing'.

> Conceiving of the interview as active means attending more to the ways in which knowledge is assembled than is usually the case in traditional approaches. In other words, understanding *how* the meaning-making process unfolds in the interview is as critical as apprehending *what* is substantively asked and conveyed. The *hows* of interviewing, of course, refer to the interactional, narrative procedures of knowledge production, not merely to interview techniques. The *whats* pertain to the issues guiding the interview, the content of questions, and the substantive information communicated by the respondent. A dual interest in the *hows* and *whats* of meaning production goes hand in hand with an appreciation of the constitutive activeness of the interview process. (Holstein & Gubrium, 1997: 114)

They mention a number of what they call 'linguistically attuned' approaches, including ethnomethodology, that can be seen as critical of interviews, which 'can emphasize the *hows* of social process at the expense of the *whats* of lived experience'. They 'want to strike a balance between these *hows* and *whats*'. Their 'aim is not to obviate interview material by deconstructing it, but to harvest it and its transactions for narrative analysis' (1997: 115).

This means that they, too, want to continue to use interviews, despite their overall endorsement of the 'constructivist' criticisms. Rather than seeing the respondent as a 'vessel of answers', as in traditional interview conceptions, they propose to see him or her as an active constructor of meaning, who is incited by the interviewer to develop meaningful stories about his or her life. The interviewer tries to 'activate the respondent's stock of knowledge' and 'bring it to bear on the discussion at hand in ways that are appropriate to the research agenda' (123). They contrast their proposal for this type of interviewing also with ethnomethodology's preference for 'naturally occurring talk and interaction', in suggesting that the contrast with interviews is relative. Furthermore, interviews may occasion narrative elaborations that are rare in casual talk. In short, interviews can be usefully exploited, according to these authors, to study 'occasioned narratives' that demonstrate and make accessible for study the cultural as well as personal resources that informants can also be supposed to use in non-interview settings in their ordinary lives.

Exemplary studies

In order to get a more solid grip on these issues, I will now discuss some exemplary interview-based studies to explore ways in which the methodological dilemmas mentioned above have been solved in actual cases. For reasons of space and topic, my presentation of these studies will be extremely selective.

A practical argument for doing interview studies, their efficiency, depends on the fact that many situations that constitute people's lives are not easily observable. It may be either because the practices of interest are scattered across a lifetime, or because they are not easily accessible for privacy reasons. Such arguments of efficiency and accessibility can be combined with others to provide a rationale for particular kinds of interviews. There are a number of interview studies, for instance, that have been focused on family life, especially on ways in which families have been coping with problematic experiences and conditions. I mentioned one example of this category in Chapter 1: Fred Davis' (1963/1991) *Passage through crisis*, a study of how families dealt with the acute paralytic poliomyelitis of a child. Other examples are Margaret Voysey's (1975) *A constant burden: the reconstitution of family life,* on the effect on family life of having a disabled child, and David Locker's (1981) *Symptoms and illness: the cognitive organization of disorder*, on the everyday medical practices of mothers. It is interesting to see how these authors formulate their topic or object(s) in analytic terms, and how interviews are being used as evidence to elaborate a representation of the chosen aspect(s) of family life.

Passage through crisis

Passage through crisis is based on data collected as part of a large, multi-disciplinary project in which Davis served as a sociologist. The major part of the data he used for the book were the interviews with children's parents, about 14 spread over a period of up to two years, which were carried out by a psychiatric social worker or by the author himself. Most of these were tape-recorded and transcribed in full. To a lesser extent, psychiatric interviews with the children were also utilized. The scheduling of both types of interview was adapted to natural points in the treatment trajectory.

Davis states that his book offers 'an account of the social-psychological impact of a serious illness (spinal paralytic poliomyelitis) on fourteen children and their families' (3). He regards it as 'a naturalistic study, characterized by a rather 'descriptive and inductive tendency', as he has 'attempted to describe and analyze certain experiences common to the families studied as they moved from one set of conditions to the next' (9). Three themes are meant to unite the book, although it is organized into separate chapters dealing with specific aspects of the family experience. These are given as 'emergence' (the gradual development of family adaptations), 'continuity of identity' (the experience of staying the same, in spite of important changes in conditions) and 'the clash of interests between hospital and home' (10–12).

The ways in which the interview materials are used is quite variable. In the core chapters that describe aspects of the experience, direct quotes from the interviews introduce the topic or illustrate particular points. Most of the time, however, the text uses the interview materials in a paraphrased or overall descriptive fashion. So a sentence may run like 'At this early stage, however, many parents (seven of the fourteen) would not even wholly admit that the child was ill' (21). Below is a paragraph that shows a mixture of usages. What is discussed here is the way the parents reacted to the first polio-specific symptoms, after having taken earlier, more general symptoms as signs of a rather innocuous ailment.

> Some parents attempted somehow to assimilate the warning cue to the commonsensical diagnosis of the child's illness that they had held from the first [warning cue]. Thus, when they first became aware of muscular weakness or rigidity in some part of the child's body, they assumed that the cold had 'settled' in the legs, abdomen, or feet, as the case might be. A strong denial component was frequently subsumed by the rationalization response. For example, although Mrs. Lawson claimed to have thought at once of polio on previous occasions when her children became ill, her awareness seemed to have deserted her at this crucial time: 'I didn't bother too much when he said his legs hurt him, because I thought that was just his weak spot, and when he gets grippe or virus like that, it probably hurts him there.' The tendency to rationalize was especially marked among parents who interpreted the child's illness in the light of some prior mishap. The injury that had

been received, actually or allegedly, afforded a ready-made point of reference for explaining away the pains and soreness of which the child complained. (Davis, 1991: 26–7)

The interview quote seems to be inserted in this part of the report to illustrate and/or substantiate the author's characterizations in the text itself. In a later part of the text, in a chapter on 'perspectives on recovery', statements of the same parents during different phases of the hospital treatment are quoted to illustrate their change of perspective (54–5), which the author subsequently tries to 'explain' (56–7).

Looking at the format of the quotes, it is remarkable that the parents' remarks are given as quasi-independent statements which have apparently been 'elicited' by an interviewer, in a way that is not included in the quote. The interviews with the children, on the other hand, are quoted as dialogues such as the following. The topic is that the children felt much better when they were moved from the treatment hospital to the convalescent hospital.

> *Interviewer:* How do you feel now compared to the way you were feeling at Eastern Hospital?
> *Marvin Harris:* Much better.
> *Interviewer:* In what way?
> *Marvin:* Well, we have more things to do, watch television, boys come in and talk to you, and have more fun.
> *Interviewer:* Any other ways that you're feeling better?
> *Marvin:* Well, your mother can kiss you, or give you things, come in and everything. And over at Eastern she couldn't. (Davis, 1991: 70)

Whatever the format, the usage of the interviews in general, and the quotes in particular, is intended to provide information on what happened to the children and their families and on the way in which they experienced these events. When quotes rather than summarizing paraphrases were chosen, that seems to have been done to provide the readers with more direct access to those experiences, by using the subjects 'own words'. What is discernible in many passages throughout the book is a kind of split or discrepancy that the author notes between what the parents say in the interview and what he apparently thinks is 'really the case'. This is also visible in the last lines of the last substantial chapter:

> As regards their over-all interpretation of the quality and meaning of their situation, all the parents were wont to claim, despite much objective evidence to the contrary, that the experience had resulted in no significant changes in their lives or in the attitudes and behavior of family members toward one another. This strong sense of continuity of identity in the midst of change doubtless betokens a high degree of social stability in these families. But from another vantage point, it perhaps also testifies to a failure of creative impulse – an excessive contentment with the familiar and known that inhibits the discovery of new meanings and purposes when important life circumstances change. (Davis, 1991: 164)

In his Introduction to the 1991 edition of the book the author seems to distance himself a bit from such a slightly condescending manner of speaking, noting the increasing sociological interest in 'the patient point of view'. But one should also take note that his book, among others, paved the way for such a change.

A constant burden

The studies by Margaret Voysey and David Locker can be seen as important further steps in the direction of taking the patient side seriously. For our present purposes, however, the major interest is in how they have used interviews as their data.

Margaret Voysey's argument in *A constant burden: the reconstitution of family life* is basically methodological – in the large sense, including theoretical aspects of interpretation and analysis. As she writes in the Introduction:

> Like most studies of disability in the family, mine is based on parents' responses to questions about what it is like to have a disabled child, and my research focus was the effects of a disabled child on family life. Two questions are then raised. Firstly, why do parents say what they say, and secondly, what, if anything, does what they say tell us about the experience of having a disabled child? Any answer to the second question depends on that given to the first. (Voysey, 1975: 1–2)

She starts by critically discussing previous studies (including Davis' *Passage through crisis*) arguing that their authors make sense of their interview materials by imputing unobserved (and unobservable) psychological processes and/or 'social factors' like supposedly shared norms and values. These are, according to her, 'constructs which typically mystify both the processes to which they refer and the methods by which they are constructed' (24).

> If an attempt to account for order or common structures in social action is to be made, then one must examine in what sense such structures 'exist'. . . . Hence, if one is to account for orderly interaction, one must examine the actual ways in which actors invoke such rules, and not impose them on the data. (Voysey, 1975: 24)

This leads her to conclude that:

> an attempt must be made to examine parents' actual statements as ways of making it so appear, to see how parents invoke normality as an adequate account of their situation. Evidently this will not refute the assumption of underlying pathology in family life. Indeed, in itself, it says nothing about family life at all. (Voysey, 1975: 25)

In a way that seems to parallel Davis' conclusions, she found that most parents claimed that the presence of a disabled child did not have 'deleterious effects on their family life' (26). The problem then becomes 'how they construct such claims in the face of questioning which implicitly asserts the contrary', and especially what is 'the relationship between objective or other-given meanings of the parents' situation and their own situational constructions' (27). Her basic argument, then, is that parents' statements 'constitute the appearance of normal family life because it is as normal parents that others, both informal and formal agencies, treat them' (27). In other words, the parents selectively used commonsense conceptions of 'the normal family' to construct (interview) accounts that pictured their life as that of 'a normal family'.

Due to a range of difficulties and problematic occurrences, the author was able to complete the intended four interviews with only 13 of her selected 22 cases. The interviews were semi-structured, tape-recorded and fully transcribed. She got the impression that almost all respondents saw her as somehow connected with an official institution, 'to whom the official morality concerning family life with a disabled child should be expressed' (73).

In the descriptive parts of the text, the interview material tends to be used in a mixture of summary statements and small quoted expressions, as in the following fragment, when describing 'effects on normal child members' of the family:

> Parents generally denied any bad effects of having a disabled child on their other normal children. If they admitted it, it was defined as past, and action as having been taken to avoid its recurrence. When the sister of a spina bifida child (F) had mumps her father expressed his horror at discovering that 'you forget she can be ill as well', and subsequently the parents made special arrangements for the child to attend dancing classes. Another child (B) was reported as having been bored at home, but as now having a neighbour's grandson to play with, and her interests were cited as the only grounds on which the mother would risk having another child, which might also be a mongol. (Conversely, the desire not to have more children may equally be presented as in the normal child's interests.) Finally, even previously agreed on actions, such as sending the normal child to nursery school, may be temporarily reversed 'in case she thinks she's being put away' (Mrs B). (Voysey, 1975: 141–2)

So we may say that Margaret Voysey is very careful indeed to treat her interview data as 'topic' in the sense of locally produced, recipient designed 'accounting practices', in which the parents were apparently keen on presenting themselves as 'a normal family'. These observed accounting practices are then subsequently interpreted in terms of a more general ideology of normal parenting as part of the ordinary social order, which is being reinforced by the agencies which 'treat' these families in various ways.

Symptoms and illness

In many ways a similar approach to interview materials is used by David Locker in his *Symptoms and illness: the cognitive organization of disorder* (1981). He has used materials from 'interviews with six women who were seen several times during the course of one year . . . to describe the way in which the cognitive resources contained within a commonsense understanding of matters of health and illness are used to make sense of experience and provide for the stable, orderly character of the world' (x). His project had to meet two methodological problems, the problematic relationship between the interview accounts and the actual practices reported; and the small number of 'cases' (six). The 'solution' to these problems could be found in the special character of the topic of the study: 'the cognitive resources contained within a commonsense understanding'. Locker claims that the knowledge and competences involved are used both in actual practical situations and in the interview itself to construct reasonable accounts. Therefore, he suggests, for this topic some general representativeness in regard to a population seems less relevant.

> I . . . provide data to illustrate and justify the view that the accounts they provide in the context of research interviews are constructed in ways such that they may be seen to be moral actors, competent persons, and adequate performers in the social status they occupy. (Locker, 1981: x–xi)

So the interviews are meant not to 'represent' the practices described, but as occasions in which the informants can display and demonstrate their everyday cognitive procedures in matters of health and illness.

Locker wanted to study the 'cognitive resources' used by members to make sense of 'problematic experiences'. Labelling the condition leading to such experiences as 'illness' is one from a range of options open to members. He speaks of a 'management sequence' to stress the time-based, career-like ways in which various sense-making activities come one after the other. The sequence starts with recognizing a problematic experience and may pass through various phases like 'wait-and-see' or consulting a professional. Locker takes these sequences as his 'analytic units' and studies the various sorts of techniques of normalization used to build them, which he assumes to be similar to the techniques available in the interview accounts. 'The aim is to use respondents' descriptions of events in order to identify the interpretive and comprehension processes via which social reality is constituted' (22).

A pervasive feature of the ways in which his informants tried to deal with problematic experiences of their family members or themselves was to 'normalize' what was happening. 'Normalization refers to that process whereby what is perceived as potentially problematic is explained in ways which show it to be normal, typical, or unworthy of further comment' (88). This is not only a cognitive or interpretive activity, however, it is also a moral one. The mothers interviewed demonstrated that they considered having the necessary knowledge of health and illness and using that knowledge to take care of their family members as a moral imperative. They recognized the limits of their obligations, including the responsibilities of the other family members and the fact that theirs was only lay knowledge, to be confirmed or corrected by professionals if need be.

Some explanations may directly involve some of the vital and moral interests of the parties concerned.

> it is easy to see that explaining a child's illness as a product of a virus infection has different implications for the public character of its mother than if it were seen to be the product of malnutrition. Because explanations may be used to impute or deny responsibility they constitute moral judgements. (Locker, 1981: 81)

Throughout most chapters the author quotes extensively from the interviews, as illustration of or grounds for his analytic summary characterizations of various features of 'lay theorizing' about illness and the management of issues of health and illness. Here is one of these quotes, in which the informant talks about her grandmother:

> [referring to an earlier exchange and its interpretation]
>
> The respondent is not only able to construe her grandmother's disorders as the direct result of motivated actions, she is also able to interpret her claim to be ill as a motivated act. In the subsequent exchange, the respondent provides further grounds for rejecting this claim:
>
> (G23) (Int.) 'Do you think she thinks of herself as being ill?'
>
>   (Mrs G) 'Oh yes, definitely. Yes.'
>   (Int.) 'Why?'
>   (Mrs G) 'Well she, you know, I mean . . . she's eighty-six and sort of a lot more fit than most people of that age. And yet you ask her if she's well and oh no, you know, she's never well. And yet she's not, you know, she's not . . . well she doesn't appear to be ill.'
>   (Int.) 'So what do you think underlies her saying that she's not well?'
>   (Mrs G) 'Well, probably she wants sympathy or something.'
>   (Int.) 'Do you give it?'
>   (Mrs G) 'No' [laughs]
>
> A claim to illness, like any other illness-relevant behaviour, is not unambiguous as an indicator. It may be taken to signify genuine illness or it may, as in this instance, be seen to be motivated by anticipated gains. In determining which of these alternatives the claim signifies, evidence must be sought to lend support to one or other interpretation. Here, two such items of evidence are offered. [continues]
> (Locker (1981: 114)

While Locker is conscious of the fact that one can never really know whether the reports given in the interview are more or less adequate depictions of the reported actions and their then-and-there local meaning, he seems quite assured of their relevance: 'While I assume that those meanings are a product of interviewer–interviewee interaction, the cognitive processes involved are not confined to that particular context but may well be employed in others' (181–2). While this seems a plausible assumption, it cannot be demonstrated.

These three studies, while here treated as exemplary, are in fact quite exceptional compared to the mass of qualitative interview research. They were similar in topic, but more importantly they all used repeated interviews with the same informants, thus being able to build up a fuller relationship than is generally possible in the more common 'one-shot–interviews'.[13] Furthermore, the last two authors proved to be extremely sensitive to the limitations and alternative analytic possibilities of their materials, being inspired in this respect by a range of interpretative and ethnomethodological approaches. Their sophistication in these matters is rare, however, and their rarely quoted studies deserve to be read more widely.

Final reflections

As noted above, interviews are an extremely popular format for generating *people displays* to be inspected by a variety of interested parties such as institutional agents, journalists, the general public and, indeed, researchers. In this way, performed texts are produced, often after an editing process, that are taken to be informative about the persons being interviewed. The information can concern events-as-experienced, actions-as-accounted-for, feelings-as-expressed, etc.; but always it is the interviewee who is – in one way or another – at stake. In the case of politicians, suspects or patients in therapy, the interviewee is talking 'in person', as a responsible actor. In research interviews, on the other hand, the interviewee's remarks are often treated as exemplary, as representing a category in a population – such as parents with a disabled child. I have suggested that interviews are so popular for two main reasons, a theoretical and a practical one. Theoretically, the interview seems an obvious way to gather information because whatever happens in society is seen as 'the product of persons': conscious, morally accountable beings. And, when this assumption is taken as self-evident, interviews are an extremely efficient method to gather the information needed. The person of interest is brought into a situation that is arranged for maximum productivity, at a time and place that allows the performance to be observed and/or recorded, and according to an agenda that is based on the interviewer's interests.

An essential theme in the practical reasonings that motivate the general preference for interviews is the issue of *control*. By arranging the interview situation and continuously managing the verbal production of the information stream through questions and reactions, the interviewer tries to control what is said according to his or her research agenda. Of course the control strategies in 'open interviews' and 'focus groups' are much looser than those in standardized survey interviews, but they are not completely absent. Informants may be explicitly invited to talk at length and use 'their own words', but still the interviewee is 'dislocated' from his or her ordinary life circumstances. Even when interviewed at home, that home is for the time being turned into a research site, a laboratory – however imperfect.

For ethnomethodology, interviews as major order-producing societal devices are of interest as a *topic*, but much less so as a resource. The reason for this indifference is that ethnomethodology does not share the assumptions and interests on which interviews are generally based. Ethnomethodology, to repeat what was stated previously, is oriented to the study of members' situated order-producing *practices*, not in 'persons' as such. Therefore, ethnomethodology generally prefers to study 'naturally occurring' situations in which such practices are observable. The concept of 'naturally occurring situations' should be understood in contrast to an 'experimentally created situation', in which a researcher creates specific circumstances in order to provoke interesting effects. And again, experiments may be studied as topics, but are generally avoided as resource.[14]

Although most qualitative research is based on interview data, not all of it is. In the next two chapters, we will encounter methods of data gathering that offer a different solution to the dilemmas of an experimental/natural mix. In Chapter 5 I will discuss documents that have been produced 'naturally', that is not as part of the research project at hand. In Chapter 6 the topic will be ethnography and field methods, which can be seen as efforts to combine a variety of methods that can be placed at different points on the natural/experimental continuum.

Some major points

The point of departure for this chapter was the observation that, while interviews are the main data source for most qualitative research projects, they are rarely used as core data in ethnomethodology. This can be related to the following points:

- Interviews of one kind or another are, in a society like ours, the major device to produce *people displays* for a wide range of purposes; that is why one uses the expression 'the interview society'.
- When interviews are used in qualitative social research, they tend to be based on the *assumptions* of the interview society, for instance that societal actions can be best understood in terms of the opinions of individual persons.
- The basic *format* for interviews is based on an asymmetrical task distribution: the interviewer asks questions, and may react to answers, while the interviewee is responsible for answering.
- An examination of actual instances of qualitative research interviews shows that the organization of interviews is quite variable:
  - during some episodes, especially factually oriented ones, the basic format can be followed quite closely – these were called *turn-by-turn* episodes;
  - but quite often, interviewers voice a number of concerns in a larger *discourse unit*, a DU, after which the interviewee gets a chance to produce an answering DU; during the production of a DU by one party, the other may insert various kinds of secondary speaker contributions, like acknowledgement tokens, questions or comments;
  - in both types of episodes it can be observed that interviewers quite often use contingent questions, questions whose content is occasioned by preceding information provided by the interviewee;
  - in short: interviewers can use a range of methods to create specific answering spaces, while interviewees can fill such spaces more or less in accord with these specifications; in so doing, the interview unfolds as a dynamically negotiated telling.
- While the basic interview format specifies an arrangement for a verbal exchange between two persons, a range of variations on that format has emerged:

- the number of members in either party can vary, as in focus groups;
- apart from more or less simple 'questions', various other elicitation techniques can be used, as in 'photo-elicitation.
- Using interviews as data-producing engines for qualitative research has been disputed and defended over the last couple of decades; apart from their conventional use to gather information about people's opinions, attitudes, etc., they can also be used to produce instances of particular kinds of practices in which a researcher is interested, such as membership categorization, story-telling, normalizing explanations and other kinds of accounting practices.

Recommended reading

On the general conception of ours being an 'interview society', read:

- Atkinson, Paul, David Silverman (1997) 'Kundera's *Immortality*: the interview society and the invention of the self', *Qualitative Inquiry* 3: 304–25

As interviews are so pervasive in qualitative research, you can open almost any book on qualitative methods to find extensive discussions of how one can organize, carry out and analyse qualitative interviews. A personal selection includes:

- Dingwall, Robert (1997) 'Accounts, interviews and observations'. In: Gale Miller, Robert Dingwall, eds. *Context and method in qualitative research*. London: Sage: 51–65
- Fontana, Andrea, James H. Frey (2000) 'The interview: from structured questions to negotiated text'. In Norman K. Denzin, Yvonna S. Lincoln, eds. *Handbook of qualitative research: second edition*. Thousand Oaks, CA: Sage: 645–72
- Holstein, James A., Jaber F. Gubrium (1995) *The active interview*. Thousand Oaks, CA Sage (Qualitative Research Methods, vol. 37)
- Holstein, James A., Jaber F. Gubrium (1997) 'Active interviewing'. In: David Silverman, ed. *Qualitative research: theory, method and practice*. London: Sage: 113–29
- Seale, Clive (1998) 'Qualitative interviewing'. In: Clive Seale, ed. *Researching society and culture*. London: Sage: 202–16
- Silverman, David (2001) 'Interviews'. In his: *Interpreting qualitative data: methods for analysing Talk, Text and Interaction*, 2nd edn. London: Sage: 83–118

Check also:

- Gubrium, Jaber F., James A. Holstein, eds (2002) *Handbook of interview research: context and method*. Thousand Oaks, CA: Sage

Notes

1   Cf. Atkinson & Silverman (1997), Silverman (1993: 19; 2001: 22, 160), who use this expression in their arguments against a 'romantic' conception of qualitative methods in which interviews are treated as offering an occasion of authentic personal expressions.

2   On the basis of the analyses to follow, I will have to nuance this rather conventional view of interviews as consisting mainly of questions followed by answers somewhat (cf. p. 62–70).

3   Cf. my earlier remarks on Conversation Analysis in Chapters 2 (pp. 18–19, 24–6) and 3 (pp. 41–51), and much more extensively Ten Have (1999a).

4   Harrie Mazeland did a project on qualitative research interviews which I supervised; cf. Mazeland (1992), Mazeland & Ten Have (1996). The transcripts quoted in this chapter were made by him. I remain responsible for the actual text as given here.

5   The English gloss has a different syntactical format than the Dutch original; for the present discussion this does not seem to be too relevant.

6   Heritage & Sorjonen (1994: 7) have coined the expression 'contingent questions' for those that 'are built so as to deal with some contingency in the prior response' and are contrasted with pre-planned 'agenda-based next question'.

7   As Pomerantz (1988) argues, a questioner may, in the way in which a question is asked, already suggest an answer, thereby providing a 'candidate answer'.

8   As discussed in the previous chapters, ethnomethodologists and conversation analysts are not interested in speculations 'upon what the interactants hypothetically or imaginably understood', but rather in their observably demonstrated normative orientations. It is to these latter orientations that an expression like 'oriented to' refers (cf. Heritage & Atkinson, 1984: 1–2).

9   The concept of 'pro-term' was developed by Harvey Sacks to indicate a class of terms which are used as indexical terms for others, as 'he' can be used to indicate a just mentioned person, or 'to do', a just specified activity (cf. Watson, 1987 for an exemplary analysis).

10 Or possibly the interviewee's wife.

11 The concept of 'recipient design' points to the observation that utterances are often formatted in special ways that take into account what the intended recipient already knows, or may be supposed to be interested in, etc. (see Sacks & Schegloff, 1979).

12 See, for instance, the *Handbook of qualitative research*, edited by Denzin & Lincoln (1994, 2nd edn 2000), and the journal *Qualitative Inquiry* which they also edit.

13 On the possible difference of first versus subsequent interviews see Baruch (1981) and Silverman's (1993: 108–14; 2001: 105–10) discussion of the implication of his findings.

14 In a recent paper, Susan Speer (2002) has objected to a strict avoidance of interviews as not being 'naturally occurring'; the paper is followed by comments from myself, Michael Lynch and Jonathan Potter, plus a rejoinder by the author. Garfinkel's 'breaching experiments', as discussed in Chapter 3 (pp. 38–41), are an obvious exception to EM's preference for the 'natural'. Ethnomethodological studies of experiments by others are available in the *oeuvre* of Michael Lynch as in Lynch (1985), Lynch et al. (1983) and Garfinkel et al. (1981).

5   Natural Documents

I will use the expression 'natural documents' to refer to various kinds of document – texts, photographs, drawings, graffiti, whatever – that are produced as part of current societal processes, that is *not* for the purpose of the research project in which they are used. As such, they differ from interviews that are a constitutive part of the very project for which they provide the data. In other words, natural documents are not 'researcher-provoked' as are most research interviews. This property may work both as an advantage and as a disadvantage, when such documents are used as evidence in a research project.

Historians, and social scientists who study past societies and long-term processes have, of course, always worked with the kind of data that are the focus of this chapter: documents and other remains of life in past ages. Among these remains, written reports have, since the development of writing systems, probably been the most important sources of information. In effect, literate societies can be seen as self-reporting systems with an enormous and still increasing production rate. Taking your own current life as an example, a bit of reflection on what you do and what you have at hand will teach you how much of it depends on and produces documents. And then, think of the major institutions of schooling, industry, trade, care, government and entertainment – they all produce an immense number of documents and could not exist without them. But reflecting on these document-based and document-producing properties of your and everybody else's life, you will also be able to conclude that an even more enormous amount of aspects of personal, institutional and public life is not reported at all – smiles and facial expressions, body movements and informal practices generally escape documentation.

Natural documents are produced for specific purposes, often to 'fix' aspects of current events and actions for future inspection. The minutes of parliamentary debates can be used to document votes on a proposal, decisions taken, arguments used. Such usages can be part of the same political process as the one being documented, referring backwards. But the documents can also be inspected much later, in a study of parliamentary change, for example. A sales slip may be needed to document a sale in case of later complaints, but it can also be used to document a timed presence. A man in whose luggage drugs had been found at Singapore airport was sentenced to death, in part because he was not able to document his claimed travels, as he said he always threw away his sales slips immediately. A further illustration of the importance of documents can be seen in the purposive shredding of documents, both as a routine practice in many organizations and occasionally as an element of suspect operations.

I will, in this chapter, consider the ways in which natural documents can be used as evidence, with special attention to the ways in which the connections between any documents and their production contexts are taken up in the analysis. Starting with some methodological arguments as well as a consideration of some exemplary studies done in a 'factist' perspective, my discussion will later switch to ethnomethodological studies of documentation, first as an organizational process, then as a job of text construction. The 'lesson is taken and used as a study policy' that documents, like any kind of research materials, should always be seen as a product of situated practices.

Contexts

The core function of documents, as summarily discussed above, is based on their transportability and their shareability. Information contained in documents can travel in space and time and can be easily shared with others, whether this was intended by the originator or not. In considering the usability of documents for research purposes, therefore, one has to distinguish types of contexts in which documents can be used, or to which documents may have been oriented. As a first approximation, one can distinguish the *production* context from various contexts of *use*. Production contexts are, in our kind of societies, often highly institutionalized, and many documents are designed to display their institutional groundings, as in the frequent use of logos, letterheads, dates, stamps and signatures. The authority of a document in many cases depends on the convincing use of such signs of origin. In other words, the sense of a document will be partly the product of an attributed production context.

Contexts of use are highly variable and, as suggested, the sense of a document may vary with these contexts. Documents may have quite specific intended main users, as in the case of a letter with one named addressee, or they may have a large, almost undefined audience, as in most media messages. Again, intended contexts may be indicated in the document itself, or assumed/suggested in a less direct fashion. A news report, for instance, will be meant to be read the same day or shortly afterwards, but it can also be read after many years and for various unsuspected purposes. In other words, presentation contexts may function as indications of preferred or primarily intended use, and therefore as interpretative frames. So we may distinguish a primary audience, projected by the presentation context, from secondary ones, foreseen or not. In secondary usage, documents are, in a way, reframed (cf. Goffman, 1974). In discussing the use of natural documents in a research setting, we are always talking about secondary usage, reframing the original document.

What documents 'do' is to re-present something. Documents refer to events, objects, persons, ideas, whatever, and make some of their aspects or features available for consideration in the same or a different context. On 22 July 2002, a newly appointed deputy minister in the Netherlands had to resign within nine hours of her swearing in, because a picture of her had been published wearing a Surinam militia uniform at a time when she had previously declared she was no longer a member of that militia. In the declaration in which she announced that she would resign, she claimed that she had remembered the date that she left the militia differently than it now turned out to have been. So while she admitted that her previous testimony had been erroneous, she also claimed that she had been 'honest'. Confrontations such as these between testimonies and documentary evidence are, of course, a central feature of judicial and other kinds of fact-finding activities. Documents produced at the time of the original event can be used to decide between conflicting present testimonies.

Documentary evidence in qualitative research

The differentiation of contexts suggested in the previous section can be used as a background in discussing the sense of using documents in qualitative social research. Again, the contrast made by Pertti Alasuutari between a *factist* and a *specimen* perspective suggests itself (cf. p. 8). We can, on the one hand, use documentary evidence to make decisions concerning factual aspects of the events to which the documents refer, or we can consider documents as specimens of their type. In the first case, the focus is on the original events or whatever is being represented. The documents themselves are only a means to get hopefully adequate information about some reality external to them. From a specimen perspective, on the other hand, the focus is on the documents themselves, and on the ways in which they are actually being used. Whatever the perspective taken, it is always advisable to consider the production context and the projected audience and intended usage of the document. In a factist perspective, features of the production context will be used to assess the truthfulness of the document. In a specimen perspective, they may be interesting in themselves, as documents are studied as part of societal processes of documentation.

Factist considerations

In his *A matter of record: documentary sources in social research*, John Scott (1990) has provided an extensive discussion of the use of documents in social research, which clearly exhibits a factist perspective. In a chapter on 'Assessing documentary sources' (pp. 19–35) he elaborates a set of criteria which offers a useful guide when considering documents as resources for studying some 'external' reality.

He labels his first criterion *authenticity,* which he further specifies in terms of both 'soundness' and 'authorship'. Soundness refers to the relation between an original document and a copy, as a copy may in various ways misrepresent the original, especially if it is copied by hand. 'Having established that a document is sound – either an original or a technically sound copy – the researcher must authenticate the identity of those responsible for its production. This is the question of authorship'(20). Even when marked on the document, it may not be at all clear who actually produced the document. This is often the case with organizational documents, which may be seen as somehow produced by a collectivity. More difficult cases involve fraudulent authorship, fictional productions passing as authentic reports, or satires. 'As in the case of assessing the soundness of a document, the authentication of authorship involves the use of both internal and external evidence' (21). This may comprise issues such as consistency of style, material properties of the document, and what is known about the usual production circumstances of documents of the type at hand.

Scott's second criterion is *credibility*, which 'involves an appraisal of how distorted its contents are likely to be' (22), and is further specified in terms of 'sincerity' and 'accuracy'. For the sincerity of the document, Scott stresses an assessment of the motives, interests and prejudices that may be involved in producing it. Apart from sincerity, one can try to estimate the possibilities for accurate reporting based especially on the proximity in time and place of the reporter and the events reported. The general preference is for 'primary reports', made by people who were able to observe the events first hand and compile the report as soon as possible afterwards.

A third consideration is a document's *representativeness*. This 'involves a judgement as to whether the documents consulted are representative of the totality of relevant documents', and even if an unrepresentative selection may be used, one has to 'know to what extent and in what respects' the documents studied are unrepresentative (24). 'The question of representativeness involves the two aspects of "survival" and "availability"' (25). The author raises a range of conditions that may have an impact on the chances of an existing documents survival, that is, its staying in existence, but then not all existing documents may be (made) available for research purposes. Many documents are destroyed, accidentally or on purpose, in order to 'clean up' or to prevent particular items of information from becoming known. And a substantial number that are preserved are not made available for similar reasons.

The fourth and final item on the agenda of the chapter under discussion, but hardly a 'criterion', is *meaning*. As Scott writes:

> The ultimate purpose of examining documents, the point to which all the preceding issues have been leading, is to arrive at an understanding of the meaning and significance of what the document contains. This problem of meaning arises at two levels: the literal and the interpretative. (Scott, 1990: 28)

Literal meaning refers to an understanding of the primary meaning of the text, depending on one's comprehension of the language, the vocabulary, and various conventional meanings associated with it, as used by the original author(s). It has often been observed that particular words in a language change in meaning over time, or have particular meanings for specific categories of people. Scott mentions terms for professions that no longer exist and different calendar systems as examples of problems of literal meaning. 'The achievement of literal understanding, however, is only the first step towards an interpretative understanding.' The latter 'is the end-product of a hermeneutic process in which the researcher relates the literal meanings to the contexts in which they were produced in order to assess the meaning of the text as a whole' (30). In other words, the researcher should try to 'place' the document 'back' into its original situation of production and presentation, and therefore should be knowledgeable about its local conventions of 'genre' and 'stylization'.

Inevitably, however, the researcher will use his or her own frame of reference in trying to understand the one used in producing the document. Therefore 'the investigator must, in effect, enter into a dialogue with the author of the documents being studied'.[1]

> Textual analysis involves mediation between the frames of reference of the researcher and those who produced the text. The aim of this dialogue is to move within the 'hermeneutic circle' in which we comprehend a text by understanding the frame of reference from which it was produced, and appreciate that frame of reference by understanding the text. The researcher's own frame of reference becomes the springboard from which the circle is entered, and so the circle reaches back to encompass the dialogue between the researcher and the text. (Scott, 1990: 31)

These considerations seem to undermine some of the factist aims that motivated Scott's considerations. After discussing other attempts at more or less objectivist approaches – semiotics, content analysis, structuralism – he has some interesting concluding remarks. He suggests that 'we must recognize three aspects of the meaning of a text – three 'moments' in the movement of the text from author to audience'. These are the *intended content* at one end and the *received content* at the other end, while the third, the *internal meaning,* is characterized as 'transient and ephemeral' and as 'intervening between the intended and received meaning'. As 'both author and audience may be socially differentiated social entities', there 'may be numerous intended and received meanings' (34).

> The interpretative meaning of the document which the researcher aims to produce therefore is, in a very real sense, a tentative and provisional judgement constantly in need of revision as new discoveries and new problems force the researcher to reappraise the evidence. (Scott, 1990:35)

I have presented John Scott's treatment of the general methodological aspects of document research so extensively because he has provided an exemplary treatment of the problems which one might encounter in a factist-oriented document-based research. Within his chosen framework, his remarks here, as well as elsewhere in his book, are quite sensible.

Texts and images

While Scott seems to target textual documents as his primary object, he claims that pictorial documents – paintings, photographs, films – can be equally treated as 'texts'. There is, I think, some merit in such a claim, as indeed such pictures are equally 'constructed' as 'texts', but there are some interesting differences as well.

There is, first of all, a difference between mechanically produced and completely human-made pictures. A drawing, a painting or a map will be easily recognized by most people as being a human-made depiction, just like a text (in the ordinary sense of the word). Photographs, film and videos, on the other hand, are – at least in part – mechanical recordings, and therefore suggest a pre-given authenticity. There are, of course, many ways in which this mechanical production can and will be managed and manipulated, but there seems to be a core impression of soundness. One would, for example, not take a posed photograph of a well-to-do 19th century family as an adequate depiction of ordinary family life, but it would be considered a reasonably sound rendering of an actually enacted scene, with 'real' backgrounds, clothes, bodies and faces. Current computer-based possibilities of picture manipulation do not seem to have completely undermined this basic 'trust'.

Secondly there is, in my experience, a hard to pin down difference between a depiction in words and through images, in the sense that for word-based texts it makes sense to talk about their 'literal meaning' in contrast to various interpretative meanings, which is not as easily applicable in the same way to images. This may have to do with the fact that texts-in-words are visibly constructed as words, sentences, etc. – identifiable elements, which is not true in the same sense for images which seem to work primarily as *gestalts*. This *gestalt*-like character is, of course, not equally prominent in all kinds of images – less so for maps, more for photographs. And of course, in textual documents *gestalt*-like effects may also play an important role.

With these remarks, I am already approaching a view closer to the *specimen* perspective, but then, these perspectives – the factist and the specimen one – are to be seen as indicating a researcher's major interest in his or her data. In effect, John Scott has, in his discussions, which seems centrally motivated by factist concerns, inevitably also included remarks on documents-as-objects and, most importantly, on processes and practices of documentation. While for him these remarks serve his factist concerns as to the usability of documents for the study of 'external realities', they may also be used in the context of studying documents as such and in research into documentation, that is document production and document use.

Some exemplary studies

It may be useful, at this point, to refer to some exemplary studies that can be placed, broadly speaking, in the factist camp.

The civilising process

In Chapter 1 I referred to the study by Norbert Elias, published in 1939 in German as *Über den Prozess der Zivilisation*, and in English in 1978 as *The civilising process*. The most clearly empirical part of this work, based on primary documents, offers a comparative study of various manner books, as well as subsequent editions of some of these, published in Germany, France, England and Italy, from the 13th through to the 19th centuries. In fact, changes in subsequent editions – at first observed accidentally – were a major source of inspiration for Elias' study as a whole. The changes observed in these texts were taken by him as indications of changes in the actual behaviour of the secular upper and later the middle classes at which these books were aimed. In a book on Norbert Elias' work, Stephen Mennell writes:

> Elias's intention is to show by the examination of empirical evidence how, factually, standards of behaviour and psychological make-up have changed in European society since the Middle Ages, and then to explain why this has happened.
>
> Elias focused particularly on the most basic, 'natural' or animalic' of human functions – eating, drinking, defecating, sleeping, blowing one's nose – because these are things that humans cannot biologically avoid doing, no matter what society, culture or age they live in. (Mennell, 1992: 30, 36–7)

The overall trend in the changes in recommendations that could be observed in these books is that the people addressed were expected to show a more extensive and more subtle restraint of their impulses. One of Elias' most remarkable findings was that what we now would consider the rougher and the most intimate kinds of activities were freely discussed in the books of earlier times, while the advice referring to them gradually disappeared from books published later. This may suggest that such recommendations had become self-evident and/or too embarrassing to mention, but in any case these changes were connected in Elias' analysis to rising levels of socially induced self-restraint – in short, civilization.[2]

It should be noted that although the manner books provided Elias with his 'core data', he used many other kinds of documents – 'literature, paintings and drawings, and historical documents depicting how people were said to have behaved' – as well as secondary literature to construct his image of the civilizing process. In the second volume of the study, dealing with the structural development of Western states and the theory of the civilizing process, Elias relies mainly on historical documents and secondary literature. Similar usage of a core set of documents and a wider range of sources used to contextualize the core data can be found in other document-based studies. I discuss some examples below.

Working-class families

My colleague Ali de Regt has based her study called *Arbeidersgezinnen en beschavingsarbeid: ontwikkelingen in Nederland 1870–1940; een historisch-sociologische studie* [Working-class families and the civilization of workers: developments in the Netherlands 1870–1940] (1984) on a wide range of historical documents. She notes that the everyday life of working-class families has hardly been documented, in comparison, say, with the more public aspects of the life of the higher classes. Therefore she had to use any documents she could find, which, when used together, would allow her to sketch an overall view of working-class family life. So besides secondary literature, she used demographic data, statistics of the composition of the working population, the growth of cities, the number of houses, the rise of juvenile delinquency, etc., family budgets, advisory books, various magazines and some autobiographies written by working-class people. Of special interest were extensive reports of various late 19th century parliamentary investigations into the living conditions of the working classes, including verbatim reports of interrogations of working-class informants. For the parts of the book in which she analyses 'organized attempts by bourgeois sectors of society to civilize working-class families', she mainly relied on the archives of various associations and foundations. These contained a variety of documents, ranging from annual reports to individual case materials. While De Regt's study targets nation-wide developments, set in terms of even more wide-ranging theories such as Elias' theory of the civilizing process, it is based on evidence depicting not only national, but also local and case-bound conditions and experiences. Inevitably, these multi-level documents are used to elaborate each other.

Complaint letters

Another colleague of mine, Rineke van Daalen, published a study called *Klaagbrieven en gemeentalijk ingrijpen: Amsterdam 1865–1920* [Public complaints and government intervention: letters to the municipal authorities of Amsterdam 1865–1920], which is based on an extensive study of 'complaint letters' written by Amsterdam citizens to the municipality (1987). Although her overall perspective is factist, there are features of a specimen perspective in her approach. In her first chapter, after the Introduction, she explicitly says that in that chapter, the letters will not be used as a resource, but instead will be the topic (16). She does indeed treat the letters as describable objects and considers letter writing to the municipal authorities as an activity. The overall framework for her observations on and interpretation of the documents, however, is formulated in terms of broad developments in city life, inter-class relationships and citizenship. The preserved letters are ultimately used as indicators of societal processes and trends. This approach dominates the other chapters, which deal with various aspects of the organization of city life and the considerable changes that were taking place at the time. Her overall thesis is that the middle classes in particular were insecure about their status and frustrated in their encounters with others and at times by the way they were treated by city personnel. They used the letters to urge the city government to take action to protect them against the various hazards of city life.

These examples should suffice to illustrate that for authors such as these the properties of the documents themselves, and the conditions and intentions of their production, while important to consider for methodological reasons, were not their primary interest. The documents were of instrumental utility to get informational access to wider ranging phenomena. In other words, the documents were tools for a job of 'constructive analysis' (cf. Chapter 3).

Documents and practices of documentation

In an ethnomethodological inquiry, documents are used not so much as resource for studying some externa realities, but as a means of providing access to the study of practices of documentation. An immensely practical interest in documentation is a dominant feature of current institutional functioning. The twin concepts of 'accountability' and 'reflexivity' – as discussed in Chapter 2 (pp. 19–20) – specify the ways in which this practical interest is taken as a topic in ethnomethodology. Harold Garfinkel's invention of the ethnomethodological programme was partly inspired by his experiences in studying accounting practices in organizational settings (cf. Rawls, 2002). His paper '"Good" organizational reasons for "bad" clinic records', written with Egon Bittner (in Garfinkel, 1967a: 186–207) is focused on the dilemmas that face a factist researcher trying to use organizational records for studying that selfsame organization. Such records are 'bad' – incomplete, biased, etc. – because they were made for specific, local and practical purposes, which are bound to be at odds with the interests of a researcher who is not a member of that organization. The chapter contrasts a researcher's external criteria of relevance for what should be recorded in a clinic's records, with internal ones apparently used by clinic personnel. It stresses the fact that recording activities are part and parcel of the very practices they are describing, that they are carried out under the auspices of 'marginal utility considerations', with an eye on future uses which may be unknown at the time. The authors suggest that the documents in the case folders may be 'read in one or the other of two contrasting and irreconcilable ways': as an *actuarial record*, or as 'the *record of a therapeutic contract* between the clinic as a medico-legal enterprise and the patient' (198). 'Contract' is here used in a large sense and it is specified that contracts need competent readers.

> In our view *the contents of clinic folders are assembled with regard for the possibility that the relationship may have to be portrayed as having been in accord with expectations of sanctionable performances by clinicians and patients.* (Garfinkel, 1967a: 199; italics in original)

'Contractual' considerations are certainly not the only ones taken into account by practitioners, but, according to the authors, they do have priority over others: 'considerations of medico-legal responsibility exercise an overriding priority of relevance as prevailing structural interests whenever procedures for the maintenance of records and their eligible contents must be decided' (200).

The information contained in the folders is said to be 'occasional and elliptical', it presupposes knowledge of typical occurrences, circumstances and relationships. And these documents are not written for 'theoretical clarity', but rather for pragmatic interests. Clinic records presuppose knowledgeable and entitled readers: 'The possibility of understanding is based on a shared, practical, and entitled understanding of common tasks between writer and reader' (201). In contrast to actuarial records, like bank accounts, clinic records do not presuppose a 'standard' reading. The folders contained material from which a 'documented representation' could be constructed, depending on the practical considerations of the reader, rather than the features of the situation of writing. Like a contract, clinic records provide materials to normalize a relationship, not a fixed description of it.

In contrast to some other essays in the *Studies*, the one on records is not extensively documented. It contains one table giving a quantitative overview of the extent to which various kinds of information were available in the folders. But no quotes from folders are given. No mention is made of any talking with the professionals who had to write the records as part of their clinic activities. It seems that the statements regarding the writing of records were based on a consideration of the problems encountered in reading the records. The essay presents a viewpoint on clinic records, but not an empirical study of a clinic's documenting activities. It does, however, raise a number of very interesting issues for such a study. It claims that medical recording activities are carried out under the prevailing auspices of medico-legal accountability. Records are reflexively tied to the occasional activities they describe. They document those activities for any future consideration.

Patient record cards in General Practice

The routine documentation of clinical encounters by physicians was later studied by Christian Heath, especially in a paper called 'Preserving the consultation: medical record cards and professional conduct' (1982). At a still later stage, he has taken up this topic again, focusing on computer usage within the consultation (Greatbatch et al., 1995; Heath & Luff, 2000: 31–60). Referring back to the Garfinkel & Bittner paper discussed above, he writes:

> The difficulties encountered when using medical records, however, are largely found when they are addressed for purposes for which they were not intended. In actual consultations, during the course of actual medical work, the contents of the records are frequently employed with no difficulty and generate little complaint Reading and writing the descriptions found in the records is an integral part of conducting professional consultative activity; the descriptions are necessary for both the assessment and management of illness. (Heath, 1982: 58)

The records report on the consultations in a way that is usable and relevant for any GP who may consult the record at a later date, as the record 'follows the patient', even when he or she moves to a different practice, or to another part of the country. It is used to decide whether the current complaint has been raised before, and to suggest the likelihood of particular diagnoses or the feasibility of particular treatments. As record entries quoted in the paper show, these tend to be very terse indeed, just a few words quoting the complaints or symptoms, and indicating an assessment and the treatment. In many cases not all of these three types of information are available, as they can be retrieved by a co-professional from the ones given: 'Items are located and part of a framework of components, each of which contributes to the overall sense of an entry and its component items' (64). Even the status of an item is dependent on its place in the 'geography' of the record card: the first item tends to indicate a complaint or symptom, while the second may depict the physician's assessment. In this way, the record provides a sequential sketch of the consultation as a whole, and is intended to invoke that whole when read at a later date. Heath refers, in this regard, both to the characteristics of *gestalt* perception and to Garfinkel's concept of 'documentary interpretation' (cf. pp. 21–2). These characterizations, which suggest that parts and wholes are mutually elaborative, not only apply to items and the entry of which they are a part, but also to entries and the series that they constitute, which may evoke the 'career' of a particular problem. In subsequent entries, an original assessment does not need to be repeated, for instance. Its absence instructs the reader to look for it in earlier entries. Again, it is the assumed similarities in the interpretative frameworks that co-professionals as writers and readers would apply that makes the extreme economy of patient records possible. And furthermore, the practical circumstances of writing and reading the records *during* the consultation make such an economy extremely advisable.[3] The ways in which the physician's reading and writing activities are coordinated with the vocal and visual activities of both doctor and patient has been touched upon by Christian Heath in many of his studies of medical consultations (cf. 1981, 1986; also Heath & Luff, 2000: 27–30 and 48–9 for very clear cases). Patients 'are sensitive to the use of the paper record during the consultation and may attempt to co-ordinate their own actions with the doctor's reading or writing' (Heath & Luff, 2000: 49). It is, therefore, quite important that the relevant information in the records is available 'at a glance'.

Seeing documents, such as patient records, as the product of sets and series of activities of documentation, and then seeing documentation practices as part and parcel of the stream of ongoing situated organizational activities, has important analytical and methodological consequences. While Garfinkel & Bittner seem to have studied the clinic records as such, in isolation from the organizational activities of which they were a part, Christian Heath's 1982 paper came out of an extensive ethnographic study of an urban health centre, which also included observing various clinic activities, interviewing, and extensive audio-visual recording of consultations. Although he does not directly quote from these non-document resources, they apparently have informed his interpretations. For ethnomethodology, then, the ideal set-up for a study of documents-as-documentation is an ethnographic one, combining various ways of collecting data, to be discussed at greater length in the next chapter, on ethnography. For the moment, the issue is that a document's practical sense depends on the intimate relationships between the properties of the document-in-itself and its use, including its writing and (projected) reading. In research based on historical records, a document's conditions of writing can only be inferred from the document itself, informed by general knowledge about similar circumstances based on other documents and secondary literature. It may be hard, however, to gain insight into contexts of use, both projected and actual, when these situations are no longer accessible.

Computer-based record systems

The 'intimate relationship' between a document's properties and its uses becomes acutely clear when established systems of document production using handwriting are transferred to computer-based systems. As a sequel to his 1982 analysis of handwritten medical records, Christian Heath has studied the ways in which a computer-based system, meant to replace handwritten documentation, was actually used by physicians in general practice. This study is reported in a chapter called 'Documents and professional practice: "bad" organisational reasons for "good" clinical records' (in Heath & Luff, 2000: 31–60; an earlier report is in Greatbatch et al., 1995). The subtitle obviously refers back to Garfinkel's chapter with Bittner. He first summarizes the 1982 findings and then goes on to describe both the new system and its actual use in the consultation. A major finding is that although the computer-based system was meant to replace the handwritten record, the two were quite often used alongside each other. The system was designed to facilitate the production of 'better' medical records, but the criteria implied in this ameliorative effort were 'external' ones, that is not based on the local usage by GPs but inspired by the project of using the data-base generated by the local use of the system for aggregate studies of topics like prescription patterns.

A number of design features of the system impeded the usages of the record that had been discovered in the earlier study. By formalizing the recording process, and separating the various classes of details to be recorded, the physicians were no longer able to use the mutually elaborative possibilities of the items forming a *gestalt*-sketch of the consultation as a whole. The subtle displays of ambiguity that the paper-based record allowed were no longer possible. Because different screens had to be filled in, the physicians often had to repeat some details, while they could not see the whole pattern 'at a glance' – either in filling in the different slots of the electronic form, or in consulting earlier records. In this way, one might say, the new system turned the recording task into a bureaucratic duty, rather than a support for the day-to-day work of the physicians in their consulting rooms. When the physicians used the two systems together, the quality of the paper records seemed to be less sure than it used to be, as some details would be only recorded in the computer system and not on paper, which undermined the completeness of the *gestalt* picture. It has too often been observed that the formalization involved in computerization ignores the informal, local and shared practices which cannot easily be caught in a limited set of 'rules'.[4] Ignoring local practices leads to studies and system designs based on an impoverished version of users, treating them – to use Garfinkel's (1967a: 68) expression – as 'judgmental dopes' rather than competent 'members'. Such a 'mistreatment' is not necessary or unavoidable, but a more 'respectful' and adequate approach requires detailed study of local practices.

Documents as such: structures and devices

While many ethnomethodological studies of documents focus on the practical interests of writers and readers, some others have studied documents as such, as structured texts. In other words, they take the products of a writer's work to investigate the textual devices that have been used.

The most famous example of an ethnomethodological study of a text is '"K is mentally ill": the anatomy of a factual account', by Dorothy Smith (1978). It is a detailed analysis of a text written by a student based on an interview she had with another, asking whether this person had ever encountered someone who was mentally ill. Because it is a rather special kind of document, I will not discuss this paper at length, except to note that Smith demonstrates the use of a crucial device, which she calls 'contrast structures'. In the text, the actions of the target person 'K' are continuously contrasted with those of others to suggest their oddity.

A perceptive, although preliminary analysis of a news report was published by Jim Schenkein under the title 'The radio raiders story' (1979). He discusses some aspects of a newspaper clipping from the *Guardian* on an announced subsequent investigation into the failure of the police to catch some bank robbers although they had been warned by a radio amateur who had intercepted walkie-talkie communications among the robbers. Schenkein discusses the 'referential puzzle' that is offered by the headline: 'POLICE INQUIRY INTO WHY THEY MISSED THE RADIO RAIDERS' and the special function of the byline 'By Our Own Reporter'. But he concentrates on the successive verbal depictions of 'Mr Rowlands', the interceptor. The first, 'an amateur radio enthusiast' is presented without quotation marks, the second description is 'a radio "ham" for many years', the third – '"an absolute fanatic" for radio and television communications' – is attributed to 'a relative', the fourth "a nut case" is reported as how he felt the police regarded him when he made his first call, while 'anyone could have picked it up' is quoted from a televised interview with Mr Rowlands himself.

> In delivering to us 'the news' of the radio raiders story, the newspaper account somehow manages, among other things, to give us glimpses of alternative existential systems interacting in the aftermath of the robbery. We are provided these glimpses through a series of alternative descriptions for the story's central character, Mr Rowlands. Each description represents another view of Mr Rowlands, each generates a comparison between itself and the other descriptions as they accumulate through the text, and each can be compared to the reader's own emerging vision of Mr Rowlands. Together they comprise a universe of discourse with densely interacting spokesmen for alternative existential systems. The spokesmen are neatly arranged, the newspaper's own characterization appearing first, Mr Rowland's own

version of himself coming last, and in between a systematically ordered presentation of three progressively vulgar colloquial versions. (Schenkein, 1979: 198)

In this essay, Schenkein demonstrates a range of possibilities for analysing newspaper documents like this. In more general terms than he uses, these can be specified as follows:

- the mutually constitutive relations between headings and texts, here formulated as a puzzle and its solution, but also possibly as an instruction and its execution, a genre characterization and a guided reading, etc.;
- the ways in which textual details can be used to suggest different sources and 'existential systems' or 'possible worlds';
- the central role of depictions of 'persons', 'actors', or 'actants' in a text.

This last analytic option can be linked to the membership categorization analysis, inspired by some of the early work of Harvey Sacks (cf. Chapter 2, pp. 24–5). While originally mostly applied in the analysis of naturally occurring talk-in-interaction (cf. Sacks, 1972a, 1992), it has also been recommended for the analysis of other textual materials, including interviews (Baker, 1997, discussed in Chapter 4, p. 75) and written texts (cf. Silverman, 2001: 139–51).

Writing and reading

It is obvious that in order to exist, documents have to be constructed, which when we consider textual documents means that they have to be written. Writing does not only involve designing words and sentences, but also arranging paragraphs, sections and chapters, making headings and sub-headings, adding notes and references, etc. As indicated in the previous section, these activities can be studied on the basis of their products: texts. But they can also be studied as activities in themselves. When writing, a writer structures an activity field for possible readers. Reading is an 'independent' activity, which is, at the same time partially pre-structured. A reader can follow the instructions embedded in the text or he or she can search out a more or less self-designed 'reading path'.[5] One can read a text from start to finish, which would constitute 'following', or one 'scan' it, dipping in here and there, returning to an earlier page, etc. A text like the one you are reading now offers various suggestions and pointers which may assist a reader in designing a reading path of their own: a table of contents, headings and sub-headings, and especially an index.

In a paper called 'Structuring writing for reading: hypertext and the reading body' (Ten Have, 1999b), I have used my experience in using HTML (HyperText Markup Language), the 'language' of the World Wide Web, as well as my reading of web-based documents, to explore some aspects of writing and reading. The core idea was that the activity of reading a text is structured by the artful use of textual devices, such as paragraphs and footnotes or end notes. Learning to read involves learning to use such devices to structure one's reading. Learning to write involves learning to produce texts which contain devices to structure readings effectively. Reading and writing are basic activities in many cultures, while the repertoire of textual devices tends to be relatively specific to (sub-)cultures. Textual devices, then, can be analysed as ethno-methods for reading and writing. Technologies for producing textual documents, like word processing software programs and HTML can be studied in order to explicate some of these methods, as they have been designed with culturally self-evident practices in mind. I argued that studying reading and writing in the practical field of electronic 'publishing', and comparing their equivalent in the field of printed exchange, helps in understanding the praxeological structures in both fields.[6] What I was trying to get at was that 'membership' – which Garfinkel and Sacks (1970: 342) have primarily explicated in terms of the ability to function adequately in oral interaction, i.e. as *orality*, in most if not all contemporary cultures – also involves *literacy*; which involves the ability not only to follow the text line by line, but also to actively 'see' the organization of the text as a structured flow of information, indicated by various design features, in order to appreciate the 'meaning-*gestalt*' of the text.

I have explored some of the practical aspects of such design features of texts as these are available in the conventions for writing scientific papers. I observed, for instance, the possibilities of knowing 'where you are' in the text when reading it in a book, as a Xerox copy, and as a text on a screen, either within a word processing program or in a WWW browser.

When reading a printed paper, a journal or a book, you have various means of locating the page you are reading in its material context, such as the paper, journal or book in its entirety. There will be page numbers, possibly head or foot texts repeating a chapter title. Furthermore, you have the physical object in your hand: feeling the thickness of the pages already read and those still ahead. It depends, of course, on whether the physical object is the same as the text unit, as with separately printed papers, and especially with books, or whether the text unit is included in a larger collection, as in a journal issue or a paper collection. But in any case, there are material possibilities for locating your current reading within the context of the reading task as a whole.

When reading a text from a screen, however, getting a similar overview can be much harder. This is partly dependent on the reading 'environment', i.e. the program used to project the text. Word processing programs will have various devices to provide some orientation and to 'scroll' the text, or, to put it in terms of a reader's perspective, to 'travel' through the text. The current page number and the line the cursor is on can be projected at the bottom of the screen. But when no section boundary or title is accidentally available on just this screen image, no clear indications of 'where one is' are available. The 'travel options' provided are general ones, like 'next screen', 'previous screen', 'next page', 'previous page', 'top of document', and 'end of document'. There will also be 'search' facilities, which allow you to type a 'string' of characters, i.e. words, to be searched for. These possibilities of 'travelling' the text, however, are largely indifferent to the typographical 'chunk marks' the writer may have provided. Furthermore, apart from scrolling by line, sentence, paragraph, screen or page, these facilities tend to leave the reader-user in the dark as to the 'distance' he or she has travelled.

When reading an HTML-document in a browser, you have even fewer resources to get an 'overview' of the text you are reading. An HTML-document does not have 'pages', such as a document in a word processor has, and no indications similar to page numbers are provided. What is called a 'page' in Internet language is the complete file. So the only guide available is the right-hand scroll bar, which provides a rough indication of the position of the current screen between the top and the bottom of the document.

In a browser such as Netscape Navigator, the general possibilities for 'travelling' within a document are limited to scrolling per line, using the 'up' and 'down' arrow keys; per screen, using 'PgUp' or 'PgDn'; and going to the start or the end of the document, using 'Ctrl-Home' and 'Ctrl-End', while extra scroll functions per line and per screen are available with the mouse on the right-hand scroll bar. Finally, you can use a 'search' facility, to search for a string. No other systematic 'browsing' functions for travelling within the document seem to be available. In short, apart from the writer-constructed extra facilities, reading an HTML-document largely consists of a line-by-line and screen-by-screen following of the text provided, lacking a general orientation to 'where one is' in relation to either the document's beginning or end.

In the paper 'Structuring writing for reading' (Ten Have, 1999b) I discussed some design features in more detail, notably the use of sections, notes and references, for each comparing the possibilities in print documents with HTML-formatted ones. Finally, I noted again that reading, as well as writing, is an embodied activity. I wrote about the eyes scanning the lines, the fingers striking a key, moving and clicking the mouse, and also marking the page. There is one bodily contrast between conventional and electronic reading that I wanted to stress in particular, however. Screen reading requires a relatively fixed body position. A book or journal can be laid on a desk, held in the hand, moved about at will, allowing the body to change its reading position frequently. The screen for most personal computer users, however, is always 'there', forcing the body, and especially the head, into a stiffness that quickly becomes uncomfortable.

These remarks should suffice to alert you to the inevitable fact that documents are not just accidentally concrete 'containers' of 'texts', which in turn provide you with abstract 'information'. In real life, documents are artifacts that need to be handled in embodied ways, first in order to come into existence – scribbling with a pen, typing at a keyboard – and then in order to be used a multitudinous ways.[7]

Final reflections

I have, in this chapter, tried to sketch some basic issues in the use of documents for research purposes. I do not pretend this is a complete overview, either of the issues or of the relevant literature.[8] As noted at the beginning of this chapter, one of documents' main functions in social life is to *fix* particular features of events for use in some other context, or more generally, to allow information to *travel* through time and space. A written report can substitute for an oral testimony; a textbook can stand in for a series of lectures, etc. The preservability of documents makes a wide range of applications possible, whether intended or not. Among the unintended usages of documents, their use as *data* in social research is in the present context of special interest. Such usage generates specific problems, which have to do with particular incompatibilities between the relevant contexts and their implied purposes. Whether one wishes to study documents as such, in a specimen perspective, or in a factist vein as a resource for researching some realities 'outside' the documents as such, one always has to consider some original contexts in relation to the present one. The relations between texts and 'their' contexts have a mutually elaborative and constitutive character. Reading some manner book in terms of its difference with preceding or subsequent specimens, rather than to learn how to behave oneself, 'changes' the meaning of the instructions contained in it. Similarly, reading some phrases from the 'radio raiders' story in order to learn about the ways in which the media constitute 'news' is different from when these were read in 1971 directly from the *Guardian* while sitting in an early morning commuter train.

In short, the serious study of documents inevitably leads to a study of *documentation*, whether as a main pursuit or as a side-activity. The biggest asset of documents, their ability to travel through time and space, also constitutes their major weakness. They may evoke features of other times and places, but inevitably some aspects of their contexts are lost in the process. Whether through invention or serious independent study, this loss has to be repaired somehow. But no method is perfect anyway, so one should try to use documents' richness as sensibly as one can.

Some major points

Documents are used to fix some aspect of life in society for future usage; they are the product of processes of documentation. Such *natural documents* can be used as research materials, but again, this is not unproblematic:

- The ultimate meaning of a document depends on the *context* in which it is considered, but there are various kinds of contexts that may be relevant, such as *production* contexts and various contexts of *use*, whether intended or not.
- One kind of generally unintended usage is to use documents in a research context.

- here the contrast between *factist* and *specimen* perspectives is again relevant: whether the document is used as a source of information on some external reality or as 'a document' in itself:
  - *factist* considerations include its authenticity, credibility and representativeness, but even if these criteria are met in a satisfactory manner, the 'problem of meaning' remains hard to solve; it requires a dialogue between various frames of reference;
  - in this way, a *factist* orientation does not exclude considering a document as a *specimen*; on the contrary it requires such a consideration in order to ground its interpretation;
  - still in a factist vein, the relation between a document and its external referent can be quite varied: the document can be the natural product of the process it documents, like a sales slip, or it can be a purposeful account of a set of events, as in a journalistic report, or it can be meant to instruct an intended audience in one way or another, as in manner books;
  - taking a *specimen* perspective, it is the document itself that is studied: its structure, the various textual devices used to construct it, etc.
- Enlarging this perspective, one can also study *writing and reading*, the first 'pre-structuring' the latter; in that case textual devices can be investigated in action.
- Studies of *documentation* transcend the factist/specimen contrast; they involve studying the actual practices in which and through which documents are produced and used, as part of more encompassing activities, as in current *workplace studies*.
- The remarks above refer primarily to *textual* documents, but many documents of course contain or consist of *images* or *sound*tracks:
  - again factist and specimen perspectives can be contrasted here, with the use of recording technologies suggesting a higher credibility than for instance drawings, which are so obviously hand-made;
  - furthermore, it is obvious that interpreting images or sounds requires more explicitly interpretive work than textual materials, which can be verbally quoted.

Recommended reading

The major overview of the uses of documents as a resource in social research is:

- Scott, John (1990) *A matter of record: documentary sources in social research*. Cambridge: Polity Press

For various styles of 'image-based' research, consult:

- Emmison, M., P. Smith (2000) *Researching the visual: images, objects, contexts and interactions in social and cultural inquiry.* London: Sage

- Prosser, Jon, ed. (1998) *Image-based research: a sourcebook for qualitative researchers*. London: Falmer
- Heath, Christian (1997) 'The analysis of activities in face to face interaction using video'. In: David Silverman, ed. *Qualitative research: theory, method and practice.* London: Sage: 183–200

For ethnomethodological studies of documentation see:

- Garfinkel, Harold, with Egon Bittner (1967) '"Good" organizational reasons for "bad" clinic records'. In: Harold Garfinkel *Studies in ethnomethodology.* Englewood Cliffs, NJ: Prentice-Hall: 186–207
- Heath, Christian, Paul Luff (2000) 'Documents and professional practice: "bad" organisational reasons for "good" clinical records'. In their: *Technology in Action.* Cambridge: Cambridge University Press: 31–60

Notes

1   This idea of interpretation as a dialogue between an original and a current frame of meaning is central to the tradition of 'hermeneutics', which emerged from 19th century biblical studies in Germany and was most influential in German historiography, philosophy and social science.

2   Cas Wouters has used 20th century manner books to study 'national differences and changes pertaining to the relationships between women and men', suggesting 'rising demands on emotion management and self-regulation'. A book is in preparation, to be published by Sage.

3   It has been observed that there is an enormous difference between the terse notes produced by physicians and the extensive ones made by social workers. This may very well be related to the fact that the latter ordinarily neither write nor read during their encounters with clients, but do so in their offices when alone.

4   Cf. Suchman (1987) and Berg (1997) for balanced observations on these matters and Button (1993), Heath & Luff (2000), and Luff, Hindmarsh & Heath (2000) for further discussions and observations based on studies in a range of practical settings.

5   A concept coined by Landow (1992: 7), cited in McHoul & Roe (1996).

6   The term 'praxeological' is often used in recent publications by Garfinkel and others. It can be glossed as referring to the actually used logic of situated actions (see for instance Garfinkel, 2002: 197–218; Coulter, 1991: 188–90).

7   This is a persistent theme in a number of 'workplace studies', such as Whalen (1995a), Hindmarsh & Heath (2000), and some chapters in Heath & Luff (2000); one of these is discussed in Chapter 8 at pp. 166–8.

8   See, for instance, Max Atkinson (1983) on devices like contrasts and lists which can be used in similar ways in oratory and written texts, Alec McHoul (1982) on texual meanings, Dorothy Smith (1987) on the importance of documents as constitutive of 'relations of ruling', Rod Watson (1997a) on 'Ethnomethodology and textual analysis', and Don Zimmerman (1969) on documentation in a public welfare agency.

6 Ethnography and Field Methods

In this chapter, I will be discussing methods that generally speaking have two basic characteristics: the researcher has to leave his or her office and other 'safe' places for what is called 'the field', where the subjects of the project are spending their lives, and the researcher will have to improvise and combine various data-gathering techniques, including some kind of observation, as well as interviewing and the collection of documents. I will, in this chapter, be talking about the various characteristics of ethnographic methods, about the problems that field researchers run into, and about the significance of ethnography in various forms of qualitative research, including ethnomethodology. As in previous chapters, I will refer to various research projects in which field methods have been used, alternating these with more general discussions. It will become clear, I hope, that, especially in ethnography research experiences, data gathering, and the development of a theoretical perspective are interwoven. This interweaving will also be a feature of my treatment of these various issues in this chapter.

On field methods

In their introductory comments on 'The nature of participant observation', George J. McCall and J.L. Simmons write that

> it refers to a characteristic blend or combination of methods and techniques that is employed in studying certain types of subject matter: primitive societies, deviant subcultures, complex organizations . . . social movements, communities, and informal groups. . . . This characteristic blend of techniques . . . involves some amount of genuinely social interaction in the field with the subjects of the study, some direct observation of relevant events, some formal and a great deal of informal interviewing, some systematic counting, some collection of documents and artifacts, and open-endedness in the direction the study takes. (McCall & Simmons, 1969:1)

From a different background and in a different setting, Jeanette Blomberg provides some additional characterizations. In the area with which she is concerned – systems design and human–computer interaction (HCI) – it 'most often refers to an approach used to develop understandings of everyday work practices and technologies in use'. Its 'practitioners share a few basic presuppositions':

These include: a commitment to studying activities in the 'natural' settings in which they occur; an interest in developing detailed descriptions of the lived experience; a focus on what people actually do, not simply on their accounts of their behaviour; and a concern with understanding the relation of particular activities to the constellation of activities that characterize a setting. (Blomberg, 1995: 175)

According to her, 'it is difficult for individuals to articulate the tacit knowledge and understandings they have of familiar activities', therefore, 'it is critical that the things people say about their own activities and about the activities of others be supplemented with firsthand observations of behaviour' in the setting in which these habitually occur (176–7).

In other words, ethnography is committed to using a variety of approaches, always including direct observation of situated activities, in order to grasp the actually lived reality of a target population.

Conflicting loyalties

As we saw in Chapter 4, doing an interview study is for many if not most qualitative researchers the obvious way to collect data, while documents may provide background information or be used as core data in historical projects. Compared to interviews and document-based research, using ethnographic field methods is extremely cumbersome. One has to spend an enormous amount of precious time waiting for interesting events that may never occur, quite often outside office hours. One has to visit places that may be uncomfortable, if not dirty and dangerous. One continuously has to improvise, as life outside is unpredictable and does not conform to a 'topic list'. So why do people do this? Or rather, for which kinds of research problems would ethnography be a solution? A short but incomplete answer would be: for all those topics and interests for which interview data and/or documents would provide unsatisfactory data, for all those situations in which what people say about their lives or what happens to be recorded in documents is too superficial, not detailed enough, too far removed from their everyday activities, or when people are just not accessible and willing to be interviewed and documents are missing. But of course there are positive reasons for ethnography as well. In my view, there are many ways in which ethnographies can be much more useful than interview studies or document-based researches, and apart from that, they tend to offer a much more lively reading experience! But, as indicated, using field methods has its problems. The practical ones are most obvious, and there is a large literature dealing with them, both in the form of general discussions and through methodological chapters and appendices, or scattered remarks in published ethnographic reports. But there are also theoretical and methodological problems, including issues of perspective, relationships, positioning, note-taking and reporting.[1]

Ethnography embodies the 'heroic' side of qualitative research: getting out into the forest or the slums, living dangerously among the natives, madmen or criminals, and coming back with stories about the *real* life that has been observed. The expression 'ethnography' designates the descriptive study of some collectivity, but it is nowadays often used to refer to any study that relies in whole or in part on 'field methods', research strategies that require the researcher to leave his or her office to visit the research subjects in the environments in which they spend the research-relevant parts of their lives. The extent to which the field researcher 'shares' the live circumstances of their subjects varies enormously, from spending a year in the bush to occasional visits, from a quasi-complete immersion to non-participatory observations and interviews. In any ethnography, however, an essential tension seems to exist between the two forms of life with which the researcher has to deal, those of the academy and in the field. From the very first ideas until years after the publication of the report, the researcher will be confronted with dilemmas and strains that can be seen as effects of the differences between these two 'worlds'. This essential tension, living with conflicting expectations and loyalties, will be the unavoidable theme of this chapter.

An important aspect of this tension is that in most settings the local repertoire of personnel categories does not contain one labelled 'ethnographer'. There may be a category 'researcher' or 'investigator', but these often carry category predicates – like doing formal interviews or searching for criminal evidence – that the ethnographer would rather not evoke. Therefore, a major task for any researcher using field methods is, in one way or another, to introduce such a category and make it acceptable to the local members. There are situations, of course, in which this task can be avoided by hiding one's categorical identity as a researcher, but quite often such a strategy has major practical and moral disadvantages. Alternatively, a researcher may use an existing category as partial 'front identity', while not denying being a researcher. In any case, some form of 'identity management' seems to be an unavoidable item on any ethnographer's agenda. In the older fieldwork literature, these issues were mainly discussed under headings like 'fieldwork roles', 'gaining access' and/or the dilemmas involved in covert versus open research. From an ethnomethodological point of view, it seems useful to approach these matters in the terms of membership categorization analysis (MCA), as originally developed by Harvey Sacks and further elaborated by other ethnomethodologists (cf. Chapter 2, p. 23–4, and the sources cited there).

In an ethnographic project, three phases or tasks can be distinguished. The researcher has first to gain permission to do the research from academic bodies and from parties in the field. This means on the one hand writing an acceptable research proposal and on the other gaining access to the field. Secondly, when in the field, various kinds of 'data' have to be gathered and recorded in ways that do not obstruct the ordinary activities in the field too much, while also producing academically adequate evidence. Thirdly, after leaving the field, a report has to be written in a way that is acceptable both to the academy and the field, the first requiring a convincing contribution to social scientific knowledge, the second a picture of life in the field that does not damage the social image of described persons and/or collectivities too much. In actual practice these phases overlap. Maintaining 'access', not only physically but also 'socially', requires constant relational management, and the gathering and recording of 'data' anticipates the report that is to be written. Doing ethnography is a demanding, stressful and time-consuming way of doing research, but it has a core value in that it resonates best with the heuristic and hermeneutic side of qualitative social research.

What I intend to do in this chapter is to discuss the basic characteristics of ethnography as field research, taking the three tasks mentioned above as major points of attention. In order to avoid undue abstraction, I will use a restricted number of exemplary ethnographic studies to explicate various aspects of doing ethnography. These include a variety of studies that could be called 'conventional' and some ethnomethodological ones. In fact, contrary to their reluctance to rely on interviews and documents, ethnomethodologists do use quite a lot of ethnography.

A classic case: *Street corner society*

The major example of ethnographic work that I will discuss in this chapter is *Street corner society: the social structure of an Italian slum*, written by William Foot Whyte, researched in the late 1930s, and first published in 1943. The book starts with Whyte's observations on the 'little guys of Cornerville'. He distinguished two categories: the lower-class 'corner boys' and the aspiring social climbers called the 'college boys'. The first category is represented by 'the Norton gang' led by Whyte's key informant, 'Doc', while his treatment of the second is focused on the Italian Community Club and its leader 'Chick Morelli'. Then he proceeds to the 'big shots', the racketeers and politicians, and concludes with some overall reflections. In the second, 1955 edition of the book, an extensive 'Appendix: On the evolution of street corner society' has been added to the original report, which recounts the story of his research project. A selective and summary paraphrase of parts of this appendix will serve as my point of departure for a discussion of some of ethnography's most relevant aspects.

Whyte starts his account of the research project with a short sketch of his 'personal background', his upbringing in an upper middle-class milieu and his college interests in economics, social reform and writing. A visit to a slum area, which made a deep impression on him, and some abortive efforts at reform during his college years contributed to his plan to do an in-depth 'community study' of a slum district. After college he received a junior fellowship from the Society of Fellows at Harvard and he decided to follow his interests by studying the 'Italian' district of nearby Boston, the North Side, called 'Cornerville' in the book. That area 'best fitted' his 'picture of what a slum district should look like' (283). He continues with an account of his preparations for the project, starting with a 'grandiose plan' for a 10-man study of the community, which was shot down by a supervisor. He wrote several less pretentious outlines, about which he writes: 'the most impressive thing about them is their remoteness from the actual study I carried on' (285).

In his preliminary reading – from community studies to Durkheim and Pareto – and especially in many personal conversations and debates in the rich intellectual community at Harvard, he developed his own approach to investigating 'social structure'. A major influence in this regard were the ideas being developed by two anthropologists, Conrad Arensberg and Eliot Chapple, who stressed the direct observation of people in interaction in order to 'establish objectively the pattern of interaction among people: how often A contacts B, how long they spend together, who originates action when A, B, and C are together, and so on' (287). But most important, it seems, was the expectation that one had to defend oneself and one's finding in a critical and competitive interdisciplinary milieu.

It is generally felt that fieldwork does require a much more intense personal involvement, and that therefore its results are much more dependent on the personality of the researcher, than other forms of social research. Background information on this may therefore be considered to be quite relevant in this context. Furthermore, the conditions of the research were such that Whyte had a lot of freedom to design his study, although he was held accountable to his colleagues and supervisors. For Whyte, then, the academy was a lively and stimulating starting point, but he still had to enter the field.

After some false starts – doing a housing survey and trying to join a couple having a drink – he approached social workers at the local 'settlement house'. It was one of these who understood what he needed and introduced him to the young man who is called 'Doc' in the book. He is quoted as saying things like:

> 'Well, any nights you want to see anything, I'll take you around. I can take you to the joints – gambling joints – I can take you around to the street corners. Just remember that you're my friend. That's all they need to know. I know these places, and, if I tell them that you're my friend, nobody will bother you. You just tell me what you want to see, and we'll arrange it.' (Whyte, 1955: 291)

So Doc proposed to help Whyte to position himself in the community using what may be called the friend-of-a-friend device, relying on a local membership category, rather than any outsider one. He suggested that taking off from such a friend-of-a-friend position, Whyte could gradually create a place for himself in the community. In later phases of the research this proved not always to be that easy. Whyte also took up a room in the district and made some efforts to learn Italian. 'My effort to learn the language probably did more to establish the sincerity of my interest in the people than anything I could have told them of myself and my work' (296).

So, at the beginning of the fieldwork, it was Doc who took Whyte around and introduced him as his friend. This worked well and he seemed to be accepted without too much difficulty, but when he left the scene, Doc had to answer a lot of questions (in Italian). Later, Whyte composed an elaborate explanation, but that didn't help very much. 'I soon found that people were developing their own explanation about me. I was writing a book about Cornerville' (300). If people liked him as a person, they thought that was a good idea, but if they didn't, they rejected it.

Over time, the relationship between Doc and Whyte developed into a collaborative one. Doc learned what was of interest to Whyte, so he started to point out scenes that might be relevant for the research, as well as discussing Whyte's emerging ideas with him. Doc also instructed Whyte in terms of his general approach and handling of field situations, such as when to talk and when to keep silent. After a particularly painful incident:

> The next day Doc explained the lesson of the previous evening. 'Go easy on that "who," "what," "why," "when," "where" stuff, Bill. You ask those questions, and people will clam up on you. If people accept you, you can just hang around, and you'll learn the answers in the long run without even having to ask the questions.' (Whyte, 1955: 303)

This proved indeed to be the case. By just hanging around and listening, Whyte learned answers to most of his questions, while later on, he also learned when he could ask which questions, depending on his personal relationships. 'When I had established my position on the street corner, the data simply came to me without very active efforts on my part' (303).

As in any field situation, Whyte encountered some difficulties while trying to 'fit into Cornerville'. He had to find a balance between adaptation and identity. When on one occasion he was using the sort of vulgar language he heard around him, this was not appreciated: 'Bill, you're not supposed to talk like that, that doesn't sound like you' (304). Maintaining good working relationships in the field inevitably engenders dilemmas that are hard to manage – between involvement and detachment, between being an outsider and simulating being a member. Whyte discusses these dilemmas in a number of areas, including language use, money spending and lending, and sport activities. Especially difficult may be encounters between antagonistic groups with which the fieldworker wants to maintain good relationship: in Whyte's case with the 'corner boys' and the 'college boys'.

Bowling

For a time, bowling played an important role in the life of Doc's corner boy gang. In the main text, Whyte describes how the bowling activities developed over time. He pays particular attention to the relation, as he sees it, between a player's place in the group hierarchy and his bowling capacities (14–25). The general idea is that the members, especially those in the higher positions, through selective encouragement maintain or undermine the various players' self-confidence to the effect that their personal scores reflect their position in the hierarchy. This was especially the case in a major session at the end of the season, an individual match among the 10 most frequently present bowlers. The men who held top positions in the hierarchy predicted that they would also be the top scorers, which indeed proved to be the case. Contrary to these predictions, however, Whyte took the number 1 position in the scoring list, but he doesn't make too much of this in the main text. He remarks that while he was on good terms with all, he was closer to the leaders. From a discussion a few days later, Whyte quotes the following remarks:

> *Long John:* I only wanted to be sure that Alec or Joe Dodge didn't win. That wouldn't have been right.
> *Doc:* That's right. We didn't want to make it tough for you, because we all liked you, and the other fellows did too. If somebody had tried to make it tough for you, we would have protected you. . . . If Joe Dodge or Alec had been out in front, it would have been different. We would have talked them out of it. We would have made plenty of noise. We would have been really vicious. . . .' (Whyte, 1955: 21)

In the appendix, he provides a more personal account, stressing both the excitement of his discovery of the connection between the predictions and the hierarchical positions and his elated feeling concerning his own playing. After recounting that after hearing the predictions he hypothesized that the general standing of a man with his group would influence his abilities when playing in their company, he writes:

> I went down to the alleys that night fascinated and just a bit awed by what I was about to witness. Here was the social structure in action right on the bowling alleys. It held the individual members in their places – and I along with them. I did not stop to reason then that, as a close friend of Doc, Danny, and Mike, I held a position close to the top of the gang and therefore should be expected to excel on this great occasion. I simply felt myself buoyed up by the situation. I felt my friends were for me, had confidence in me, wanted me to bowl well. As my turn came and I stepped up to bowl, I felt supremely confident that I was going to hit the pins that I was aiming at. I have never felt quite that way before – or since. Here at the bowling alley I was experiencing subjectively the impact of the group structure upon the individual. It was a strange feeling, as if something larger than myself was controlling the ball as I went through my swing and released it toward the pins. (Whyte, 1955: 318–19)

Writing about his reflections on this experience later, he not only mentions his major finding about 'the relationship between individual performance and group structure', but also that up until that night he had considered his bowling activities as 'simply recreation for myself and my friends' (320) and also as a part of building a position for himself with the men, and therefore had never taken notes about the scores and other game-related events. The lesson he takes from this experience is:

> Instead of bowling in order to be able to observe something else, I should have been bowling in order to observe bowling. I learned then that the day-to-day routine activities of these men constituted the basic data of my study. (Whyte, 1955: 320)

One can say, however, that, at least in the main text, Whyte is still not taking 'bowling' as his *topic*, but rather something like 'social-structure-in-action', or 'a hierarchy-maintaining mechanism'.[2]

'Objective structures' and a leadership perspective

In more general terms, these passages raise important issues of the interconnections between (subjective) experiences, (objective) observations, and analytic preferences. It is clear from Whyte's 'confessions' that he was defensive of his overall approach in terms of the objectivist and quantitative critiques he was receiving from his Harvard colleagues and supervisors. He regretted, therefore, that he discovered the possible analytic usage of the 'objective' bowling scores when it was too late. Indeed, he tries at various point in his main text to 'objectify' his observations, using schematic depictions of status relations and interactional networks (13, 95, 156, 184, 188, 222), and also by counts of who was talking with whom (333–5), etc. This is part of the Arensberg & Chapple approach, to which I referred earlier (p. 111), stressing objectifiable aspects of interactions.

A further consideration of his approach, not only methodologically, but also theoretically, allows one to discern even more involved and consequential connections. As noted, Whyte observed the interactions in terms of their 'structure', operationalized in terms of who interacts with whom and who initiates interaction for whom. It is also clear that he was closest to Doc, who was the 'leader' of his chosen gang of corner boys. These two circumstances seem to have contributed to his taking what I will call a 'leadership perspective' on the life he observed, in which leadership is conceived in terms of establishing relatively stable relationships among group members and with various other leaders.

Here is how Whyte summarized the development of Doc's gang, 'the Nortons':

> The men became accustomed to acting together. They were also tied to one another by mutual obligations. In their experiences together there were innumerable occasions when one man would feel called upon to help another, and the man who was aided would want to return the favor. Strong group loyalties were supported by these reciprocal activities. (Whyte, 1955: 12)

And he adds that 'there were distinctions in rank' among the members. The top positions were taken by some slightly older ones, who 'possessed a greater capacity for social movement', that is they had a wider circle of friends. 'The leadership three were also respected for their intelligence and powers of self-expression', and 'Doc in particular was noted for his skill in argument' (12).

And talking about bowling as a group activity:

> The origination of group action is another factor in the situation. The Community Club match really inaugurated bowling as a group activity, and that match was arranged by Doc. Group activities are originated by the men with highest standing in the group, and it is natural for a man to encourage an activity in which he excels and discourage one in which he does not excel. (Whyte, 1955: 24)

Whyte not only took a leadership perspective in the sense that he considered it a key element in the group life he observed, but also as a sort of methodological preference in his choice of informants. As he explains:

> While I worked more closely with Doc than with any other individual, I always sought out the leader in whatever group I was studying. I wanted not only sponsorship from him but also more active collaboration with the study. Since these leaders had the sort of position in the community that enabled them to observe much better than the followers what was going on and since they were in general

more skilful observers than the followers, I found that I had much to learn from a more active collaboration with them. (Whyte, 1955: 302)

So it is in many ways not surprising, and quite consistent, that Whyte took such a leader-like view of life in the district.

In a later part of the book, which I will not discuss here, Whyte reports his research on two 'higher' levels in the community, first the college boys and later the racketeers and politicians. The leader of the college boys, Chick, is described as more individualistic and ambitious than Doc. In organizing the Italian Community Club he tended to take a formalistic, 'parliamentarian' approach to leadership, relying on argumentation and voting rather than seeking consensus in an informal fashion. This accounts, according to Whyte, for the rather conflictual history of that organization. What we can discern here is the contrast between what later became known as formal and informal leadership, and the idea that a too formal approach, relying only on positions and procedures, is not enough for successful leadership. These ideas played a central role in the industrial sociology that emerged after the war, to which Whyte made a significant contribution.

In his conclusion Whyte again goes to some lengths to develop his perspective on leadership in terms of the dynamics of intragroup relationships, stressing again that the leader is the one to initiate group action, the role of spending money and even the function an active and successful leadership has for the leader's well-being (257–63). In fact, he explains some later psychological problems of Doc and one of his friends as resulting from their inability to live up to the leadership position, and adds:

> The type of explanation suggested to account for the difficulties of Long John and Doc has the advantage that it rests upon the objective study of actions. A man's attitudes cannot be observed but instead must be inferred from his behavior. Since actions are directly subject to observation and may be recorded like other scientific data, it seems wise to try to understand man through studying his actions. This approach not only provides information upon the nature of informal group relations but it also offers a framework for the understanding of the individual's adjustment to his society. (Whyte, 1955: 268)

And towards the end of the book, he states:

> The corner gang, the racket and police organizations, the political organization, and now the social structure have all been described and analyzed in terms of a hierarchy of personal relations based upon a system of reciprocal obligations. These are the fundamental elements out of which all Cornerville institutions are constructed. (Whyte, 1955: 273)

What we see displayed in these quotes is a particular perspective on 'structural' aspects of social life, which sees them as a product of group activities resulting in personal relationships of some stability, which in turn are actively managed by people with leadership capacities. It is remarkable that Whyte's perspective as displayed in these concluding remarks is rather similar to the one suggested by his reflections on fieldwork. 'Method' and 'substance' seem to be mutually constitutive.

Effects of publication

The final topic that I will discuss in this section refers back to my earlier remarks on the ambivalence of the researcher-informant relationship: what happens after publication of the report. In his appendix, Whyte describes his visits to various informants after the book had been published, mentioning both their later careers and their reactions to the book (342–56). He characterizes Doc's reaction, some five years after the publication, as 'a combination of pride and embarrassment'. Doc seems to have actively discouraged people from reading the book as well as further publicity. Chick, the college boy leader was also rather ambivalent, protesting that he was depicted as a bit too rough, for instance in his manner of speaking. He is quoted as saying: 'The trouble is, Bill, you caught people with their hair down. It's a true picture, yes; but people feel it's a little too personal' (347). Whyte agrees that, contrary to a formal interview, using field methods does not allow people to offer only a 'public performance' to the researcher. So he catches them in a range of situations and therefore also in less flattering moments. While this may be unavoidable, a researcher still has the opportunity to select what he will report. But then, there's another dilemma, or should we say clash, between the requirements of research and everyday living: the first requires full and honest reporting, the latter may make tactful avoidance of painful matters desirable. And what will turn out to be painful may not always be easy to predict. Whyte reports that Doc had read every page of the book before it was published, but apparently he still had some misgivings about it afterwards.[3] The feeling of being 'used' by the researcher may be hard to avoid.

Institutional ethnography

I have spent so many pages on this classic instance of ethnography because it provides a glimpse of the many aspects and dilemmas of actually doing an ethnographic study. I am aware, of course, that it is just one, unique case, so while useful as an illustration, it does not offer a nearly complete picture of the ethnographic adventure. What is especially lacking in my treatment of this case is a sense of the difficulties one may run into when investigating the working of an organization. What I did not discuss were Whyte's rather critical observations on social work in the district, organized in two settlement houses. And indeed some of the more negative reactions he received to his book came from people associated with those institutions. To do some justice to these kinds of issues, I will focus, in this section, on what I want to call 'institutional ethnography'.[4] I use this term to indicate a genre of ethnographic studies in which the ethnographer enters an organization, quite often a service institution, to study particular aspects of the daily workings of (a part or aspect of) that organization. Examples are Erving Goffman's *Asylums: essays on the social situation of mental patients and other inmates* (1961) and two studies of euthanasia in Dutch hospitals by Robert Pool (1996) and Anne-Mei The (1997).

Such ethnographies not only tend to elaborate particular analytic themes, but they also engender particular strategic problems. A first and major point is that such studies require the official approval of the authorities in charge of the institution, and experience shows that these are often extremely reluctant to allow researchers in. The situation tends to be roughly as follows. One can distinguish three parties in the arena the researcher would like to investigate: management, workers and clients. The relation among these parties, and also within the first two mentioned collectives, may be tense. There may be conflicts and wherever you look long enough you are bound to encounter secrets, things that are done in ways that one wouldn't like to be made public. For example, management may fear 'negative publicity' – information becoming known that might damage the image of the organization that it would like to protect. Workers, in turn, may dislike the idea that the corner-cutting aspects of their daily practices might become known to management and then lead to management action. It seems unavoidable that detailed information on a practice leads to, or is at least associated with, criticism, debunking, exposure.

In Goffman's *Asylums* and in other institutional ethnographies of service institutions, a discrepancy has been noted between the officially maintained 'ideological' version of institutional practices and a much less flattering, down-to-earth version which arises from the ethnographic descriptions. And in the case of *Asylums*, this debunking report seems to have made a major contribution to a world-wide reconsideration of institutional psychiatry.

So rather than being surprised that a researcher is not allowed to enter an institution to explore its workings, one should be surprised that at times ethnographers are indeed accepted. On the other hand, refusing research is an accountable action: it suggests that one has something to hide. So authorities wanting to refuse entry need arguments. Here are some of the commonly used ones. The presence of a researcher would disrupt the workings of the institution. The organization is currently in flux because of a reorganization and research would confuse these delicate processes. The clients could object for privacy reasons, and even if they would not do so, management wants to protect them anyway. A researcher's counter-arguments could be that no real disturbance is to be expected, that the time investment requested of the workers will be minimal, that the intentions are not critical at all, but just scientific, that both the name of the organization and of all persons eventually mentioned in the report will be changed, etc. Unavoidably, when researchers are allowed in, there will be some disruption of ordinary routines. There will be claims on the time of workers. People will feel 'observed', at least for some time. And when a report is published, there will be objectified depictions of situated practices, which – because of this reframing in a different context – will be somehow 'strange'.

The ways in which an institutional arena is divided into various 'parties' or 'categories' will also have an impact on the fieldworker's research activities, loyalties and understandings. The split between workers and clients is an obvious case in point, but within the workers there may also be deep-cutting divisions, such as between physicians and nurses in a hospital setting. In the two euthanasia studies by Pool and The, the first was intentionally focused more on physicians, the second on nurses, while both report at times intense involvement with the patient-side as well.

Perspectives

In ethnography, as well as in other kinds of qualitative social research, it is often stated that the overall purpose of the research project is to get at the participants' own perspective, their particular, local, native vision of the world. In ethnography, this overall aim to study the world of the research subjects 'from the inside' is taken more or less literally as the researcher tries to get as close as feasible to the actually lived action scenes of the natives, whether coral reefs, street corners or hospital beds. But then, the idea of studying the native perspective goes deeper than just a physical approximation.

In anthropology, a distinction is often made between what are called *emic* and *etic* descriptions, concepts or meanings. These terms were developed in linguistic anthropology by Kenneth Pike (1967):

> It proves convenient - though partially arbitrary – to describe behavior from two different standpoints, which lead to results which shade into one another. The etic viewpoint studies behavior as from outside of a particular system, and as an essential initial approach to an alien system. The emic viewpoint results from studying behavior as from inside the system. (Pike, 1967: 37)

These terms were constructed by analogy with 'phonetic' and 'phonemic' from linguistics, but they have a wider relevance. *Etic* categories are in principle universal. They can be formulated prior to any particular analysis, to be applied afterwards to cases at hand. *Emic* categories, on the other hand, emerge from one culture in particular and are 'discovered' during an investigation into that particular culture.

> Descriptions or analyses from the etic standpoint are 'alien' in view, with criteria external to the system. Emic descriptions provide an internal view, with criteria chosen from within the system. They represent to us the view of one familiar with the system and who knows how to function within it himself. (Pike, 1967: 38)

The last clause in this quote suggests an affinity with the notion of 'membership knowledge', as used in ethnomethodology (cf. Chapter 2 and Ten Have, 2002a), but it is most often conceived of in terms of empathizing with or imaginative immersion in the subjects' experiences and intentions. The emic/etic distinction is not unproblematic (cf. Duranti, 1997: 172–4), but it seems useful to alert one to some of the ideas associated with 'perspective' as applied to ethnography.

Note-taking

Ethnographers seem to agree that taking notes is a crucial activity in any ethnographic endeavour, an essential step in the process of moving from the informal and intuitive knowledge that comes with experience and observation on to an analytic grasp of the forms of life being studied. As John and Lyn Lofland write in their 'guide to qualitative observation and analysis':

> Without continually writing down what has gone on, the observer is hardly in a better position to analyze and comprehend the workings of a world than are the members themselves. Writing, in the form of continued notes by which the past is retained in the present, is an absolutely necessary if not sufficient condition for comprehending the objects of observation. Aside from getting along in the setting, the fundamental concrete task of the observer is the taking of field notes. If you are not doing so, you might as well not be in the setting. (Lofland & Lofland, 1984: 62–3)

This admonition does not specify, of course, what one should note down, how much, in which terms, etc. The Loflands distinguish successively 'mental notes', 'jotted notes' and 'full field notes'. 'Mental notes' are what you try to 'fix' in your mind when something happens, 'jotted notes' are the few words one scribbles in a notebook as reminders, while 'full notes' consist of a report, written as soon as possible after the events recorded, as a 'more or less chronological log of' what is happening to and in the setting and to or in the observer' (65). Besides urging promptness, they recommend that the researcher 'be concrete' and typographically distinguish verbatim quotes from free paraphrases. They also advise the fieldworker to take down any additional information or thoughts that the activity of descriptive note-taking may work up in the researcher's mind: memories, changes and contrasts compared to earlier notes, theoretical and methodological ideas, etc. Such additional comments should be marked as such (for instance by putting them in parentheses). Schatzman and Strauss (1973: 99–101) even recommend a separation into three types of notes, marked in the margin as such: 'observational notes' (ON), 'theoretical notes' (TN) and 'methodological notes' (MN). In short, note-takers are advised on the one hand to stay close to the actual events, in time and in being concrete, while on the other hand also permitting themselves to write in a free-flowing fashion, memoing any ideas that the evidence being recorded raises in their minds – but still maintaining the distinction between the two. In order to keep this distinction in mind, the ethnographer may choose to divide a writing session into two parts, the first describing the observed scene in a rather spontaneous mode, using plain – possibly native – language; the second, based on re-reading the products of the first, in a reflective mode, adding comments and suggestions – in short first ONs, and later TNs and MNs.

Note-taking is not only a 'recording' activity, it is 'transformative' as well. As Emerson et al. say in their *Writing ethnographic fieldnotes*:

> In writing a fieldnote [one] does not simply put happenings into words. Rather, such writing is an interpretive process: it is the very first act of textualizing. Indeed, this often 'invisible' work – *writing ethnographic fieldnotes* – is the primordial

textualization that creates a world on the page and ultimately shapes the final ethnographic, published text. (Emerson, Fretz and Shaw, 1995: 16)

In this way, the note-taking activity reinforces the observer-side of ethnographic presence, which is quite often experienced as in tension, if not in conflict, with the participant-side. Any writing can be seen as resulting from specific, even if not completely conscious, writing choices (105–7), which, therefore, are features of the 'constructive' process of ethnography.

The contrast between *emic* and *etic* depictions is also relevant in note-taking. The words and categories that constitute the 'emic' perspective will not be immediately available to the researcher/note-taker. It is part of the ethnographic learning task to acquire the competencies and sensitivities that make the emic features of scenes and discourses available. This requires an open mind and entering a continuous dialogue – both actual and virtual – between the emic and the etic, based on the close observation of naturally occurring scenes of what might be called the emic-in-action: research subjects actually and without provocation (researcher questions) using the emic words and categories (cf. Emerson et al., 1995: 108–41).

The ultimate purpose of writing field notes is, of course, for them to be used as evidence, to be analysed, leading to an informative social scientific report. It can be noted again that 'description' and 'analysis' cannot ultimately be separated while they mutually implicate one another.[5]

More exemplary studies

For the moment, I want to return to some exemplary studies in 'institutional ethnography', in order to flesh out the preceding remarks a bit. I earlier mentioned Erving Goffman's *Asylums* as a major example, but that book is in many ways exceptional, and therefore not typical of the genre I want to discuss here. As many commentators have remarked, the core activity in Goffman's many essays is the development of a conceptual framework, starting with one or another metaphor, followed by an elaboration of a growing number of distinctions. These conceptual constructions are then abundantly illustrated with a range of examples of varying empirical status, including his own fieldwork observations. In *Asylums* the basic idea is that of a 'total institution', for which the large mental hospital he studied provided ample illustrative materials. In comparison with most ethnographies, this way of working represents an atypical kind of dialogue between ideas and evidence. Furthermore, Goffman hardly mentions how he actually worked in the field.[6]

Euthanasia practices in two hospitals

Two more typical examples – although quite special in terms of their topic – are the studies by Robert Pool (1996, 2000) and Anne-Mei The (1997) of euthanasia practices in two Dutch hospitals. The studies were part of a larger, government financed, research project that was intended to clarify the actual practices which led to various decisions regarding the end of life of very ill patients, in a period – the early 1990s – when opinions about euthanasia were in flux and heavily debated. Both researchers report that it took them many months to find a place that would let them in and both say that they finally succeeded only by a friend-of-a-friend kind of personal recommendation. Anne-Mei The focuses her report on the role of the nursing staff in the decision-making process, while Robert Pool was better able to represent the role of the physicians. This was not just a matter of personal interest or preference, but seems more or less unavoidable. Pool 'followed' the doctors, both literally and in terms of studying their perspective, while The associated herself with the nurses, feeling that this was almost a 'political' choice. In ethnography, research relations are at the same time social relations: socializing with the members of one category may be frowned upon by members of the other one. Furthermore, the relations that physicians and nurses have with patients and their associates tend to be rather different in many respects: in duration, intimacy and content. Doctors have a more technical and focused perspective, while the contacts that nurses have are more 'social' in character. These differences in relationship and perspective are reinforced by various organizational differences, in tasks and responsibilities but also in terms of the organization of work shifts, leading to communication barriers, which tend to be especially urgent in crisis situations. One could even speak of two 'cultures', each with its own kinds of acceptable discourse, offering differing possibilities for technical elaboration or emotional expression.

Both authors stress the complexity of decision-making processes regarding the end of life and ultimate care. It takes time to reach a final decision in a field in which so many parties with different perspectives, information, responsibilities and emotions are involved. Both authors have chosen a strategy of presenting in detail a relatively small number of cases (10) which are considered to be illustrative of a range of issues and trajectories. These are described in detail, stressing the multitude of viewpoints and feelings of the parties involved as the case develops. Pool is more restrictive in providing general reflections than The. Both authors used audio recordings of various scenes which are quoted – in edited form – as part of the case presentations. In this way, the authors have produced reports which demonstrate the extreme complexity of euthanasia problems as these are experienced in actual hospital practices, in contrast to the inevitable simplifications in public debates about these matters. In a way, such debates and the general political and moral arguments that constitute them lose their relevance as people are faced with the tasks involved in the care of dying patients. As such they provide a major argument for the sense of doing ethnographic studies.

Before I leave these two studies, let me say a few words about their authors. Robert Pool is an anthropologist who wrote a PhD thesis on folk ideas about illness among villagers in Cameroon in West Africa. He stresses that he sees meanings not as fixed entities to be discovered by the ethnographer, but as 'performed' in actual situations, so his overall orientation seems to be close to some types of post-modernism. Still, his insistence on making audio recordings whenever that seemed feasible also suggests a certain 'realism', at least in the collection of evidence. Anne-Mei The studied both law and anthropology. She does not express affinities with a particular theoretical or methodological 'school', but she is firm in stressing the importance of fieldwork and of her personal involvement in the cases that she describes.

Passing on

In line with the general purpose of this book, I will now present two ethnographies that demonstrate a clear ethnomethodological perspective.[7] The first of these is David Sudnow's *Passing on: the social organization of dying* (1967). It is, as far as I know, the first ethnomethodological ethnography that has been published as a book. The study is based on observations in two hospitals, one he called County, 'a large, urban West Coast charity institution', and another Cohen, 'a Midwestern, private, general hospital'. Sudnow characterizes his book in the Preface as follows:

> This study is, first and foremost, an ethnography. It seeks to depict the heretofore undescribed social organization of 'death work' and to do so from the perspective of those persons in our society intimately involved, as a matter of daily occupational life, in caring for the 'dying' and the 'dead' – members of a hospital staff. (Sudnow, 1967: V)

A little further on, he writes:

> A central theoretical and methodological perspective guides much of the study to follow. That perspective says that the categories of hospital life, e.g., 'life,' 'illness,' 'patient,' 'dying,' 'death,' or whatever, are to be seen as *constituted by the practices of hospital personnel* as they engage in their daily routinized interactions within an organizational milieu. (Sudnow, 1967: 8)

He reports his core observations in two chapters, 'The occurrence and visibility of death' and 'Death and dying as social states of affairs', adding a chapter 'On bad news' about the organization of death announcements.

Essential to a sociological study of death and dying is, of course, a distinction between the social and the biological. What is called 'clinical death' is marked by 'the appearance of "death signs" upon physical examination'; 'biological death' involves 'the cessation of cellular activity'. These two should be distinguished, then, from 'social death', 'which, within the hospital setting, is marked by that point at which a patient is treated essentially as a corpse, though perhaps still "clinically" and "biologically" alive' (74). These distinctions became crucial at those moments when some discrepancy manifested itself, for instance when a nurse tried to feed a person who was already 'really' dead, or more commonly, when someone about to die was already treated as essentially a corpse. Whether someone was treated as socially dead or still 'possibly alive' could be related to various conditions and local evaluations of that person, rather than being simply a 'medical' decision. The observations reported in this study often have the character of summary characterization of routines, being at times substantiated by description of critical incidents. The stress on routines is especially prominent in his descriptions of County, while a dominant theme throughout the book is accountability, as in the following:

> No matter how firmly grounded in experience the physician's assessment of inevitable death within specifiable time periods, no matter how deteriorated and beyond repair the patient's condition, the reluctance or hesitancy or willingness to orient to the patient as one who is dying can often be located by reference to the pressures that confront the physician, and particularly by reference to the extent and manner in which he finds his activities accountable to others. Within the course of a hospital admission that is felt to be the patient's last, the timing of the proclamation – or if not an outright proclamation then the institution of 'merely palliative care' – can be seen as largely a function of the various audiences that the physician faces and attends as audiences he might be obliged to face. (Sudnow, 1967: 91–2)

In other words, decisions taken in the last phase of a patient's life are also practical decisions embedded in the social setting in which workers are implicated. In County, an essential part of the practical context was a relative absence of parties to which the staff risked being held accountable. Most patients were very ill indeed and did not have a very 'active' family. So practical considerations of work organization and medical interest could easily take the upper hand, while routinization was a prominent feature of the work. Exceptional cases provided a contrast to this overall picture of indifference:

> On those occasions when a nontypical death caused staff members to step outside their regularly maintained attitudes of indifference and efficiency, one could glimpse a capacity for emotional involvement which ordinary work activities did not provide proper occasions for displaying. The maintenance of appropriate levels of affect in the hospital requires standardization to the types of events and persons which personnel confront. (Sudnow, 1967: 171)

These few glimpses of this impressive study should suffice, in this context, to show that a study based on detached observation can bear strong ethnomethodological fruits, to mention a few: descriptions of routines and exceptional incidents, demonstrations of the significance of accountability and 'respecifications' of common sociological concepts like 'differential treatment' or even 'medical care' and 'social class' as situated practices. Sudnow's observations are especially focused on the workers, which corresponds to my earlier remarks to the effect that it is hard to study the world of more than one category at a time. In the second ethnomethodological ethnography that I will present here, the researcher tried to avoid such a category-bound perspective.

'Telling the code'

In his *Language and social reality: the case of telling the convict code*, D. Lawrence Wieder (1974a) reports an ethnographic study of a 'half-way house for paroled (ex-)addicts'. His ethnography, however, is not just a description of a local culture or the workings of an organization. It is rather the case that he 'treat(s) the ethnographic occasion itself as an object of study'(43). As he explains:

> The formal structures of everyday life in general, and the place of norms in these structures in particular, may be made accessible to study by embarking on a traditional ethnography of a normative culture and then turning our attention to the production of that ethnography as an accomplishment in the context of the ethnographer's interactions with his informants and the informants' folk use of 'ethnographies'. (Wieder, 1974a: 43)

Wieder's text is divided into two parts. In the first, he offers an overview of the patterns of resident behaviour which he observed in the 'half-way house' which he studied, and the explanations for these patterns that were available in the talk of residents and staff members, as well as in the established literature on similar institutions. Such explanations were usually given in terms of a 'convict code' that normatively obliged the residents to refuse to cooperate in the programme that was designed to assist their rehabilitation. The first part, then, offers a kind of standard sociological way in which action patterns are explained in terms of independently existing norm sets. In the second part, on the other hand, these kinds of explanation are themselves taken as topics of investigation, as situated practices. That is the idea expressed in the subtitle's 'telling the code'. In other words, what in the first part was treated as a *resource* for sociological analysis, is now turned into a *topic* for an ethnomethodological investigation. It now 'becomes his [Wieder's] problematic phenomenon: How do parties to the setting find the code to be the source of, and hence the ready explanation for, the distinctive patterns of behavior found in the halfway house?' (Zimmerman, in Wieder, 1974a: 16).

The overall structure of Wieder's report is, then, closely tied to the specifics of his argument. In Part One he describes a number of 'patterns of resident behavior', for instance what he calls 'doing distance'. This became visible in seating arrangements, conversational patterns and language choice (Spanish or English). Other patterns include: 'doing disinterest', 'doing disrespect', 'doing unreliability as informants', and especially 'doing violations'. So, the residents continuously showed that they were unwilling to cooperate with staff and to follow the official rules and regulations. Both residents and staff related these behaviours quite explicitly to 'the code', an informal set of norms that were said to be learned in prison, if not even earlier, on the streets. Wieder provides a summary version in a number of rules, like 'do not snitch', 'do not cop out', 'help other residents', 'do not trust staff', etc. In a similar way, such conceptions of a 'prison code' have been used in the sociological literature to 'explain' observed behavioural patterns.

In Part Two of the book, Wieder recounts how he was, from very early on in his research, 'instructed' in the code.

> In the third to fourth week of the study, my understanding of the code as it applied to me (that it applied to me and how it applied to me) was strengthened by some residents who explicitly pointed out the relevance of the code in and for their dealings with me. . . . resident recitations of the code, or some element of it, were done in such a way that the residents were not simply describing a set of rules to me, but were also simultaneously sanctioning my conduct by such a recitation. I experienced their 'telling the code' as an attempt to constrain my conduct by telling me what I could and could not appropriately do. In particular, they were often engaged in persuading me that some questions I might ask and some questions I did ask were 'out of order' and that there were some areas of resident 'under-life' that I should not attempt to explore. (Wieder, 1974a: 138)

Here we see how the evolving research experience not only produces 'findings', but at the same time conditions the research itself. In a similar fashion, Wieder shows how 'telling the code' and seeing things happening in terms of 'the code' served residents and staff in handling the situations they were facing as somehow rational and general. It allowed members of both parties to take the troubles they were having with each other as 'nothing personal'.

> 'Telling the code' provided staff with a useful way of talking about residents and themselves which portrayed both teams as more or less reasonable and more or less helpless to change the character of the relationship between the teams, because of the social-fact character (in Durkheim's sense) of the regularities made available by 'telling the code' which were none of anybody's specific doing or responsibility. (Wieder, 1974a: 157)

Becoming a member of the organization, whether as resident, staff member or researcher, involved 'seeing' things in terms of the code, explaining whatever happened in its terms, including the general failure to enact the programme as planned or to reach the project's official goals. Wieder does not fail to note, of course, that the relation of 'the code' to the particulars of life in the half-way house was one of 'reflexivity', in Garfinkel's sense: the explanation was part of what it was explaining. These themes are elaborated in the text of the second part in great detail, empirically and conceptually, making this book one of the most instructive in earlier ethnomethodology.[8]

Categorical issues

Let me add a few words on Wieder's study as an institutional ethnography. As noted above, he uses his own research-strategic troubles as a learning experience as he continuously refers to his 'being instructed' in using the code as an order-producing device and to his own growing competence to use it in this fashion. At first he tried to associate himself with the residents. He dressed informally to distinguish himself from staff, he avoided being seen with staff, and tried to strike up conversations with residents as much as he could. He was not very successful in these endeavours, however. When they were not required to be in the house, the residents tended to be out. And when he succeeded in talking with them, they would break off the conversation as soon as he tried to talk about particular kinds of topics such as deviant activities and relations within the resident group. Again, these frustrating experiences were accounted for and explained to him in terms of 'the code'. So he felt that he was not getting anywhere with his research. He did some formal interviews with residents, avoiding all tabu areas, and he interviewed staff members, while continuing his informal observations wherever and whenever he could. In this way, he was finally able to describe and analyse how the code was used, and write his report.

In my earlier section on 'institutional ethnography', I suggested that the division of an institutional population into categories which often have tense relations with each other tends to condition such ethnographies in particular and often spectacular ways. Management often plays a crucial role in 'getting in', while it may be hard for researchers to study both workers and clients. Furthermore, there may be deep categorical divisions within the worker category, as between physicians and nurses. In the case studied by Wieder, it became clear that not only was the division between staff and residents deep and full of distrust, but also it was in a way *accepted* by both parties as an inevitable fact of institutional life. In other words, categorical divisions are not only a strategic research problem, but also a major research topic, and furthermore such divisions not only factually exist – *à la* Durkheim, but are continuously 'accomplished' in and as situated practices – *à la* Garfinkel.

Returning to Whyte's experiences, we saw that in his case too, categorical tensions played a part in 'obstructing' his efforts to gain access to certain kinds of information. It took time to become 'accepted' in the neighbourhood, but still he never became 'just one of the boys'. No ethnographer will be able to transcend the social limitations of his basic categories completely without losing the capacities to observe and be an ethnographer – what anthropologists call 'going native'. Wieder's study offers a procedural analysis of how such categorical limitations are enacted and accounted for in an actual case.

Field recordings

In the section on note-taking the general presupposition was that data will be recorded by writing notes. This was in all probability the only way in which data were preserved in the studies by Whyte and Sudnow. Wieder reported that he was able to tape-record some interviews with staff, while in the studies by The and especially Pool, both interviews and 'naturally-occurring' events seem to have been audio-recorded as a more or less routine matter. Over the last few decades the facilities for making audio recordings have become much more easily available and therefore their use has become much more common. The same is now happening with video recording. So researchers can more often use these facilities, both because they have become materially available (and smaller!) and because resistance to their use has lessened. It should be realized however that such resistance still exists, depending on various circumstances, such as the researcher/researched relationship and the character of the activity being recorded.

In the examples encountered so far, audio recordings were made as a matter of convenience, because note-taking would have been cumbersome and much less precise than making a transcription of a recording after the event or the interview. This is different from the use of recorded material as *core data* in disciplines like conversation analysis (cf. Chapter 3, pp. 41–51, especially pp. 41–3; also Ten Have, 1999a: 47–73). In those cases, the audio and/or video recordings, and the transcripts made of those, constitute the actually analysed data, while other kinds of data can be used as supportive evidence. The distinction between core data and supportive evidence is a gradual one, of course, varying from case to case. Combining the general strategy of ethnography with the making of field recordings has a number of advantages over just one or the other. Researchers often report that they started making recordings only after having been 'around' doing ordinary field observations for quite some time. The familiarity and 'rapport' that has resulted from this has probably made the recording easier and more acceptable. Furthermore, it is evident that the ethnographic phase provided the researcher with local knowledge that was extremely useful for selecting scenes to record, and for understanding the recorded events. On the other hand, recorded evidence enables a much more detailed analysis than would have been possible with ordinary ethnographic data alone, that is field notes and interviews. As noted in Chapter 3, this latter advantage is essential for ethnomethodological studies.

A clear example of using audio recordings as core data and ethnography as a resource for background knowledge is Douglas Maynard's (1984) *Inside plea bargaining: the language of negotiation*. A variety of data collected through field methods – observations and note-taking, interviews and court documents – are used to sketch the overall features of the setting, the main characters and the general proceedings, while the audio recordings and the transcripts made of them are analysed in detail to identify the conversational structures used to actually *do* the plea bargaining, including specific conversational practices such as person descriptions and character assessments.

While Maynard used rather detached observation and audio recordings, a study by Jack Whalen, 'A technology of order production: computer-aided dispatch in public safety communication' (1995), reports on a study using participant observation and video recording. After having studied audio-recorded emergency calls, often in collaboration with Marilyn Whalen and Don Zimmerman (Whalen et al., 1988), he studied the activity of call-taking and message dispatching itself. As he explains:

My resources for developing this analysis include extensive field observations undertaken *while working as* a call-taker and dispatcher at a police and fire communications facility – Central Lane Communications Center in Eugene, Oregon – for fifteen months, as well as video recordings of call-takers at work that were collected at Central Lane. The discussion is also informed by field work at other public safety dispatch facilities. (Whalen, 1995a: 187; italics added)

In the paper he analyses a single case of a call being taken, demonstrating the extent to which the call's progression depends on the tasks that the call-taker has to perform at her computer, in relation to the structure of the computer-aided dispatch system she has to work with. It seems impossible that he could have analysed these intricate connections without the intimate working knowledge gained by his participant observation work. While most of the other 'workplace studies' that I have seen use less intensive fieldwork, they all seem to require a certain amount of local and technical knowledge, in order to be able to understand what is going on in technologically saturated workplaces.[9]

Instructed hearing/viewing

The notion that one might need to have some ethnographic background knowledge in order to be able to adequately understand what is happening on the recorded scene is not limited to the field of 'workplace studies'. A telling illustration of the importance of an instructed hearing/seeing of a tape is provided by David Goode (1994:160–2). He gives the following description of an incident in his study of Christina, a girl born deaf and blind who stayed in a state institution, which will be more fully discussed in Chapter 8.

> I was videotaping Chris playing with a record player, laughing hysterically as she dragged her tongue across the record and made the sound in the speaker 'slur'. . . . Without any external change in the conditions of her play, she suddenly began to cry hysterically. This abrupt change in affect was something that I had seen with several children and that I had termed behavioral non sequiturs. (Goode, 1994: 160)

He later played the tape to some colleagues at UCLA, 'detail-oriented observers by training', evidently without instructions about what they were to see. No one reacted to the sudden crying, the 'abrupt change in affect'. And he adds: 'As I watched the tape, *I* saw the whole behavioral non sequitur sequence in detail, but they did not!' After that, he did instruct the viewers in what he saw, and then, at a repeated playing, they now saw exactly what Goode had seen. As he writes:

> The seeable features of the tape were the products of the interaction between me, the expert on deaf-blindness present at the actual scene, and colleagues who were trying to serve as helpful coresearchers. But however understandable the process through which the 'proper' interpretation was established, this was nonetheless an alchemical 'now you see it, now it is gone and has become something else' affair. (Goode, 1994: 161)

There have been related disputes as to the sense of providing 'ethnographic particulars' when quoting transcripts in publications. Authors may choose to identify speakers in a quoted transcript by a letter, by initials, by name or by an 'institutional' categorization. Rod Watson (1997b), in his essay on the relation between sequential analysis as prominent in CA and membership categorization analysis (MCA) has objected to this practice. He notes (1997b: 51–3), for instance, that CA studies of medical interaction are in the habit of presenting their data in the format:

Dr: Did y'feel sick.
       (0.6)
Pt: A little bit. Yes

He argues that such a presentation seems to be 'instructing' the reader to 'hear' the utterances transcribed as being produced by 'the doctor' and 'the patient' respectively, without providing or inviting an MCA of the utterances under consideration. This critique is part of a general argument which favours a re-involvement of MCA in the CA enterprise at large. Watson suggests that in later CA categorical aspects tend to recede to a background status, while sequential organization is 'foregrounded'. This, he suggests, impoverishes the analysis and may lead to a 'constructive analytic' reification and stabilization of the categories involved. Analysts would do better, he thinks, to 'combine' categorical and sequential analyses and include the interactional relevance of various categories into their analytic problematic (cf. Schegloff, 1991: 49–52). Similar arguments can be raised concerning the common practice in CA of providing short sketches of the situation in which a particular bit of quoted talk occurred, or more generally the analysis of recorded materials informed by ethnographic fieldwork (cf. Ten Have, 1999a: 53–60). My general preference would be to search for a 'dialogical' solution to these dilemmas. It seems a bit artificial to use identifications like 'John' and 'Mary', or 'Mr Jones' and 'Mrs Peterson', while one knows that they 'are' doctor and patient to each other. But the warnings against 'imposing' external presuppositions like gender relations or institutionally fixed tasks and right/duties also have a pointed methodological validity (cf. Schegloff, 1991, 1997).

Virtual ethnography

In recent years the preference for recorded data has taken a new twist in the field provisionally known as 'virtual ethnography', that is the 'ethnographic' study of online activities as in newsgroups, chat rooms, etcetera. In such studies one can in principle have a complete (electronic) record of all the scenes observed and possibly additional online interviews, while note-taking may be limited to recording one's own experiences, upcoming ideas and summary conclusions. For two non-ethnomethodological examples, see Annette Markham's very lively *Life online: researching real experience in virtual space* (1998), which focuses on users' experiences and is based on online interviews as well as participant observations, and Frank Schaap's (2002) ethnography of a role-playing community. Rhyll Vallis (2001a, 2001b) has studied the use of chat-specific categories – such as Founders, OPS, Users, Regulars, and Newbies – in the maintenance of chat room moral orders, while I have made an inquiry into the use of general categories – Age, Sex and

Location – in the opening phases of chat room conversations, as in the opening request 'ASL please?' (Ten Have, 2000).

Ethnography and ethnomethodology[10]

In the last section of Chapter 1, I commented on the ways in which ethnography – exemplified by Whyte's *Street corner society* – can be seen as a way to overcome the limitations of time and place. It offers descriptions of local, time-bound events to readers who are themselves situated 'far away' in time and place. In various ways, these descriptions suggest that they reflect events as they actually took place then and there. They are named, detailed and contextualized to evoke the original scenes as somehow still witnessable. But it is of course the ethnographer, as both observer and author, who is mediating the message, 'transporting' it from the original then-and-there to the current here-and-now of reading. Field notes and recordings can be used as vehicles for this transportation, but it is ultimately the ethnographer-as-author who uses a range of literary devices to evoke the scenes observed, the remarks heard as well as their significance for the form of life under study. The ethnographer may be said to use a collection of practices, which Garfinkel & Sacks characterized as 'glossing practices', which in ethnomethodology constitute a topic, rather than just a resource:

> The interests of ethnomethodological research are directed to provide, through detailed analyses, that account-able phenomena are through and through practical accomplishments. We shall speak of 'the work' of that accomplishment in order to gain the emphasis for it of an ongoing course of action. The work is done as assemblages of practices whereby speakers in the situated particulars of speech mean something different from what they can say in just so many words, that is, as 'glossing practices'. (Garfinkel & Sacks, 1970: 342)

It follows from programmatic statements like the one above that ethnomethodologists tend to be a bit reluctant to use ethnography in a naïve fashion, as an unexamined data-producing engine. The preference for the usage of mechanical recordings as core data, noted above, can be seen as an effort to at least partially repair the unsatisfactory qualities of ordinary ethnographic descriptions. In addition to these records, ethnography is then used to acquire at least a minimum of membership knowledge in order to be able to make sense of what is recorded, for instance the function of particular technical operations as in Whalen's work referred to above. In his later writings, Garfinkel has suggested that such acquired knowledge is often not enough to gain access to some of the more specialized activities, leading him to formulate the 'unique adequacy requirement of methods' (Garfinkel & Wieder, 1992). This would ultimately necessitate a kind of double membership, in the professional culture being studied and in ethnomethodology. Here the old anthropological sin of 'going native' would become a required virtue. In actual practice, this does not seem feasible as a general way of doing ethnomethodological studies.[11] Furthermore, it might be argued that it would require *readers* to acquire the relevant membership competence as well. I don't think that most people will be able to follow the details reported in Eric Livingston's (1986, 1999) studies of mathematical proofing, for instance. In short, Garfinkel's invocations, although defensible in principle, do not seem to be often taken to their extreme in practice: we may be condemned to live with compromise solutions.

In ethnography, the original is no longer accessible; some of its features may be invoked in one way or another, through verbal descriptions, photographs, audio or visual recordings, but one will always need additional or embedded *instructions* to 'see' what is available in the materials. But at the same time, ethnography has some essential virtues, especially when combined with field recordings, which are currently just beginning to get exploited in full: it offers access to the *embodied* and *materially contexted* character of human existence. In interview studies, the words spoken tend to be analysed as 'text'. Documents also are mostly considered as verbal reports or constructions. But ethnography and field recordings offer possibilities to study talk *as* an embodied activity, documents *as* having a material existence – being handled, pointed at, etc. What we see these days is a rising interest in the body and materiality, which takes rather different forms in various intellectual pursuits. For ethnomethodologists, it makes it possible to 'flesh out' notions like situated actions and indexical expressions in ways that are not restricted to the purely verbal. In workplace studies, aspects like body postures, things noticed in peripheral vision and pointing gestures aid the researcher to gain a more complete understanding of actual work practices.[12]

Ethnography and ethnomethodology are related to each other in complex ways. Ethnomethodology seems to teach ethnography to be careful in its descriptive ambitions; it teaches a particular kind of 'distrust'. In order to get its message across, however, ethnomethodology will also need ethnography, verbal depictions and characterizations of events in particular places and at particular times, if only to instruct its readers about what is to be seen/heard in the records – an issue to which I will return (in Chapter 9, pp. 173–81).

Some major points

- Ethnography involves the field study of the *ways of life* of a delimited set of people or people acting in a restricted area or setting.
- The core strategy in the field methods used in ethnography is the *direct observation* of naturally occurring *in situ* actions; additional strategies include informal and formal interviewing, the collection of documents and artifacts, and the making of field recordings. The researcher's own experiences inevitably also play a role, whether explicit or implicit.
- As the ethnographer stays in the field for a considerable amount of time, and has to find his or her way amongst a range of changing circumstances,

he or she acquires knowledge about the topics of interest in an *improvised* and *incremental* manner.

- Furthermore, and equally inevitably, the researcher has to be able to manage a difficult combination of *categories* and associated *loyalties*: some 'located' in the academy, others in the field.
- Further problems for ethnography can be related to the possibly *illegitimate* and *private* character of observed activities and the possibilities for local members to *hide* such activities, or for gate-keepers to prevent or obstruct observations in various ways, especially by *denying access* to the field.
- The analytic perspective of the researcher, his or her choice of theoretical objects, is often related on the one hand to his or her *biography* and basic social *categories* (gender, class, etc.), while the ways in which these categories are taken up by the local participants may further delimit his or her observational possibilities.
- Daily *note-taking* is an essential part of fieldwork. More than 'recording what happened', it is a first step in constructing results; it should, therefore, be done with great care, including self-reflection on all aspects of the project.
- Because of their overall characteristic as person-bound productions, adding *field recordings* to field notes is of great interest; this is especially the case for ethnomethodological studies, for the reasons explicated in Chapter 3.
- *Combining* ethnographic fieldwork with the analysis of field recordings has proven to be a very fruitful strategy in ethnomethodological studies of work, in which these two kinds of data are *mutually instructive* in complex ways.

Recommended reading

On ethnography, there are two kinds of resource: on the one hand reports of actual ethnographic studies and special chapters or appendices in which ethnographers reflect on their own research experience, and, on the other hand, more practical or methodological discussions of (aspects of) ethnography and field methods. Publications of the first type are too numerous to be mentioned here. Just search for field studies that seem to be interesting for your own purposes.

Here is my personal selection from the second type:

- Blomberg, Jeanette L. (1995) 'Ethnography: aligning field studies of work and system design'. In: Andrew Monk, Nigel Gilbert, eds. *Perspectives on HCI: diverse approaches.* New York: Academic Press: 175–97
- Emerson, Robert M., Rachel I. Fretz, Linda L. Shaw (1995) *Writing ethnographic field notes.* Chicago: University of Chicago Press
- Goffman, Erving (1989) 'On fieldwork', transcribed and edited by Lyn H. Lofland), *Journal of Contemporary Ethnography*, 18: 123–32

- Hammersley, Martyn, Paul Atkinson (1983) *Ethnography: principles in practice*. London: Tavistock
- McCall, George J., J.L. Simmons (1969) *Issues in participant observation: a text and reader*. Reading, MA: Addison-Wesley
- Schatzman, Leonard, Anselm L. Strauss (1973) *Field research: strategies for a natural sociology*. Englewood Cliffs, NJ: Prentice-Hall
- Walsh, David (1998) 'Doing ethnography'. In: Clive Seale, ed. *Researching society and culture*. London: Sage: 217–32

Also consult:

- Atkinson, Paul, Amanda Coffey, Sara Delamont, John Lofland, Lyn H. Lofland, eds. (2001) *Handbook of ethnography*. London, etc.: Sage

For discussions of field recordings, see:

- Goodwin, Charles (1994) 'Recording human interaction in natural settings', *Pragmatics*, 3: 181–209
- Heath, Christian (1997) 'The analysis of activities in face to face interaction using video'. In: David Silverman, ed. *Qualitative research: theory, method and practice*. London: Sage: 183–200
- Lomax, H., N. Casey (1998) ' Recording social life: reflexivity and video methodology' *Sociological Research Online*, 3(2) [http://www.soc.surrey.ac.uk/socresonline/3/2/1.html]

Some major examples of the fruitful combination of ethnographic fieldwork and the analysis of recordings made in the field are:

- Goodwin, Charles (1995) 'Seeing in depth', *Social Studies of Science*, 25: 237–74
- Goodwin, Charles (2000) 'Action and embodiment within situated human interaction', *Journal of Pragmatics*, 32, 1489–522
- Goodwin, Charles, Marjorie Harness Goodwin (1996) 'Seeing as situated activity: formulating planes'. In: Y. Engeström, D. Middleton, eds. *Cognition and communication at work*. Cambridge: Cambridge University Press: 61–95
- Goodwin, Marjorie Harness (1990) *He-said-she-said: talk as social organization among black children*. Bloomington: Indiana University Press.
- Heath, Christian (1986) *Body movement and speech in medical interaction*. Cambridge: Cambridge University Press
- Heath, Christian, Paul Luff (2000) *Technology in action*. Cambridge: Cambridge University Press
- Lynch, Michael (1985) *Art and artifact in laboratory science: a study of shop work and shop talk*. London: Routledge & Kegan Paul
- Whalen, Jack (1995) 'A technology of order production: computer-aided dispatch in public safety communication'. In: Paul ten Have, George Psathas, eds. *Situated order: Studies in the social organization of talk and*

embodied activities. Washington, DC: University Press of America: 187–230

● Whalen, Jack, Eric Vinkhuyzen (2000) 'Expert systems in (inter)action: diagnosing document machine problems over the telephone'. In Paul Luff, Jon Hindmarsh, Christian Heath, eds. *Workplace studies: recovering work practice and informing systems design.* Cambridge: Cambridge University Press: 92–140 [discussed in Chapter 8]

Notes

1   Some major sources are: Atkinson et al. (eds) (2001), Douglas (1976), Emerson et al. (1995), Hammersley & Atkinson (1983), Johnson (1975), McCall & Simmons (1969), Schatzman & Strauss (1973), Van Maanen, ed. (1995), Walsh (1998).

2   I owe this observation to a remark made by Michael Lynch during a discussion of a paper I presented in Manchester, July 2001, in which he referred to Garfinkel's teaching.

3   See also a rather aggressive report by Marianne Boelen reporting some reactions 30 years later, as well as Whyte's rebuttal, in a special issue of the *Journal of Contemporary Ethnography* on '*Street corner society* revisited', 21(1), April 1992.

4   I am a bit reluctant to use this term, as it has been used with rather different meanings by Dorothy Smith (1987).

5   For observations on the use of field notes in publications, cf. Ten Have (2001b).

6   But see a transcription of an informal talk on his fieldwork methods, published after his death (Goffman, 1989), in which he stresses the immersion aspect of fieldwork: experiencing a form of life by submitting oneself to its conditions, in order to understand what it means to the natives.

7   The fact that I have here chosen two examples from the early years of ethnomethodology should not be seen as suggesting that later studies are less valuable. It is the case, however, that later studies tend to use video- or audio-taped data as the core materials, and ethnography for background information, while these two are mainly observation-based.

8   This is illustrated by the fact that it has so often been taken as a case in introductions to ethnomethodology, as in Heritage (1984a: 200–9) and Sharrock & Anderson (1986: 49–57). Some extract from Wieder's monograph (1974a) were published as a chapter in Roy Turner's 1974 collection (cf. Wieder, 1974b).

9   Cf. Whalen (1995b) for another report from the same project and Whalen & Vinkhuyzen (2000) for a later project (to be discussed in Chapter 8); also the introductions to Button (1993), Heath & Luff (2000), Luff et al. (2000), and Arminen (2001) and Heath, Knoblauch, & Luff (2000), for reviews.

10   For more on the relation between ethnography and ethnomethodology, see Pollner & Emerson (2001) and Ball (1998).

11   Cf. Lynch (1993: 271–308) for a more extensive discussion, in which he mentions that even in his own work he has not been able to fulfil this requirement.

12   See C. Goodwin (2000, in press), M.H. Goodwin (1996) and Hindmarsh & Heath (2000), for examples.

7 Qualitative Analysis

In Chapter 1, I referred to Charles Ragin's conception of social research in terms of a dialogue between ideas and evidence in order to produce a representation of social life. Then, after an introduction to ethnomethodology as an 'alternate sociology', in Chapter 2, and its research practices, in Chapter 3, I discussed various styles of doing qualitative social research in Chapters 4, 5, and 6. Although these later chapters were differentiated one from the other in terms of types of data collection, I did not limit my discussions to something like 'data gathering'. It doesn't make sense, in a qualitative inquiry, to gather data without taking into consideration what is to be done with them. In the same vein, it wouldn't seem to make sense to discuss 'analysis' completely separate from other aspects of qualitative social research. There has been, however, over the last 30 years or so, an increasing tendency in the literature on qualitative research methods to treat 'analysis' as a separate topic. This may be related to a relative neglect of analysis in the earlier literature (which was strongly focused on 'relational' issues), but also to the development in the 1950s and 1960s of *generalized* analytic strategies, such as 'analytic induction', and most prominently the 'grounded theory' approach.

The original idea of analytic induction emerged as early as the 1930s and was developed further in the 1950s and 1960s. Some of these ideas are still discernible in various current approaches to qualitative analysis.[1] The general idea is to start with an examination of a single case from a predefined 'population' in order to formulate a general statement about that population, a concept or a hypothesis. Then the analyst examines another case to see whether it fits the statement. If it does, a further case is selected. If it does not fit, there are two options: either the statement is changed to fit both cases, or the definition of the population is changed in such a way that the case is no longer a member of the newly defined population. Then another case is selected and the process continues. In this way, one should be able to arrive at a statement that fits all cases of a population-as-defined, for instance all cases of recreational marihuana use (Becker, 1963). Many qualitative researchers take it that this method is only appropriate for a limited set of analytic problems: those that can be solved with some general overall statement. It has, however, in its weaker forms a very useful spin-off as it raises interest in 'deviant cases', which should not be discarded as rare exceptions to a 'rule', but rather should be studied in depth as challenges to some (over-)generalization. In this way, there are some affinities with strands in ethnomethodological studies, especially conversation analysis.[2]

The grounded theory approach was formulated in the 1960s by Barney Glaser and Anselm Strauss (1967), and has been elaborated in various and increasingly conflicting ways by these authors in later years. It is currently probably the most popular way of doing (and accounting for) qualitative analysis, especially in the version promoted by Strauss in collaboration with Juliet Corbin (1990, 1998). The notion that one could use a general strategy for qualitative analysis, independent of the kinds of data and the research topic(s), has probably been reinforced by the development of specialized software to assist in qualitative analysis (cf. Fielding & Lee, 1998 for a general discussion). The current chapter will not be a comprehensive overview. I will focus, instead, on selected aspects of the grounded theory strategy that provide an interesting confrontation with ethnomethodology.

The general GT approach

In essence, the *grounded theory* approach (hereafter often labelled GT),[3] involves two phases in the analysis of qualitative data. In the first, 'incidents' (data fragments) are compared in order to derive general descriptors (concepts; categories) which catch their analytically relevant properties. Comparing incidents and concepts should be continued until the concepts are 'saturated', i.e. they don't change through new comparisons. This is called 'the constant comparative method'. This first phase has been characterized as one of 'open coding', as incidents are considered as indicators of the concepts they exemplify, but the process is still 'open': data-driven rather than guided by preconceived theoretical ideas. The second phase is used to elaborate, refine and reduce the results of the first phase. This involves, on the one hand, connecting codes in the form of hypothesized propositions specifying conditions, and on the other a process of abstraction in which similar codes and the properties of phenomena they point to are grouped under more general headings. These processes still involve comparisons with data, but their selection is guided by considerations of theory development, which is therefore called 'theoretical sampling'. Coding in order to develop a category further has been called 'axial coding' by Strauss, while later coding in order to elaborate and test specific hypotheses is called 'selective coding' (Strauss, 1987; Strauss & Corbin, 1990). Two important aspects of the coding process should be mentioned here. The first one is that by selecting parts of the data as incidents to be coded, the analyst breaks up the data – interview transcripts, texts, field notes – in their original form, re-contextualizing them as in principle separate 'bits', which get a new significance as 'indicators' of concepts. The second aspect is that the GT originators stress that the coding process involves more than just constructing concept/indicator pairs, as the analyst should record any ideas that are generated as part of the coding process in a separate 'memo', a process called memoing and considered essential to the GT-approach.

The purpose of the two phases taken together is to generate and at the same time test 'theory' based on empirical data, therefore it is called the *grounded theory* approach. It is contrasted with previous conceptions of the function of theory in research, which stress (quantitative) verification of hypotheses derived from general theoretical ideas, whatever their source. Grounded theories are, in the first instance, 'substantive', focused on a specific empirical field, but can later be developed into 'formal' ones, which have a wider application by formulating similar aspects or processes relevant to a wider range of situations.

As noted, the GT approach was developed in the 1960s by Barney Glaser in collaboration with Anselm Strauss. Glaser had been trained at Columbia, at that time the centre of verificational quantitative methodology as elaborated by Paul Lazarsfeld, while Strauss was a participant in the Chicago-based tradition of qualitative research. The approach was, on the one hand, a codification of the actual analytic practices they had used in their study of the treatment of dying patients in hospitals (cf. Glaser & Strauss, 1965, 1968), and, on the other, quite strongly polemical in relation to the then current stress on verification using quantitative methods and to various procedures of qualitative analysis such as 'analytic induction' which were also current at the time. Until the mid 1980s, the approach had been developed and used mostly in books and papers by Glaser and Strauss together, with Glaser as senior author, or by Glaser alone, especially *Theoretical sensitivity* (1978). In 1987, however, Strauss published his own book on GT, *Qualitative analysis for social scientists*, which, in its first chapter quotes extensively from Glaser's *Theoretical sensitivity*, but after that develops various illustrations and elaborations of procedures that seem to depart from his colleague's ideas. If this was already a split, it became a more or less open fight, at least from Glaser's side, with the publication in 1990 of *Basics of qualitative research: grounded theory procedures and techniques,* written by Strauss with a former student, Juliet Corbin. As documented in a fiercely polemical book by Glaser, *Emergence vs forcing: basics of grounded theory analysis* (1992), Glaser tried to persuade Strauss to withdraw the book with Corbin, which Strauss refused. As the title *Emergence vs forcing* makes clear, the thrust of Glaser's criticism is that in Strauss' hands the GT approach has degenerated from a methodology to a set of methods, with a 'focus on preconceived, forced conceptual description' (9). From that time onwards, Glaser has continued the battle, while Strauss has largely ignored it (cf. Glaser, 1998; Strauss & Corbin, 1994, 1998). In the mean time, Strauss seems to have been much more successful in terms of publishing his books and creating many followers, while Glaser has to publish his own books and has a smaller, more closed group of followers (cf. http://www.groundedtheory.com).

GT's 'theory'

In *The discovery of grounded theory* (1967) Glaser & Strauss stress that their approach should be seen as an effort to close the continuing gap between 'theory' and 'research' by supplementing the then current stress on verification with a focus on discovering theory from data, especially qualitative data. As they say:

> (S)uch a [grounded] theory fits empirical situations, and is understandable to sociologists and layman alike. Most important, it works – provides us with relevant predictions, explanations, interpretations and applications. (Glaser & Strauss, 1967: 1)

What I want to do here is to explicate their conception of 'theory', focusing on 'conceptualization' as an essential part of it, in order to be able to make some critical observations on the implied conception of an accountable social science.

A first question, then, is: what is the conception of 'theory' in the grounded theory approach? In the initial pages of the 1967 book, Glaser & Strauss enumerate a collection of functions 'theory' should have:

> The interrelated jobs of theory in sociology are: (1) to enable prediction and explanation of behavior; (2) to be useful in theoretical advance in sociology; (3) to be usable in practical applications – prediction and explanation should be able to give the practitioner understanding and some control of situations; (4) to provide a perspective on behavior – a stance to be taken toward data; and (5) to guide and provide a style for research on particular areas of behavior. Thus theory in sociology is a strategy for handling data in research, providing modes of conceptualization for describing and explaining. The theory should provide clear enough categories and hypotheses so that crucial ones can be verified in present and future research; they must be clear enough to be readily operationalized in quantitative studies when these are appropriate. The theory must also be readily understandable to sociologists of any viewpoint, to students and to significant laymen. Theory that can meet these requirements must fit the situation being researched, and work when put into use. By 'fit' we mean that the categories must be readily (not forcibly) applicable to and indicated by the data under study; by 'work' we mean that they must be meaningfully relevant to and be able to explain the behavior under study. (Glaser & Strauss, 1967: 3)

So a theory provides 'modes of conceptualization for describing and explaining', while it should be 'clear' and 'understandable' to a wide range of people, including 'sociologists of any viewpoint' as well as lay people. In a footnote to a later part of the same page, they add a caveat: 'Of course, the researcher does not approach reality as a tabula rasa. He must have a perspective that will help him see relevant data and abstract significant categories from his scrutiny of the data.' In their view, a 'perspective' precedes 'theory'; while 'generating a theory involves a process of research', 'the source of certain ideas or even "models," can come from sources other than the data' (6). In other words, while they concede the role of a pre-existing viewpoint or 'perspective', as a source of 'ideas' and 'insights', they maintain that reworking those in close connection with the data would result in a theory that is clear and understandable to people 'of any viewpoint'. To my mind, this conception of 'theory', while conceding that ideas can function as a source of inspiration, but stressing the role of data to generate the ultimate theory which should be understandable (acceptable?) to virtually 'anybody', can be said to be 'empiricist'. It suggests that data speak a unified language, understandable by a general or, one might say, commonsense audience.

They also say, however, that the 'production' of theory is a unique task for professional sociologists: 'the task of generating theory from the data of social research' is 'a job that can be done only by the sociologist, and that offers a significant product to laymen and colleagues alike (30). Furthermore, they stress that the major preoccupation of research sociologists should not be to get the facts right, as 'the distinctive offering of sociology to our society is sociological theory, not researched description' (30–1). Here, then, the authors seem to retreat a bit from the suggestion evident in other parts of their writings that 'anyone' who follows the GT strategy can 'see' concepts in the data. We also see their polemical attitude against 'a-theoretical' or purely descriptive research, whether quantitative or qualitative.

Glaser and Strauss suggest that a 'theory' can be presented in two different forms: 'as a well-codified set of propositions or in a running theoretical discussion, using conceptual categories and their properties' (31). But they prefer the 'discussional' format as it more clearly displays the processional character of theoretical development, while the propositional format would suggest a stable 'product'. In a 'theory' they distinguish different kinds of 'elements': (1) 'conceptual categories and their conceptual properties', and (2) 'hypotheses or generalized relations among the categories and their properties' (35). They make an important distinction, when they write:

> It must be kept in mind that *both* categories and properties are concepts indicated by data (and not the data itself); also that both vary in degree of conceptual abstraction. . . . conceptual categories and properties have a life apart from the evidence that gave rise to them. (Glaser & Strauss, 1967: 35–6)

In other words, in Glaser & Strauss' view, 'theory' involves the abstract naming of properties of 'objects', i.e. conceptualization, and the formulation of 'relations' between such conceptualized objects, in order to 'explain' phenomena. In that respect, there is hardly any difference between their conception of 'theory' and the one that was and is current in many otherwise different kinds of empirical/analytic sociology. What *is* different from those other approaches is their stress on 'generation' versus 'verification', culminating in a preference for locally generated as against abstractly deduced or 'borrowed' theory and concepts. They claim that 'our focus on the emergence of categories solves the problems of fit, relevance, forcing, and richness':

> An effective strategy is, at first, literally to ignore the literature of theory and fact on the area under study, in order to assure that the emergence of categories will not be contaminated by concepts more suited to different areas. Similarities and convergences with the literature can be established after the analytic core of categories has emerged. (Glaser & Strauss, 1967: 37)

So they go as far as recommending 'theoretical ignorance' as a strategy to foster open-mindedness. Furthermore, they also stress a diversified kind of theory, in order to provide a better 'fit' with a local field.

> While the verification of theory aims at establishing a relatively few major uniformities and variations on the same conceptual level, we believe that the

generation of theory should aim at achieving much *diversity* in emergent categories, synthesized at as *many levels* of conceptual and hypothetical generalization as possible. The synthesis provides readily apparent connections between data and lower and higher level conceptual abstractions of categories and properties. (Glaser & Strauss, 1967: 37)

Therefore, the researcher is even encouraged to select 'non-traditional areas', for which not too much technical literature is available.

'Theory' and 'meta-theory'

From my earliest confrontation with the GT approach, my reaction to it was ambivalent. On the one hand there was, I felt, much that made sense in its approach to qualitative analysis, like the stress on detailed inspection of data through constant comparisons, theoretical sampling and memoing. But I was very sceptical of GT's inductivist and empiricist rhetoric – as in the almost ritually repeated notions of 'emergence' and 'discovery'. In my view, analysis always involves a creative confrontation of already present 'theoretical' ideas and newly produced or considered evidence, leading to some kind of change in these ideas, be it confirmation, specification, elaboration or refutation.[4] Following Ragin's (1994) suggestions, 'analysis' can be seen as a constructive action of connecting ideas and evidence in an argumentative fashion, producing a new and insightful depiction of some aspect or part of social life.

If one wants to elucidate analytic processes, a necessary step, therefore, would be to make one's pre-existing but changing ideas explicit. GT writings do not deny the analyst's reliance on pre-existing knowledge, including his or her professional training, but the overall tendency is to present this pre-knowledge as a danger, especially as concerns any specific concepts or hypotheses, rather than an asset. Although one can endorse the general principle that the analyst should be 'open minded', GT's rhetoric seems to deny or at least downplay the importance and usefulness of orienting oneself broadly in terms of existing ideas, theories and literature.

Part of the problem may be related to different conceptions of what one means by 'theory'. When Glaser and Strauss talk about 'theories' they seem to be thinking in terms of rather concrete, specific and elaborate sets of statements regarding phenomena and their relationships, as hypotheses about multivariate relationships.[5] In that sense, their thinking is quite similar to that of quantitative social scientists' conceptions current at the time they were developing their approach, the mid-1960s. My own thinking on these matters, however, was formed at a later period, the early 1970s, when 'theory' was gaining a more abstract usage close to the Kuhnian conception of 'paradigm', as a specific way of thinking and arguing about certain aspects of reality and ways of doing research on the phenomena specified in such a framework. One could also talk about 'meta-theory': a framework within which specific theories can be formulated and can gain their meaning.

It may be the case that for Glaser & Strauss the 'meta-theory' that frames their approach was so self-evident that they did not even think of explicating it. Their polemic is not *with* the conventional multivariate paradigm, but *within* it. They oppose the *deductive*, verificational style of work – verifying pre-existing hypotheses – by stressing methods for *inductive* theory generation. Their adherence to the multivariate paradigm is perhaps clearest in their use of the concept/indicator model, as demonstrated in the following quotes.

Glaser writes:[6]

> Grounded theory is based on a *concept-indicator model*, which directs the conceptual coding of a set of empirical indicators.[7] This model provides the essential link between data and concept, which results in a theory generated from data. . . .
>
> Our concept indicator model is based on constant comparing of (1) indicator to indicator, and then when a conceptual code is generated (2) also comparing indicators to the emerging concept. From the comparisons of indicator to indicator the analyst is forced into confronting similarities, differences and degrees of consistency of meaning between indicators which generates an underlying uniformity which in turn results in a coded category and the beginning of properties of it. From the comparisons of further indicators to the conceptual codes, the code is sharpened to achieve its best fit while further properties are generated until the code is verified and saturated. (Glaser, 1978: 62)

Although they do not endorse the *top down* reasoning model implied in the idea of an 'operationalization' of concepts, as in the usual quantitative approaches, the notion of *coding*, as used in GT, can be seen as a 'flipped' analogue to it. While in 'operationalization' indicators are seen as representing theoretical concepts at the level of data properties, the GT coding amounts to a *bottom up* translation of data properties into 'emerging' theoretical concepts. In both approaches, a distinction is made between two 'levels', an abstract theoretical one, at which 'concepts' are formulated (either before or during the analysis of data), and the more concrete level at which relevant properties of the data are treated as 'indicators' of those concepts. Furthermore, both models explicitly state that a particular concept can be 'indicated' by several different data properties, while particular data may be used to indicate different concepts.[8]

Noting an analogous underlying model for both the conventional, quantitative multivariate methods and GT should not obscure the important differences, of course. The major difference is probably that the concept/indicator link is constituted differently in the two traditions. In the quantitative style it is stipulated beforehand, on the basis of plausible reasoning, and researched in aggregate forms afterwards, in terms of various correlational measures of 'validity' and 'reliability'. In the GT tradition, it is supposedly based on an in-depth case-by-case consideration by carefully executed comparisons. GT notions like 'emergence' and 'discovery' suggest a 'natural' relationship, existing, so to speak, independently of any research project as such, while in the quantitative traditions choosing an indicator seems to be a matter of convenience. But this may also be a matter of rhetorical style.

In short, the basic model or meta-theory for Glaser and Strauss is a kind of qualitative multivariate conception of theory. While the core job for quantitative researchers is to find order in the aggregate of objects measured in terms of empirically indicated variables, the GT approach is oriented to 'discovering' relations *in* the data and elaborating those on the basis of data comparisons. For GT, constituting the concept/indicator relationship is not a matter of objectified measurement, but of careful 'seeing' which concepts are able to catch what an incident signifies in terms of the emerging theory. After having been coded up to a satisfactory level of 'saturation', however, the data are no longer important to the GT researcher.

The process of discovery

Working with codes, comparisons and memos is essential within the GT style. About coding, Glaser writes:

> Coding gets the analyst off the empirical level by fracturing the data, then conceptually grouping it into codes that then become the theory which explains what is happening in the data. Coding for conceptual ideas is a sure way to free analysts from the empirical bond of the data. It allows the researcher to transcend the empirical nature of the data – which is so easy to get lost in – while at the same time conceptually accounting for the processes within the data in a theoretically sensitive way. The code gives the researcher a condensed, abstract view with scope of the data that includes otherwise seemingly disparate phenomenon[sic]. This conceptual scope transcends the empirical arguments often surrounding disparate data on the same level. (Glaser, 1978: 55)

Here the second polemical aspect of the GT approach surfaces again: its opposition to the 'descriptivist' kind of qualitative research. The crux of this opposition is that the empirical findings are not primarily seen as parts of a locally contextualized phenomenon, but as more or less useful indicators in the service of theory development. Therefore, the data are to be 'fractured' and the analyst has to be 'freed' from their grip on his or her mind. It is almost as if the concrete level of contextual phenomena is a sensuous world of temptation from which the analytic monk has to free himself through the purifying rituals of abstract conceptualization. Coding and comparison are essential 'transcending' strategies here: by seeing and abstractly naming patterns of similarities and differences, the spell of the concrete can be broken. So the attitude of GT towards data can be characterized as 'ambivalent'. On the one hand the data are continuously presented as the major source and criterion, while they are also presented as a temptation that might prevent theoretical transcendence.[9]

The 'transcending' aspect of codes is stressed by adding qualifiers such as 'conceptual' (as in many quotes above), or 'ideational'. Furthermore, Glaser writes:

There are basically two types of codes to generate: substantive and theoretical. Substantive codes conceptualize the empirical substance of the area of research. Theoretical codes conceptualize how the substantive codes may relate to each other as hypotheses to be integrated into the theory. (Glaser, 1978: 55)

And he adds:

The two types of coding most often go on simultaneously, and this should be brought out in memos. But the analyst will focus relatively more on substantive coding when discovering codes within the data, and more on theoretical coding when theoretically sorting and integrating his memos. (Glaser, 1978: 56)

The analyst, it is suggested, has to 'know' many theoretical codes and not stick to a few 'pet codes'. Glaser elaborates their variety by discussing 18 'coding families', more or less overlapping sets of concepts which can be used to 'connect' coded phenomena (Glaser, 1978: 73–82). The first one ('the "bread and butter" theoretical code of sociology') is called 'The Six C's: Causes, Contexts, Contingencies, Consequences, Covariances and Conditions' (74). Others are: Process, Degree, Dimension, Type, Strategy, etc. So Glaser suggests a wide range of ways in which coded phenomena might be theoretically related in the analysis. One of his most important objections to the later writing of Strauss is that he selected only the first of these 'coding families' as the basis of his 'coding paradigm' (Strauss, 1987: 27–8; Strauss & Corbin, 1990: 99–107; 1998: 127–35). For Glaser, this signified Strauss' tendency to promote 'forcing the data', rather than letting theory 'emerge'.

Discussion

For the purpose of the overall argument of the present chapter, these critical observations on the grounded theory approach should suffice for the moment. Although I have limited my discussion mostly to the earlier programmatic statements, I do think that present GT publications and practices – however diversified and popularized they may be – are still founded on the assumptions contained in these earlier writings. In a way, the grounded theory approach can be seen as a 'mixed marriage' (Dey, 1999) of two contrasting traditions: the Columbia University tradition of variable analysis, and the Chicago-based tradition of interactionist, naturalistic inquiry. Combining inspiration of and polemical opposition to these two approaches seems to have created ambiguities in GT's overall approach that could, in turn, easily lead to misunderstandings and disputes. It does not seem to be the case, however, that Glaser and Strauss in their conflict were simply returning to their respective pasts. In fact, Glaser reproaches Strauss for importing too many deductive and verificational elements into his rendition of grounded theory, which in themselves would be associated with Columbia rather than Chicago.

The grounded theory approach has over the years become very popular indeed. There are probably many reasons for this, of which I will just mention a few here. A major appeal of the GT approach could be that it offers a set of guidelines for analysing qualitative data that seems to make this elusive activity 'do-able' and its results 'respectable'. Making qualitative analysis 'do-able' is especially prominent in Strauss' later publications, which offer extensive examples and many visualized schemes to clarify both the steps to be taken and the connections between various abstract concepts. The results of the analysis – a 'grounded theory' – gain in respectability because they transcend 'mere description', while also being presented as the product of a systematic 'method' rather than just a set of personal impressions. The rhetoric of 'discovery', 'emergence', etc. further downplays the interpretative and subjective implications and suggestions that tend to make qualitative reports less convincing in the perception of outsiders, including of course people with money, power and/or practical interests.

During the period that GT gained its present prominence in qualitative analysis, a parallel development was the creation of a number of software packages to 'assist' or 'support' qualitative data analysis.[10] The core activity in these programs is the coding of data fragments, which seems to fit seamlessly with the central position of 'coding' in the GT approach, while most offer the possibilities to add 'memos' to codes and/or coded fragments. In this way, the 'fracturing' of the data and their 'transcendence' through rising to the conceptual level, while keeping track of the connections between concepts and indicators, as well as between concepts, is eminently supported. There has been some debate as to the extent to which the developers of these programs were inspired by, or even limited to, the GT approach, and whether the construction of the programs can be seen as 'biasing' users to use GT procedures rather than alternatives (cf. Lonkila, 1995; Fielding & Lee, 1998: 177–80). One way in which such programs can help in overcoming some of 'dangers' of the GT approach should also be mentioned, however. Offering the possibilities of creating multiple links between the original data and various kinds of analytic reworkings of the data – such as codes and memos – makes it easy to 'return' to the data' at any moment, which allows repeated inspections of both the data-fragments themselves and the context from which they have been taken.

Apart from the rhetorical advantages, mentioned before, the GT movement has made an important contribution to qualitative research for a number of further reasons. It has, indeed, reinforced the notion that qualitative social research involves an explicit 'dialogue of ideas and evidence', and not just a possibly subjective description. It has also, in its concept of theoretical sampling, loosened the grip of representativeness as a general criterion of social research. In the next sections, I want to build a contrast between the grounded theory approach and ethnomethodology, which may provide us with a sharper focus on both.

Ethnomethodology versus grounded theory

Although grounded theory and ethnomethodology emerged in the same period – the respective ground-laying books were both published in 1967 – and both can be seen as a pointed reaction and alternative to the then current academic practices in American sociology, the differences between the two seem to be quite deep. The situation is rather complicated, however, so a black-and-white contrast will not be helpful.

While the GT approach was developed as a combination of opposition and continuity with the research traditions associated with Columbia and Chicago, Garfinkel's ethnomethodology ultimately grew out of a confrontation with the theoretical work of Talcott Parsons at Harvard University, inspired by a variety of alternative sociological and philosophical approaches.[11] Although there are some continuities between Parsons and Garfinkel, such as the focus on membership and social order, the break with Parsons seems to have been more radical. In essence, the Parsonian enterprise is based on the idea that one would need an elaborate analytic pre-given construction in order to be able to understand and explain the 'raw stream of experience'. For Parsons, social order is not to be found in the concrete activities of members, but in intricate theoretical constructions that explain those activities. Taken together, these constructions constitute an analytic framework, based on a set of preconceptions which are in themselves no longer scrutinized. What Garfinkel did was to use phenomenology to turn his attention to these very foundational assumptions, such as the rationality of action and a shared culture. For him, social order, rationality and mutual understanding are continuously achieved 'in and as' members' concerted activities. While Parsons largely ignores members' 'applied knowledge' – the practical notions which we take for granted in our everyday lives – the application of such knowledge is, for Garfinkel, the very foundation of the social order. Members of society should not be taken as 'cultural dopes', who in a quasi-automatic way enact the scripts of their culture, but rather as active creators of the very life they live together (Garfinkel, 1967a: 68). The switch which is implied in these differences has important consequences for one's conception of sociology. For Parsons, the sociological analyst has a unique position and a very special task, analytically explaining the social order, which is basically different from the position and tasks of ordinary members. For Garfinkel on the other hand, ordinary members are practical analysts, lay sociologists, as they use their situated analyses of local social orders to live their lives. The task of professional sociologists is then to describe in active, procedural terms the ways in which they do this.

This summary sketch of the Parsons/Garfinkel contrast[12] can now be used to elucidate the differences between the GT approach and ethnomethodology. The crucial issue seems to be the different conceptions of the analytic task. In both Parsons, and Glaser & Strauss, there is a fundamental split between a conceptual level and the level of concreteness, which leads to the notion that ultimately it is the task of the analyst to elaborate concepts and conceptual relations in such a way that what happens at the concrete level of human action can be explained in conceptual (analytic, theoretical) terms. The differences between Parsons on the one hand and Glaser & Strauss on the other, concern the ways in which one should arrive at one's concepts and theories, through analytic construction or through empirical generation. For ethnomethodology, a split between levels of concreteness is not assumed to exist as such; it is, rather, a feature of some kinds of lay or professional theorizing – a product, one could say. The concepts that ethnomethodologists use are not part of a causal *explanation* of events and action, but of a procedural *explication*; they are 'procedurally descriptive'.

In a serious way, then, ethnomethodology does not strive to 'add' anything to the social life it studies, no 'theory', no 'concepts', not a different level of reality. It just brings to light what is already available for all to see; it is, then, just an eye-opener. The suggestions that one can find in the ethnomethodological literature, such as the 'study policies', 'pedagogies' or 'tutorials' that Garfinkel has offered, are not methods, in the ordinary sense of the term, as an inquiry has to be fitted to its circumstances in each and every way (cf. Garfinkel, 1967a: 31–4; 2002 *passim*). There is in ethnomethodology nothing like a generalized analytic strategy, comparable to what is promised in the GT approach. There are only hints as to how one might try to gain access to the phenomena of interest. Some of these were discussed in Chapter 3. In the next chapter, I will offer some more sketches of exemplary ethnomethodological studies.

To conclude

Generalized analytic strategies, like analytic induction and especially grounded theory, can be seen as specifying a trajectory of first taking the data into account, and then leaving the data behind by moving up to a conceptual level. In the activity of 'coding', so central to GT, the significance of the data – which in themselves are already representations of some original events – is reduced to their function of providing an indication of a concept. Most of the data to which the GT strategy is applied are in themselves already what Harold Garfinkel (2002) has called 'signed objects', that is collections of signs that are used as stand-ins for some original phenomenon. Codes can then be considered as 'signed objects' to the second degree. The analytic process can be seen, therefore, as a stepwise loosening of signed objects from their time- and place-bound character, to gain a new significance in terms of an emergent time- and place-free 'grounded theory'. In other words, GT is devoted to the substitution of objective for indexical expressions (cf. Chapter 2).

My remarks on the GT approach may have been read as 'criticism', as fault finding, but they are meant as a characterization of the essential ways in which it is a member of the family of conventional social sciences, of what in ethnomethodology used to be called 'constructive analysis' and is now discussed as 'formal analysis' (Garfinkel, 2002). Ethnomethodology offers to be an 'alternate' to formal analysis, as I hope to make clear up to a point in the next two chapters.

Some major points

As I have limited my discussion to *analytic induction* and the *grounded theory* approach, the points below are limited in this way as well, while their contrast with ethnomethodology is stressed.

- The strategy of *analytic induction* involves a rather strict way of steering the fit between ideas and evidence, through adapting any generally formulated conclusion to what can be said about *all* cases in a relevant population of cases.
- The major strength of this strategy, even if used in a less strict manner, seems to be its stress on taking *deviant cases* seriously as challenges to any abstract conclusion.
- The core property of the *grounded theory* approach is its stress on the *generation* and refinement of *concepts* and categories through inspection and systematic comparison of 'instances' – data fragments selected from a variety of sources.
- GT's originators – Glaser and Strauss – have presented their approach in a double polemic: on the one hand with methodologies that stress empirical *verification* of theories, while they promote empirical *generation*, and on the other with what they consider mere *a-theoretical* description.
- The basic methodological framework underlying the GT approach is the *concept-indicator model*; in this model the research materials are scrutinized for fragments which might serve as *indicators* of to be generated or refined *concepts*, in which concepts are names for *variables* or their *values*; this latter notion is taken over in a self-evident and unaccounted-for manner from qualitative (Lazarsfeldian) methodology.
- The GT approach has had a major *effect* on the development of qualitative analysis in raising its status as a systematic and theory-oriented approach of equal although different standing in comparison with established quantitative methodologies.
- It has, furthermore, encouraged serious and detailed consideration of the data, purpose-oriented selection procedures in its notion of *theoretical sampling*, and constant record-keeping of the analytic process in *memo-writing*.
- In a later phase of the development of GT the originators have taken *different pathways*: Strauss, the most successful propagator, suggesting one particular (and rather conventional) framework for coding events – a *coding paradigm*, while Glaser, the more conscious methodologist, objecting to the *forcing* of the data that might result from this strategy.
- In its Straussian version, GT seems to have inspired the development and widespread use of *software programs* to assist in qualitative data analysis; while being very useful for code-and-retrieve and memo-linking purposes, such programs may also have led to a kind of conventionalizing and routinization of qualitative analysis.

- On a number of points, the GT strategy can be contrasted with the preferences that characterize ethnomethodology:
  - many ethnomethodologists would reject the *decontextualizing* tendency in GT, its breaking up of data into small pieces to be analysed independently of their original context (although some conversation analysts might be seen to be doing just that);
  - ethnomethodologists tend *not* to be interested in building the kinds of *generalized theories*, separated from the data, to which GT aspires;
  - ethnomethodology, then, represents a much more *radical* departure from the conventional conception of the sociological mission than GT, which, in a way, represents only a minor correction to the verificational ethos of current methodologies; ethnomethodology's radicalism is probably best caught in its ideal or *re-specification*.

Recommended reading

General sources on qualitative analysis include:

- Becker, Howard S. (1998) *Tricks of the trade: how to think about your research while you're doing it.* Chicago: University of Chicago Press
- Silverman, David (2001) *Interpreting qualitative data: methods for analysing Talk, Text and Interaction*, 2nd edn. London: Sage

On the grounded theory approach, the classic sources are:

- Glaser, Barney G., Anselm L. Strauss (1967) *The discovery of grounded theory: strategies for qualitative research.* Chicago: Aldine
- Glaser, Barney G. (1978) *Theoretical sensitivity: advances in the methodology of grounded theory.* Mill Valley, CA:The Sociology Press
- Strauss, Anselm L. (1987) *Qualitative analysis for social scientists.* Cambridge: Cambridge University Press

Current usage is mostly based on:

- Strauss, Anselm, Juliet Corbin (1990) *Basics of qualitative research: grounded theory procedures and techniques.* London: Sage
- Strauss, Anselm, Juliet Corbin (1998) *Basics of qualitative research: techniques and procedures for developing grounded theory*, 2nd edn. London: Sage

Glaser's alternative version is voiced in publications like:

- Glaser, Barney G. (1992) *Emergence vs forcing: basics of grounded theory analysis.* Mill Valley, CA:The Sociology Press
- Glaser, Barney (1998) *Doing grounded theory. issues and discussions.* Mill Valley, CA:The Sociology Press

For critical overviews of the GT approach see:

- Dey, Ian (1999) *Grounding grounded theory*. Orlando, FL: Academic Press
- Dey, Ian (forthcoming) 'Grounded theory analysis'. In: Clive Seale, David Silverman, Jay Gubrium, Giampietro Gobo, eds. *Inside Qualitative Research: craft, practice, context*. London: Sage

On computer-assisted qualitative data analysis, consult:

- Fielding, Nigel G., Raymond L. Lee (1998) *Computer analysis and qualitative research*. London, etc.: Sage
- Weitzman, Eben A. (2000) 'Software and qualitative research'. In: Norman K. Denzin, Yvonna S. Lincoln, eds (2000) *Handbook of qualitative research: second edition*. Thousand Oaks, CA: Sage: 803–20

Notes

1   See the papers by Robinson and Turner in McCall & Simmons (1969: 169–216); also Ragin (1994: 93–8), Becker (1998: 194–212), Silverman (2001: 237–8) for summaries, applications and discussions.

2   Cf. Ten Have (1999a: 129–56), also Clayman & Maynard (1995), Peräkylä (1997).

3   The reader is referred to the quoted publications of Glaser and/or Strauss. Strauss' (1987: 1–39) 'Introduction' provides an accessible inside overview, Fielding and Lee's (1998: 21–55) 'Approaches to qualitative data analysis' discusses the GT approach in a larger comparative context, while Dey (1999) offers a book-length critical discussion.

4   The 'creativity' of the analyst is not denied as such in GT writings (cf. Strauss & Corbin, 1998: 12–14, for instance), and the same goes for the notion of 'construction' of theories (cf. Straus & Corbin, 1998: 24–5), but the rhetoric of 'discovery' and 'emergence', as well as various technical elaborations of procedures, seems to hide these a bit.

5   Herbert Blumer has in his 'Sociological analysis and the "variable"' (1956, reprinted in 1969) depicted some of the limitations of 'variable analysis', most notably its inability to capture the essentially interpretative and processual character of 'human group life'. But – although Blumer's work is at times cited as related and a source of inspiration for GT, at least for Strauss – this particular paper of his is not, as far as I know, discussed in the GT literature.

6   Cf. Strauss (1987: 25) for an echo of this.

7   At this point, Glaser has a footnote to three publications of Paul Lazarsfeld!

8   See the following quote:

> Any concept is indicated by what may be called a reasonable set of indicators which therefore may be seen as interchangeable. . . . All that is required is a broad concensus [*sic*] of what may be included in the reasonable set of indicators for the concept. . . . It is important to remember that the analyst is collecting facts as indicators to be compared and coded into ideas, he is not collecting facts to be rendered empirically in descriptions.
>
> By the same token, the interchangeability applies to the same indicator indicating more than one concept. So different analysts may see a different

concept in the same datum. . . . Each indicator therefore can have more than one meaning. The point is, always, to achieve the cogency of indicator–concept meaning so others can see (and judge) it for themselves, that is how well the concept fits and work [*sic*] using the indicator. (Glaser, 1978: 42–3)

9   This theme is still prominent in Glaser's current polemical contributions. In a recent paper (Glaser, 2002), he criticizes Kathy Charmaz (2000) for ignoring GT's conceptual character in favour of descriptivist concerns, as in the following:

Remember again, the product will be transcending abstraction, NOT accurate description. The product, a GT, will be an abstraction from time, place and people that frees the researcher from the tyranny of normal distortion by humans trying to get an accurate description to solve the worrisome accuracy problem. Abstraction frees the researcher from data worry and data doubts, and puts the focus on concepts that fit and are relevant. (Glaser, 2002: para. 3)

10 Two acronyms are being used for this field: QDA-programs, where QDA stands for Qualitative Data Analysis, or CAQDAS for Computer Assisted Qualitative Data Analysis Software. For an extensive overview see Fielding & Lee (1998) and the CAQDAS website at: http://www.soc.surrey.ac.uk/caqdas/.

11 Cf. Chapter 2, and the overviews mentioned there; Rawls (2002) offers some interesting information on Garfinkel's pre-Parsons period.

12 For further elaborations, the reader is again referred to Heritage (1984a) and Sharrock & Anderson (1986).

8 Doing Ethnomethodological Studies

In this chapter, I will consider the practice of ethnomethodological studies: how to proceed, how to report, how to train one's sensibilities in order to do such studies. I will do so by presenting a variety of practical activities, exercises and strategies. This chapter is not meant as a how-to-do manual, but rather, and hopefully, as a source of inspiration.

At various places in his writings, Harold Garfinkel has wonderful enumerations of concrete activities that ethnomethodologists might study. Here is one of them, followed by some advice on how to analyse those activities.

> No inquiries can be excluded no matter where or when they occur, no matter how vast or trivial their scope, organization, cost, duration, consequences, whatever their successes, whatever their repute, their practitioners, their claims, their philosophies or philosophers. Procedures and results of water witching, divination, mathematics, sociology – whether done by lay persons or professionals – are addressed according to the policy that every feature of sense, of fact, of method, for every particular case of inquiry without exception, is the managed accomplishment of organized settings of practical actions, and that particular determinations in members' practices of consistency, planfulness, relevance, or re-producibility of their practices and results – from witchcraft to topology – are acquired and assured only through particular, located organizations of artful practices. (Garfinkel, 1967a: 32)

In short, any activity can be studied as concrete, lived, socially organized, naturally occurring, situated inquiry or order creating action. You can take some exotic activity and make it ordinary, or you can take an ordinary activity and make it strange, at least strange enough to study it. You can start where you are: sitting and reading this book – that's already two topics: 'sitting' and 'reading'. Observe yourself doing those two. Observing here means to 'see' those activities in procedural terms: how you 'do sitting' or 'do reading'. The first would be considered a bodily activity, the second a mental one, but – just for the fun of it – you might turn that around, as if you are sitting with your mind and reading with your body. Ethnomethodological observation, then, is an effort to catch what's going one without presuppositions, or rather, by 'bracketing' what you already know, taking what you bring to the observation itself as an observable.

Instructed actions

As Harold Garfinkel stresses in his recent book (2002), there has been a shift in ethnomethodology's conception of its own task, which he dates as occurring around 1972 (2002: 106). A central theme in his later writing, as well as in those of some of his later students such as Livingston and Lynch, is the local, each-time-again, embodied character of practical order-producing activities, conceived of as an achieved relationship between on the one hand descriptions and instructions and on the other hand the actual activities to which these descriptions and instructions refer. In the pre-1972 publications, this relationship was mostly formulated as an interpretative one, as in 'the documentary method of interpretation', 'etcetera' provisions or the prospective–retrospective properties of sense-making. In various programmatic statements from the post-1972 period (such as Garfinkel & Wieder, 1992; Garfinkel, 2002), the focus is often elaborated in contrast to what is then called the 'formal analysis' (FA) that is typical of 'the world-wide social science movement'. Both FA and EM are confronted with a problem: connecting the description or instruction with the actual events or activities, which in any actual case is achieved *somehow*. 'Both seek to replace *somehow* with an instructably observable *just how*'. FA tends to do so 'by designing and administering generically theorized formats', leading to 'generically represented relations of correspondence' (Garfinkel, 2002: 106). In contrast to this generalizing solution, ethnomethodological studies of work focus on the 'just this-nesses', the *haecceities* of actual activities. In any actual work situation in which the activities are done under the auspices of FA's generic strategies, these have to be supplied by a range of *ad hoc*, local and concrete practices. These are, however, while practically recognized officially ignored as uninteresting and not really relevant.

As Lynch (2002: 128–9) explains, Garfinkel uses the concept of *Lebenswelt*-pair as a formal device 'to elucidate the relationship between formulations and local actions'. It 'teases apart the primordial unity of, for example, actions performed in accordance with instructions, by distinguishing such actions into two parts'. 'The first part of the pair is a formal set of instructions', the 'second part consists in an actual course of "lived work"'.

> This order can be schematically represented by using the term *instructions* to stand for the various texts, rules, models, and so forth that make up the formal part of the pair:
>
> ```
> [instructions]  →  {Lived course of action}
> ```
>
> The arrow denotes the situated work of using the instructions, making out what they say, finding fault with them, re-reading them in light of what is happening *just now*, and other contingent uses and readings. Despite the directionality of the arrow, the route traveled from instructions to lived course of action is not a one-way street, nor does the 'lived work' follow a single pattern. Instead, the formal account of the *Lebenswelt* pair itself acts as a gloss that requires the (re)discovery of the local work of *doing* what the pair formulates. The point of juxtaposing the two pair parts is neither to generate ironies nor to celebrate indeterminacy; instead, the point is to encourage investigations of *just how* the lived work of any given pair is achieved. (Lynch, 2002: 129)

In other words, the concept is meant as a reminder, or as an invitation to study actual instances of the lived work of following instructions in detail.

Do-it-yourself

In order to discover for yourself what this is all about, I would advise the reader to take any upcoming case of practical work that can be conceived of as 'instructed action' as an occasion for a do-it-yourself ethnomethodological study. You may, for instance, have bought a chair, a bookcase or wardrobe or whatever, that comes in separate parts that need to be fitted together in order to produce a usable object. So what you may have at hand are:

- a collection of parts
- a set of instructions, both verbal and visual
- an image of the object to be constructed.

As you consider your work, you may start with inspecting the parts, probably aided by a list or drawings of the various types, with an indication of how many of each type should be present. The instructions may also mention which kinds of instruments you need to have at hand: a hammer, a screwdriver, etc. When all you need is there, the instructions may specify a series of sequentially ordered steps to be followed, in an ordered list or by giving a numbered series of instructive drawings. As you proceed, you may discover that while some of these sequential orderings are necessary, others may be considered optional – but it is often only afterwards that you can see which is which, whether (a) must or may precede (b). Each time you encounter a new item in the list, you will have to go from the instructions (description or drawing) to the parts at hand and/or the object-so-far-produced, and back again, to see how to proceed exactly, here and now. That is, you will have to construct a recognizably fitting pair of instruction and action.

Another aspect to be discovered concerns the limitations of the instructions. There will be aspects of the actions which will not be elaborated, but just mentioned or taken for granted. When you have to use a screwdriver, the instructions will not tell you how to do that. And when you have to fit pieces together, you will have to find out how to hold and move them in action, as an arrow indicating an overall direction may be all that is given. Another crucial aspect concerns the recognizability of the parts, both singly and in being fitted together, in terms of the target image of the finished object, either as given in a picture or 'in your mind'. These are but some of the aspects of your work that you may attend to, practically, and for the purpose of your DIY study also explicitly.

It may be helpful, in doing this ethnomethodological exercise, to 'think out loud', that is to verbalize what you are doing and taking into consideration. You might record this in audio, or – even better – make a video of both your actions and comments. And then afterwards, you might write a report on your findings. In this way, the work of doing ethnomethodology may come alive for you.

Instructed hearing of bird songs

Like 'following instructions', situations of 'learning' and 'teaching' can provide occasions in which generally unnoticed qualities of actions can be more easily 'seen'. Therefore, I will now present some reflections on a learning task – recognizing species of birds by their songs and calls – based on my own experiences and observations.

As part of your general membership you know that life forms are differentiated into multi-layered systems of classification. Plants are considered to be basically different from animal forms, mammals are different from birds and insects, etc. Depending on the circumstances of your upbringing and personal interests, you may learn to make some finer distinctions. At age 10, for instance, I could distinguish a number of common bird species, say *merel* (blackbird), *ekster* (magpie), *koolmees* (great tit), *roodborst* (robin), *huismus* (house sparrow), *vink* (chaffinch), and even some less common ones like *goudvink* (bullfinch), which happened to visit our garden at times. I acquired most of this knowledge by looking at the birds and having their names mentioned to me by others. I learned to distinguish the species by sight, acquiring the ability to *connect* properties of form, colour and behaviour to names. Gradually, I also learned to recognize some birds by their songs. The blackbird was probably among the earliest to be known in this way, as he sang from our rooftop in spring. Seeing a bird you know by sight sing his song is one method of building a repertoire of recognizable bird songs. Over the years I was able to enlarge my repertoire by a variety of means, including having a song I heard 'named' for me by a co-listener, consulting descriptions in field guides and comparing what I had heard outdoors to a specimen song recorded on tape or CD.

According to my experience, the main difficulty in this learning process is to remember the details of what you hear, in order to be able to connect those with a name, on the spot or later. For colours we have names, forms can be described and behaviours characterized, but sounds are more difficult to 'catch'.[1] There are, of course, easy cases, like the *koekoek* (cuckoo) who was given its name after its call – so-called onomatopoeia. There are a number of onomatopoetic bird names, as for instance – in Dutch – *grutto, tureluur, kievit, kauw* and *karekiet*. Often the recognizability of onomatopoeia in the field is not an easy matter. It may take repeated 'connection work' before the sound of, say, the black-tailed godwit (*limosa limosa*) is effectively recognized as *grutto*. What you do is 'sing' (in your mind) what you hear in the field or on the record, using the Dutch pronunciation of ↑*grutto* ↑*grutto* ↑*grutto*. In field guides more complicated renderings are given, for instance *rieta-rieta-rieta*, and *gr-wieto* (Peterson et al., 1984). Such renderings could be called 'transcriptions' and they are often given in combination with ordinary descriptions.[2] Here's an example for the song of the *kleine karekiet* (reed warbler):

> babbelend' in laag tempo, bestaand uit nerveuze, 2–4 keer herhaalde noten (onomatopoëtisch), af en toe onderbroken door imitaties of fluittonen, *trett trett*

trett TIRri TIRri truu truu TIe tre tre wi-wuu-wu tre tre truu truu TIRri TIRri. . . .
Tempo af en toe hoger, maar nooit met crescendo van Rietzanger.

['babbling' at a slow tempo, consisting of nervous, 2–4 time repeated notes
(onomatopoetic), now and then interrupted by imitations or whistlings, *trett trett
trett TIRri TIRri truu truu TIe tre tre wi-wuu-wu tre tre truu truu TIRri TIRri. . . .*
Tempo now and then higher, but never in crescendo like the sedge warbler.]
(Mullarney, et al., 2000: 296)

Apart from such published transcriptions and descriptions, birders use a
variety of informal tricks to assist their connection work. For instance, two
small birds that inhabit the same types of environments and that sing not only
in spring but also during the autumn and winter months, when most others
are elsewhere or silent, are the *roodborst* (robin) and the *winterkoning* (wren).
The song of the robin can be described as 'pearling', and a memory-aid for the
wren is to pronounce the Dutch name in the following way:
winterrrrrrrrrrrrrkoning, with the repeated *rrr*'s representing the rattle-like part
which wrens produce in the middle of their song. So when I hear a 'small' bird
in wintertime, I try to fit these two tricks to the sound and make my decision
whether it's a robin or a wren that I'm hearing. Birders exchange such tricks
among themselves. The *grasmus* (whitethroat, literally 'grass-sparrow'), for
instance, is informally called *krasmus* ('scratch-sparrow'), after its 'scratchy'
song. Once birders have acquired a more solid kind of knowledge of a
particular bird's song, they don't need these tricks any more (except when they
teach newbies). Experienced birders do what might be called an instant *gestalt*
recognition: they will need only a small fragment of a song to immediately
recognize the bird that produced it, mostly on the basis of the tone-quality of
what they hear, together with contextual knowledge of which birds sing where
and when. Having that ability for a substantial number of birds is a mark of
expert membership. Instead of just enjoying the singing of birds in spring,
they hear an ecological soundscape, a natural order.

In terms of the concepts used by Garfinkel, species names may function as
instructions for an accountable seeing and/or hearing of a specimen as an
authentic and accountable 'observation' of a member of a particular species.
In a name like blackbird, the instruction is a visual one, while in cuckoo or
karekiet it is aural: listen for this sound. In a trick like *winterrrrrrrrrrrrrkoning*,
mentioned above, the name is 'extended' in order to produce an aural
instruction: listen for an extended *rrrrrrrr*. For other tricks, there may be no
direct connection with the name, as in the characterization of the robin as
having a 'pearling' song. You have to remember that this is a property of a bird
for which the name just offers a visual instruction, not an aural one. In short,
names and tricks may assist in local identification work, but that work still has
to be done, on the spot and in real time, during or just after hearing the song.

A descriptive sketch such as this one could be turned into a demonstration
for a live audience, since recordings of bird songs are widely available, so I
could play a record of an isolated bird song, teach some of the tricks like those
mentioned above, and have the audience recognize the bird as part of a

recording on which a number of birds are singing at the same time. Or I could take some people out in the wood, the dunes or the polder to do some live teaching. In that case, the audience would be transformed into a group actively participating in the activity under investigation. In this way, we would be able to approximate what Garfinkel (cf. 2002) has called a 'hybrid science', partly the practical science of field biology with special reference to birds and bird songs, for example doing an inventory project, and partly an inquiry into the ethno-methods of birding.[3]

Teaching 'observation'

For my next example, I have selected another learning situation, but this time as seen from the teaching side. This example is more elaborate, as I touch on a number of research dilemmas and possible solutions.

For a number of years, I have been teaching short courses in 'observation' for first and second year sociology students. They had to do three assignments, first one using 'direct observation', a second using 'indirect observation'– that is by using a camera – and finally a small research project based on direct and/or indirect observation. In most cases, they observed scenes of public or semi-public life. The 'indirect observation' was mostly done by making photographs of situations like waiting in line or leaving/entering trains, but some used a video camera. They had to write a descriptive and analytic report, and turn in the photographs or videotapes as well. I will use these experiences – theirs and mine – to discuss 'observation' as an accountable activity.

For most students, the first assignment – direct observation – was not too problematic. Most of the time, they chose to do covert observations, passing as innocent participants or bystanders while observing some scenes of social life. They therefore showed a marked preference for situations in which their presence and their looking around seemed to be not unusual. In my instructions, I stressed that observing one's surroundings is a normal aspect of being in a public area, that everybody looks around, even if often in a furtive manner, so that doing observations for an assignment would not be visibly deviant in such areas. They had to do two observations, lasting 15 minutes each, on two different occasions. I encouraged them not to take notes during those periods, but scribble some keywords soon afterwards and write their report later in a quiet place. A substantial proportion of the students did not trust their ability to remember enough details and therefore tried to make some notes during the observation periods. They selected scenes which would allow such note-taking, like a library, or they simulated some reading-and-writing activity while sitting in the train, for instance. But even then, the alternation of looking around and making notes made some of their victims suspicious. While doing their observations, the students also observed how other participants in the scene managed to look around. They observed, for example how males used the reflections in train windows to look at female passengers, or how people used scanning eye movements for hiding their selection of 'interesting objects'. The students, of course, used the same kinds of strategies to do their assignments.

Observations such as these can be analysed in terms like the following.[4] As part of their ordinary membership, people 'know' what kinds of activities are to be expected in the various scenes in which they find themselves. Different scenes have different repertoires of more or less 'fitting' activities and people adapt their actions to these repertoires in one way or another. Some may choose to restrict their activities closely to the suitable repertoire, trying not to draw attention to themselves. Others may choose to do things that do not fit very well, putting up with any negative inferences that may be drawn. Looking around is ambiguous because it is on the one hand a normal and necessary aspect of being with people, while being on the other suspicious if it suggests a distribution of attention that deviates from current expectations. Looking intensely at someone may fit a situation of 'focused interaction' – although it may make the other uncomfortable if it lasts too long – but will be felt to be out of place when the interaction is expected to be 'unfocused'. When in a conversation, by contrast, it would be continuously looking around that would be seen as deviant, as 'doing disattention'.

Using a camera

Returning to my students, the problems they feared or experienced with their first assignment became much more intense with the second, requiring 'indirect observation', using a camera. When I discussed this, many students voiced their reluctance to do so. They expected to be embarrassed and encounter various kinds of objections from the people who were to be observed. After doing the assignment, most students reported with relief that the experience wasn't too bad after all, but some encountered fierce opposition to their visible intention to use a camera or their actual shooting. Many of the students had taken various kinds of precautions, hiding their use of the camera in order to avoid embarrassment and open difficulties. Some acted as if they were making pictures of tourist objects or of a friend who was visibly posing for a picture, while in between these they were shooting the street or market situation. Others took a tourist scene as (part of) their target object, for instance studying the interaction between a 'living statue' or a man operating a street organ and his public. Many pictures and videos were taken from quite a distance, or from behind the people being targeted. In their pictures and tapes, the students constituted themselves as onlookers at a distance. In our discussions of these experiences, it became clear that the students expected their victims to wonder why they were taking pictures or making a video. Using a camera in public is apparently considered an accountable action. In fact, when occasionally asked 'what it was for', an answer like 'an assignment for school' proved to be sufficient in most cases. When the students simulated that they were taking a picture of a friend or of a tourist scene, the motive for doing so seemed so obvious that no questions were asked or accounts required.

One persistent theme in students' reactions to the assignments, especially concerning the analytic parts, was that they would have liked to interview the people they observed in order to understand their 'motives' better. That is, they thought that observation without talking to people made it more difficult to understand what these people were up to. For example after they had observed that passengers in trains avoided sitting next to people when there were still places where one could sit alone, they wrote in their reports that for a deeper understanding of this avoidance, one would have to interview passengers about this preference.

My defence of requiring a restriction to observation was that social life in the public realm is in large part organized on the basis of visual displays and their silent interpretation, so that in order to grasp that organization, one did not need to have access to 'motives' as verbalized by the subjects themselves. It would be sufficient, I said, to use one's membership resources oriented to visual displays in order to analyse the visual organization of everyday life.

As the students themselves realized, their distancing strategies caused their pictures – photographs and videos – to provide less access to various interactional details – such as facial expressions and gaze direction – than might be desirable for some kinds of sociological analysis. In fact, they often analysed their data in terms of overall 'patterns' that made such details less important. In my general instructions, however, I had encouraged them not only to look for overall patterns, but also to consider the ways in which actual, concrete instances were accomplished in and through such details. So there were rather sharp discrepancies between my analytic suggestions and their data collection methods.

The purpose of the course was to train students in making observations that could be analysed sociologically. And because the time available was extremely limited, I suggested that they select scenes of public or semi-public life, in order to minimize time loss due to entry negotiations, etc. Over the years, a number of scene types emerged as most popular with the students, mostly because of their accessibility. These included: seating arrangements in public transport, open-air markets, service lines, leaving/entering trains, pedestrian crossings and, less commonly, library use, waiting rooms, playgrounds, parties and club scenes. In the next subsections I will discuss the discrepancies mentioned before, and how we dealt with them, as regards one particular topic, what I call pedestrian traffic streams.

Pedestrian traffic streams

Quite a number of students studied pedestrian crossings, especially 'zebra crossings'. They employed direct observation, photographs and/or videos to study how people used such facilities, often focusing on the fact that many pedestrians (in Amsterdam!) did not follow the official rules that stipulate that they should only cross when the lights are green. Most of the time the students took a 'side position', which would minimize the chances of their observing presence being noticed: they were acting as people 'just standing there'.

There was some variation, however, in their distance from the crossing. Some made a video from a large distance, while others took it from a position right beside one end of the zebra crossing. In the first case, their materials could only be used for a global pattern analysis, noting for instance that when one person started crossing when the light was red, others tended to follow. In the second case, this could also be done, but one could additionally analyse particular incidents. One could observe, for instance, 'non-vocal negotiations' in a multi-person party about whether to cross at a red light, or the bodily ways in which a crosser reacted to a horn signal evidently used as a complaint about his action.

I often commented on such choices and their practical and analytic implications after the fact, when the students reported their findings and showed their materials. The idea was to have them discover these things from their own experience, so that they might choose a different tactic when working on the next assignment. This was particularly successful in one case which I will discuss at some length. As her first assignment, one student, Irene, had observed pedestrians in a busy shopping street from a table at the first floor of a fast-food restaurant. In my comments, I referred to a seven-page chapter in Eric Livingston's book, *Making sense of ethnomethodology* (1987) on 'Pedestrian traffic flow'. He contrasts the social order of pedestrian crossing, as depicted by a sociologist filming the behaviour of people crossing a busy intersection *from above*, with the order that is created by the pedestrians who actually do the crossing together, *on the ground*.[5]

Seen from above, a crossing cycle starts with two rows of pedestrians facing each other. When the lights for the pedestrians turn green, both rows move forward and the 'pedestrians form themselves into "wedges" and "fronts" behind "point people"' (21). What remains mysterious, however, is *how* exactly the participants themselves get this complicated job done.

> The perspective of 'wedges,' 'fronts' and 'point people' is, of course, from a vantage point that none of the participants had or could have. Pedestrians do not use these documented, geometrically described alignments of physical bodies; they are engaged in a much more dynamic forging of their paths. They are engaged in locally building, together, the developing organization of their mutual passage. That organization is, and accommodates itself to, the witnessable structures of accountable action as they develop over the course of their journey. To understand how pedestrians manage their crossing we must, metaphorically, move the camera to eye level. (Livingston, 1987: 22)

Of the two contrastive depictions of pedestrians crossing, one based on an observer's image from above and one from a participant perspective on the ground, only the latter, he suggests, is able to show the actual lived work of pedestrians crossing. He provides a verbal sketch of the actions and orientations of a crosser in visual interactions with the others engaged in crossing from the other side, but he does not seem to ground his 'observations' in concrete instances observed directly or indirectly. Here is one fragment of his sketch:

Even before a 'front runner' or 'scout' comes into physical proximity with the opposing flow, the small group of people in front of her observable path begin to move so as to allow a place for her passage. The people behind the bifurcating interface see this directed movement and begin to orient themselves toward following those in front, continuing their motion in that direction. While this is going on, the 'scout' has already headed for, and moved into, the opening that is being provided for her. (Livingston, 1987: 22)

In other words, the idea is that people on both sides of the street continuously orient to what the others are doing, seizing any opportunity provided by the others, or even suggested as upcoming by the pace and directions of their movements.

Referring again to the contrast between his sketch and the film images, Livingston writes:

During the ongoing course of the crossing, the pedestrians are intrinsically building the interface between their two conflicting currents. That interface as it is seen and produced by the pedestrians is quite different from the way it appeared on the sociologist's films. When it is seen on films made from above, the interface itself provides the films' witnessable phenomenon. Through his interest in accounting for pedestrians' behavior in terms of documented, regular, repeating structures of practical action, the sociologist attempted to render that interface through the use of geometric figures. The phenomenal basis of his theorizing – the pedestrians' production and maintenance of an interface between the two oppositely directed currents of walkers – was hidden by his methods of analysis and his natural theorizing. (Livingston, 1987: 23)

In other words, Livingston connects the contrast in depicting methods – filming from above and at eye level – with a contrast in analytic interests. Filming from above, one gains access to social life as a *product*, but at the same time the lived-work of *production* is hidden from view. He does not claim that his verbal sketch provides an analysis of this work: 'It gives an idea – or, as an ethnomethodologist would say, technical access to – the intrinsic, locally produced, *in situ* organization of the walk across the crowded intersection'. It could be used as a 'invitation', so to speak, to go out on the street and 'elaborate the description in terms of the actual lived-details of the organizational work of pedestrian street crossings'.

Inspired by my discussion of Livingston's example, Irene did take his suggestion – to move the camera to eye level – not just metaphorically, but almost literally. For her next assignment, she wrapped a video camera in a bag, held it under her arm, and walked the streets with the camera running. Looking at the tape she could infer how she manoeuvred, avoiding people who walked slower than she did, seeking opportunities to keep her pace, etc. In short, she had an image that represented both what she saw and what she did on that basis. This image was, of course, not complete, as the camera, tied to her body, was less flexible than her head and eyes, but it provided a useful approximation of a *participant's perspective*, and as such it can be contrasted with the *onlooker's perspective* that was available in the pictures and videos shot by the other students. For her last assignment, Irene decided not to use video again, because she wanted to have the complete bodies of the other pedestrians in view, not just the limited part available with a camera at a rather short distance. So now she used a more traditional kind of participant observation, walking the streets and making 'mental notes' of what she observed.

As an aside, I note that at a recent conference I saw a video based on pictures shot with a miniature camera that was hidden in a pair of glasses, sending its images to a receiver at the back of the wearer. It was used as evidence in an exploration by Marc Relieu, a French ethnomethodologist, of online text-based chatting on a mobile phone while conversing with a friend. The image of this camera corresponds more closely to the view of the person wearing the glasses than in the arrangement used by Irene, but as Paul McIlvenny, who was present at the showing, remarked, it still does not catch the actual sight since it does not follow the eye movements. Furthermore, the scope of the image is extremely limited, which may not be a serious problem when studying mobile phone use, but makes it hardly useful for studying pedestrian manoeuvring on the streets.

Discussion

The upshot of these experiences is, I think, that each of these 'methods' – observing from above, using the arm-held camera, and actual participant observation – has its own possibilities and limitations. It might be suggested that for a topic like pedestrian traffic, a combination of 'perspectives', as embodied in and realized through various ways of doing visual studies, might provide the best results.

In the case of Irene, for instance, it is my impression that her two first assignments contributed to the richness of her final 'traditional' participant observations. These exercises had alerted her to a range of phenomena that she could now study as part of the overall action stream. Now she could, for instance, shadow people, both those who walked alone and others who were 'with' someone else.[6] What she discovered was, among other things, that within a couple walking on a busy shopping street, a kind of division of labour tended to emerge. One partner – often the male, often walking in the left position – would watch the traffic straight ahead and initiate changes in pace and direction to fit with the stream. In this way, he seemed to free his companion – often female, walking to his right – from these tasks, which allowed her to look around at people and shop windows. So he acted as the driver of the 'circulation unit', she as the passenger. This pattern, it seems to me, is immediately recognizable as 'the way we act'. Just as in Livingston's sketch, it depicts a set of obvious solutions to common problems of modern city life.

Another phenomenon, which might be called 'a preference for movement', was also observable with a variety of methods. When walkers were faced with a temporary blockage – whether a red light, some people standing, or a car crossing their path – they would tend to adjust their direction or their pace, whichever was most convenient, rather than stop and wait for the blockage to be removed. So they might walk around a group standing before them or adjust their walking, slowing down or even running, when another 'circulation unit' was about to cross their path. Such patterns were clearly 'demonstrated' in Irene's tape from her arm-held camera, but these could also be observed by a camera looking from a side position, or through direct observation.

As Livingston stresses, pattern descriptions like the ones given above do not constitute 'detailed ethnomethodological analyses', but they can be seen as a first step, or 'a pedagogy' (cf. Garfinkel, 2002) for anyone caring to go out and see for themselves, not only *that* it is done in the ways indicated, but *how* this is actually accomplished.[7] In such an activity, the 'methods' of visual observation discussed above may have different functions. The 'arm-camera method', for instance, is instructive in demonstrating a walker's body movement, because one sees and can vicariously experience those movements and the actual situations which have provoked them. Methods of direct observation or tapes made from a side position may provide access to multi-party accommodations in body movements, gestures and/or positionings. But whatever the method, the observer still has to do inferential work in order to see the systematics of the movements in relation to their environments, as well as the work of their accomplishment. The types of inference to be made may be different, but inferential work as such seems unavoidable. While a 'body-held camera' can be quite instructive, it has its limitations too. The usual way to videotape interactive activities, using a 'side position' may often be the best solution, as can be seen for instance in Christian Heath's studies (1986, with Luff, 2000). And as he has stated (1997) and demonstrated, additional fieldwork will often be required in order to enable the analyst to make sense of the taped events. In this regard, pedestrian traffic is different from many other kinds of setting, as one can observe and experience this kind of collective action without bothering anyone.

After these discussion of what anyone could do, or of situations in which I myself was implicated – as a birder or a teacher – I will now turn to some ethnomethodological studies done by others, and as reported by them. I will start with some aspects of David Goode's exceptional studies of the life of severely handicapped children.

Gaining understanding of a closed world

As part of his graduate work at UCLA, Goode studied children born deaf and blind, who were also retarded and without formal language, due to a rubella infection during pregnancy. This specifically involved the in-depth study of two of such children, one hospitalized in a state institution and another living with her parents (Goode, 1994). An important overall theme of these explorations is the continuously emerging observation that the assessment of the capabilities of these children was dependent on the character, format and frequency of the assessor's interaction with those children. In the state hospital, Goode observed that the assessments made by various specialized clinicians were markedly different from those made by members of the 'direct-care' staff. The first saw the children only incidentally, for brief periods, and in terms of their practical-professional frameworks, such as medical or educational tests, while the second had to deal with the children every day in a variety of practical contexts.

When Goode started to communicate his observation-based ideas that these children might have their own perspective on things and were even 'smart' in their own ways, the very possibility of the children having such capacities tended to be denied by the clinicians and accepted by the direct-care staff. He therefore planned to undertake an intensive study of one child's 'world' through a period of frequent and intense interactions. Most of these interactions with 'Christina' had a playful character in that he could more and more leave his normal seeing/hearing self-evident presuppositions behind and let the child initiate a variety of forms of play. This involved, for instance bracketing the usual functions of various objects, such as musical instruments, to see her use of those objects as sensible-for-her, in terms of her perceptual possibilities. In other words, he had to discard the remedial attitude that was so natural for all able seeers/hearers when confronted with seemingly bizarre behaviour, since this led inevitably to the application of 'fault-finding procedures'. Here is what he did:

> I decided to *mimic her actions* in order to gain more direct access to what such activities were providing her. I used wax ear stops (placed more securely in the left ear, since Chris has a 'better' right ear than left ear) and gauzed my left eye with a single layer of lightweight gauze to simulate the scar tissue that covers Chris's left eye. I began to imitate Chris's behaviors. . . . While the procedure had its obvious inadequacies with respect to my gaining access to Chris's experience of these activities, I did learn a number of interesting things in this way. (Goode, 1994: 33–4)

By 'imitating' her condition in this way he could, for instance, understand that she would get some auditory or visual stimulation by moving parts of her body rhythmically in certain positions *vis-à-vis* particular sources of sound or light. In fact, a lot of her bizarre movements appeared to be 'rational' as effective means of self-stimulation in terms of her particular sensory restrictions. By way of this partial imitation of her conditions and action, Goode was able to get at least a sense of the significance *in her own terms* of these acts. A major overall condition for these possibilities, however, was that he was free from custodial or pedagogical obligations and therefore free to play with her, allowing her to show him how she was striving for at least some 'primitive' gratifications. By becoming a 'superplaymate' to her, he was able to 'meet her' in ways that staff members could only rarely achieve. In this way, Goode has given a very creative demonstration of what 'procedural immersion' might mean.

Using 'paired novices'

I would like to switch now to a rather different field of inquiry, that of people working in technologically complex environments. Some of the labels that are used to denote this field and some sub-fields are human-computer interaction (HCI) and computer-supported cooperative work (CSCW), but now 'workplace studies' seems to have become the overall label. For a long time this field has been dominated by cognitivist and individualistic approaches, like Artificial Intelligence (AI), but over the last decade ethnographic and ethnomethodological inspirations and inquiries have gained a substantial position as well (Blomberg, 1995). A most important contribution to this development has been the work of Lucy Suchman, whose 1987 book, *Plans and situated action: the problem of human–machine communication* embodied a crucial challenge to the AI-based approaches to software design.

As her title makes clear, she builds up a contrast between 'plans' and 'situated action'. She starts with discussing 'The planning model . . . [which] treats a plan as a sequence of actions designed to accomplish some preconceived end' (28), and elaborates a contrasting view which stresses 'situated action'. 'The coherence of situated action is tied in essential ways not to individual predispositions or conventional rules but to local interactions contingent on the actor's particular circumstances' (27–8). In this view, plans never suffice as prescriptions for action. They have to be locally realized by changing or adding to the prescriptions in various ways. She suggests, however, that plans continue to be used to frame the actions, and that as such they are the basis for reports on and accounts of the actions, even if these have departed significantly from the plans.

The contrast involves two conceptions of practical action, one seeing it as following a systematic sequence of pre-planned steps leading to a goal, and another as a series of consecutive 'situated actions', which while broadly oriented towards a goal, are basically improvised on the spot, taking into account what seems to be the locally relevant knowledge available. Starting off from some anthropological studies of navigation at sea, Suchman presents an in-depth study of people working at an experimental copying machine, which had an 'instruction component' attached to it. She invited couples of novice users to carry out certain complicated copying tasks, on the basis of the 'instructions' provided by the machine. She chose first-time users because the machine was intended to be self-explanatory and she used a pair in order to get a record of their reasoning:

> In each of the sessions two people, neither of whom had ever used the system before, worked together in pairs. Two people asked to collaborate in using a relatively simple machine like a photocopier are faced with the problem of doing together what either could do alone. In the interest of the collaboration, each makes available to the other what she believes to be going on: what the task is, how it is to be accomplished, what has already been done and what remains, rationales for this way of proceeding over that, and so forth. Through the ways in which each collaborator works to provide her sense of what is going on to the other, she

provides that sense to the researcher as well. An artifact of such a collaboration, therefore, is naturally generated protocol. (Suchman, 1987: 115)

These trials were videotaped and analysed using a special kind of transcript, which was organized in four columns, two for the users and two for the machine. The first user column contained the talk between the users, under the heading 'Not available to the machine', while the second recorded their actions on the machine as 'Available to the machine'. The machine columns were similarly divided, one 'Available to the user' mentioning the displays provided for the users' information, and the last 'Design rationale', explicating the 'reasoning' that was implemented in the design of the machine. The crux of the matter was that the machine had been designed on the basis of a rationalistic, systematic step-like *plan*, which was not available to the users, while they operated in terms of *situated action*, i.e. locally improvised guesses at what might have to be done next and what the machine displays and activities could 'mean'.

Suchman refers to the empirical findings of CA in order to explore the *repertoire* of communicational resources that might be available in a communicative situation. She notes that face-to-face interaction can be considered to be 'the richest form of human communication', 'with other forms of interaction being characterizable in terms of particular resource limitations or additional constraints' (69). She discusses some basic properties of face-to-face interaction, like local control, sequence-based coherence and especially the possibilities for 'locating and remedying communicative trouble'. Then she turns to 'specialized forms of interaction', referring to interaction in institutional settings and specifically to issues of 'pre-allocation of turn-types' and 'the prescription of the substantive content and direction of the interaction, or the *agenda*' (88).

It is from this background that she analyses a number of cases of 'trouble' in the interaction between the users and the machine. These troubles can be seen as produced by particular 'misunderstandings' between the users and the machine, which are hard to detect for either party, and therefore hard to repair. The machine is designed in terms of a collection of step-wise plans, and checks its various parts in order to 'know' which is the current plan and which its current phase. The users' action on the machine are 'interpreted' accordingly. The users, however, may be mistaken as to either the current plan or the current action-state. As Suchman writes:

> The new user of a system . . . is engaged in ongoing, situated inquiries regarding the appropriate next action. While the instructions of the expert help system are designed in anticipation of the user's inquiries, problems arise from the user's ability to move easily between a simple request for a next action, 'meta' inquiries about the appropriateness of the procedure itself, and embedded requests for clarification of the actions described within a procedure. (Suchman, 1987: 169)

In other words, the new user has a wider range of informational needs than has been, or maybe can be, anticipated by a pre-programmed system. Therefore, while the user may 'read' the machine's (non-)response as a reaction to her own inquiries, the machine does react in terms of what her actions suggest when seen in terms of the current procedure as planned.

> In reading the machine's response to her situated inquiries and taking the actions prescribed, the user imports certain expectations from human communication: specifically, that a new instruction in response to an action effectively confirms the adequacy of that action, while a non-response is evidence that the action is incomplete. (Suchman, 1987: 169)

This can lead to various kinds of ambiguities and impasses, which in themselves may be hard to detect. The overall message of this book, then, is that in order to understand what can go wrong when users work with pre-planned action systems, one should study their *actual situated activity* in detail, i.e. the local rationality of users' activities, rather than see it as faulty operation based on misconceptions regarding a rational system.

In terms of research strategy, this study offers some interesting ideas. It uses videotapes providing a record of the sessions, as I discussed in Chapter 3. Those sessions had an 'experimental' quality, in that the users had some pre-specified tasks to do, but it was not a 'controlled' experiment as they had to work the tasks on their own. Furthermore, the study used an interesting variation of the strategy of the novice (cf. p. 23), which might be called the novice pair, as the two first-time users had to work together. A similar strategy was apparently used in an unpublished study by one of Garfinkel's students named Friedrich Schrecker, to which Lynch et al. (1983) refer. He did a study of laboratory work in an undergraduate chemistry lab in which he assisted a partially paralysed chemistry student with his lab exercises for a course in 'quantitative analysis'. The two had to develop a rather special division of labour and responsibilities, where Schrecker had to do what the student instructed him to do, which made observable 'the mutual dependence of chemical reasoning and embodied action' (225).

A workplace study

As a final example, I have selected a case that seems quite representative of current ethnomethodological work in the applied field of 'workplace studies', combining field methods with recordings. It is called 'Expert systems in (inter)action: diagnosing document machine problems over the telephone' and was written by Jack Whalen and Eric Vinkhuyzen (2000). It is a study of 'naturally occurring expert system use' in which customers call a support centre of a company that designs and manufactures document machines, such as copiers and printers. The call takers at the centre – customer service and support representatives (or CSSRs) – have to process the requests and dispatch service technicians. The work is done by entering information about the customer and the problem in a computer system in order to produce a job ticket for the relevant group of technicians. In some cases, the call takers could assist the callers in solving their problems, although they did not receive any special training to do so. Furthermore, it would be most efficient if they could assist in differentiating hardware and software problems, as the latter could be solved over the phone by specialists. In order to support these functions, an expert system was developed which would provide the technical knowledge required for these tasks, without having to train the call takers. After having entered customer information and any fault codes that customers might report, they were to type in a problem description, as given by the caller, using ordinary, non-technical terms. The system would then provide questions which would have to be answered by the caller and entered by the call taker, leading to one or another pertinent action to be taken by the call taker or the customer.

The authors 'observed and listened in to conversations between CSSRs and customers for two months before recording approximately thirty-six hours of work activity, involving twelve different CSSRs at two centres'. The 'recorded data include the phone conversation between CSSRs and customers, the CSSRs' actions on their computer screens, and interactions between these CSSRs and their colleagues in the center'. They did additional ethnographic observations at one of the centres, discussed the system's design with the developers, and talked with some of the 'managers about their views on telephone customer support operations and the corporation's technology strategy' (94).

They describe the complexity of their task in the following terms:

> These data and methods allow us to analyse a particular situated activity system – a customer service and support telephone centre – in its interactional, socio-technical and organisational dimensions; respectively, the encounters between customers and CSSRs on the telephone, the expert system used by CSSRs during these encounters and their work practices around that technology, and the corporation's policies and practices that shape both the work of CSSRs and the design of their expert system. To examine the history of a particular set of actions in this complex social/organisational/technical matrix, one must use several different, complementary types of data: audio-visual recordings of CSSRs at work and on the phone with customers, video records of their interactions with the expert system during these telephone conversations, and fieldnotes collected through traditional observational methods and informant interviews. (Whalen & Vinkhuyzen, 2000: 94)

In other words, they maintain that their complex data-gathering strategy fits the complexity of the work situation to be studied. In effect, their study is a multi-faceted ethnomethodological ethnography, using transcribed phone interactions and screen displays to illustrate their findings.

Recall that the system, while designed to support the call takers, was also designed to process problem descriptions in ordinary terms and did not suppose that the call takers would have any specific expertise on the machines and their problems. In other words, the call takers were 'designed' to be blind transmitters of customer-provided information, and in the next phase to be readers of the machine-generated questions, and again transmitters, this time of the answers. The necessary technical expertise was supposed to be provided by the expert system. Observing actual cases of call takers at work tells a different story, however. It is not an easy task for customers and call takers to assemble a useful problem description. The examples show that they often struggle to find the seemingly 'right' description. In the process, the call takers try to distil a concise summary characterization, often using different words from those used by the customer. This is linked by the authors to, among other things, the time pressure they are working under and their efforts to gain at least some control over the system. There is, then, a clear *discrepancy* between the designers' 'user model' and the actual *in situ* use made of the system by the call takers. In other words, as is so often the case, the planned rationality of the designers does not fit well with the reasonable work practices of the users.

The authors note and illustrate a range of other problems which are, in some ways, similar to other reports of users who have to work with 'intelligent machines' which have, however, a rather limited vocabulary, and therefore limited 'interpretative flexibility'. This may lead, for instance, to misunderstandings between the worker and the machine, which are not 'visible' to either party, and therefore not repairable (cf. Suchman, 1987). Furthermore, the worker has to 'mediate' between a system which provides 'instructions' and another human with whom they have to interact *as if* that was a conversation. The authors show, for instance, that the call takers at times change the wording of the system-generated questions, and in so doing 'project' particular responses which may not be accurate descriptions. This is similar to what has been found in interviewing practices where scripted questions are changed to fit the interactive situation, for instance in light of rapport considerations (Houtkoop-Steenstra, 2000). The authors conclude that:

> the detailed series of observations we have presented on interrogating the customer suggests that an expert system strategy that fails to recognise the active participation of the user in the questioning of customers has fundamentally misconceived the ways in which those users actually participate in the diagnosis. In diverse but systematic ways, discrepancies may arise between the 'context' invoked by the system to diagnose a machine problem by generating questions and using answers to then eliminate or select cases, and the interactional context invoked by the CSSR in asking, not asking, or modifying those questions and entering those answers. (Whalen & Vinkhuyzen, 2000: 126)

This discrepancy may be less troublesome if the call taker does have some technical expertise and is supported by a system for elaboration of his or her hunches. In such a case, technical expertise combined with interactional flexibility can lead to much more efficient case handling than in the majority of the studied events. This would amount to a strategy which the authors call a 'system for experts', instead of an 'expert system'.

In the final section of their paper, Whalen and Vinkhuyzen discuss the possibilities to offering an alternative approach to systems design on the basis of their observations – a rather unique step: to think about the 'application' of ethnomethodological findings. As they write:

Developing tools and technology systems to support or enhance work performance, or to enable people to work together more effectively, is not sufficient. We need to devote equal attention to questions of how people learn to use that technology to do their work, and how they learn about and strive to master their work projects and tasks more generally. This is not simply a 'training' problem. It is rather a problem in understanding the foundations of work practice, including the epistemological history behind that practice. (Whalen & Vinkhuyzen, 2000: 133)

They therefore developed an approach which integrated 'a learning strategy with a technology strategy', which stressed the possibility for call takers to learn about the document machines, their most common problems and the ways in which these could be solved. In effect, they recommended generalizing the peer-to-peer learning which they had observed in a few successful cases, as well as learning from the technicians. Both would have to be on-the-spot learning, rather than in a classroom format. On the technology side, they proposed to make the system more transparent for the users, in the sense that they would be informed about what the system was doing and why, so that the users would be able to use the system in a more purposeful manner. System design should also be based on information about the actual work practices, rather than on abstract presuppositions developed at a distance, and system use should be evaluated and results fed back to the developers.

The reactions to these proposals were mixed, with the overall tendency being that managers and developers at a distance from the actual work-site were resisting, while those more directly involved were more easily convinced and willing to try to implement parts of the proposals, especially learning strategies to help call takers to develop their expertise.[8]

Access and rendition

As ethnomethodology studies the accomplishment of concrete lived orders, any EM study has to come to terms with the requirement of getting access to the detailed specifics or local order-producing activities. The cases discussed in this chapter illustrate a variety of access strategies, which can be summed up as:

- do-it-yourself experiences, both novice and routine;
- observing co-member and novice instruction, instruction-following, and learning;
- intensive interaction with, observing/recording of, and mimicking 'incomprehensible' actors/activities;
- observing/recording 'paired novices' at a learning task;
- combining ethnography and on-the-spot recording.

Choosing a strategy for an ethnomethodological study involves a complex set of choices. One has to choose a setting and the activities on which one wants to focus, but one also has to construct ways in which the activities to be studied will be represented as 'data'. The latter issue includes the relationship between the competences required to do the activity and those of the would-be analyst. In my proposal that the researcher him- or herself would do a DIY-activity in order to study the required ordering work, I suggested that one might study one's own activities – in this case one's struggle to 'connect' instructions, parts-at-hand, and objects to be constructed. In a similar vein, I used my own experiences in learning to recognize bird songs to describe how group-based tricks could be applied in that particular task. For the study of DIY jobs, I recommended recording one's activities and 'thoughts', in order to be able to study them in detail. For the section on bird song recognition, I relied on my own memories, turning my previous experiences into a post-hoc ethnography, so to speak. But I added the suggestion that the exercise could be turned into a collective demonstration or teaching event. For the section on observation, I again relied on my own experiences, but this time as a teacher, while I also referred to the learning experiences of my students, as evident in their oral and written reports and their recordings.

From the studies by David Goode and Lucy Suchman, as discussed above, one can learn that various kinds of 'manipulation' may be necessary to make the phenomena of interest 'visible': Goode's 'mimicry' of his subject's perceptual limitations, and Suchman's novice-pair set-up. For Goode, his actual 'data' were his own observations and experiences, while he also made videotapes. Suchman videotaped her novice pairs at work. In her report, she uses a special way to represent her data, in which she places the information – transcripts, displays, actions and design rationales – in different columns, according to their local accessibility for the two parties, the users and the machine. In other words, she uses an instructive way in which readers can discern the analytic significance of the data.

On reflection, this is only one of the many ways in which 'data' can be provided to readers in such a way that they are 'instructed' in seeing their significance. Jefferson-styled transcripts, like the ones that Suchman provides in one of her columns, are *themselves* examples of an instructive way to read data in a conversation-analytic way. They *foreground* particular aspects, such as sequential ones, while ignoring others. Inevitably, it seems, researchers engage in specialized order-producing activities, reifying aspects of the lived-orders studied. This is a persistent theme in ethnomethodological critiques of conversation-analytic practices.[9]

In the study by Whalen and Vinkhuyzen, discussed above, we encountered again, the use of ethnographic background information to instruct the reader how to understand what is happening in the transcribed fragments.

As noted before, methods used in ethnomethodological studies retain a somewhat ambivalent and paradoxical character. While resisting the reduction of lived orders to one or another kind of formal account, their focus on 'the missing what', 'indexical features' and *haecceities* seems to lead inevitably to an alternate kind of reification, depending on different sets of rendering technologies, such as transcripts, videoclips, etc., which ultimately require some kind of suggestive 'evocation'of their topics.

There is, in a way, no one ethnomethodological method. With the disputed exception of conversation analysis, every ethnomethodological study requires the creative *invention* of a unique approach to the problems of gaining access to the phenomena of interest and ways to render them inspectable for others. My discussion of examples is intended to provide inspiration for anyone trying his or her hand in ethnomethodological studies. Therefore, no 'major points' section concludes this chapter.

Recommended reading

It seems rather arbitrary to select further 'exemplary' ethnomethodological studies to recommend, apart from the ones mentioned at various places in the book, so here I just repeat the details of the ones I have already discussed at some length, and add a few more of my personal favourites, concentrating on book-length reports.[10]

- Anderson, R.J., John A. Hughes, Wes W. Sharrock (1989) *Working for profit: the social organization of calculation in an entrepreneurial firm.* Aldershot: Avebury
- Clayman, Steven, John Heritage (2002) *The news interview: journalists and public figures on the air.* Cambridge: Cambridge University Press
- Crist, Eileen (2000) *Images of animals: anthropomorphism and animal mind.* Philadelphia: Temple University Press
- Goode, David (1994) *A word without words: the social construction of children born deaf and blind.* Philadelphia: Temple University Press
- Heath, Christian, Paul Luff (2000) *Technology in action.* Cambridge: Cambridge University Press
- Lynch, Michael (1985) *Art and artifact in laboratory science: a study of shop work and shop talk.* London: Routledge & Kegan Paul
- Lynch, Michael, David Bogen (1996) *The spectacle of history: speech, text, and memory at the Iran-Contra hearings.* Durham, DC: Duke University Press
- Maynard, Douglas W. (1984) *Inside plea bargaining: the language of negotiation.* New York: Plenum
- Maynard, Douglas W. (2003) *Bad news, good news: conversational order in everyday talk and clinical settings.* Chicago: University of Chicago Press
- Suchman, Lucy (1987) *Plans and situated action: the problem of human–machine communication.* Cambridge: Cambridge University Press
- Sudnow, David (1967) *Passing on: the social organization of dying.* Englewood Cliffs, NJ: Prentice-Hall
- Whalen, Jack (1995a) 'A technology of order production: computer-aided dispatch in public safety communication'. In. Paul ten Have, George Psathas, eds. *Situated order: studies in the social organization of talk and embodied activities.* Washington, DC: University Press of America: 187–230

- Whalen, Jack, Eric Vinkhuyzen (2000) 'Expert systems in (inter)action: diagnosing document machine problems over the telephone'. In Paul Luff, Jon Hindmarsh, Christian Heath, eds. *Workplace studies: recovering work practice and informing systems design.* Cambridge: Cambridge University Press: 92–140
- Wieder, D. Lawrence (1974) *Language and social reality: the case of telling the convict code.* The Hague: Mouton
- Wieder, D. Lawrence (1980) 'Behavioristic operationalism and the lifeworld: chimpanzees and chimpanzee researchers in face-to-face interaction', *Sociological Inquiry* 50: 75–103

Notes

1   It seems that people with some formal musical training are often better at it than others.
2   As discussed in Chapter 3, section on transcription, pp. 44–5.
3   Cf. Bjelic & Lynch (1992) for a much more elaborate example of such a 'hybrid' demonstration, in a different field.
4   My perspective here and elsewhere in this example is of course deeply indebted to the writings of Erving Goffman, most notably *Behavior in public places* (1963).
5   A similar set of remarks, but this time concerning highway traffic, has been made in a short excursus by Michael Lynch (1993: 154–8), who refers to concrete inspirations from Harold Garfinkel's lectures and unpublished writings. Some of this is now available in Garfinkel (2002: 162–5).
6   Some previous studies on walking-in-company include Goffman (1972: 40–50) on 'Participation units' and Ryave & Schenkein (1974) in 'Notes on the art of walking'. The first is probably based on dispersed field observations, the second on two video recordings; no information on their 'positionings' are given.
7   This caveat is similar to the last sentence in the quote on p. 152 above, from Lynch (2002: 129).
8   There seems to be an interesting parallel between this 'pattern of resistance' and the one observed by Goode (1994), as summarized above, p. 162–3.
9   As in Bogen (1999: 90–3); for a more extended analysis of the rendition of talk-in-interaction by recordings and transcripts, see Ashmore & Reed, 2000 – both critiques are discussed in Ten Have (forthcoming).
10   I have not included strictly conversation-analytic ones, as these are available in Ten Have (1999a).

9 Reflections

In this final chapter, I will present some general and abstract reflections on qualitative research methods and ethnomethodological studies. In doing an actual study, the ways in which one proceeds will depend on many different kinds of circumstances, but the leading consideration should be what one is trying to accomplish in one's inquiry. That is the major item on the agenda. One key element in a research's purposes is often the aspiration to come up with something 'larger' than the research itself, with results of a more general relevance, but such generalizations may lead to losing one's grip on the data at hand. I will discuss this as the problem of 'generalities'. Among the doubts that probably remain concerning ethnomethodology, some may be glossed as having to do with its 'position' in various intellectual debates. I have therefore formulated some tentative reflections on its position in terms of epistemology and morality. 'Final reflections' on the book's central themes round off this last chapter.

Three types of research purpose

For the sake of argument I want to distinguish three broad types of research purpose, which can be related to three overall types of research: quantitative, qualitative as usually done, and ethnomethodological. As suggested in Chapter 1, and following Charles Ragin (1994), quantitative research investigates the covariation within large data-sets, that is, a relatively small number of features is studied across a considerable number of cases. So the focus is on 'variables and relationships among variables in an effort to identify general patterns of covariation'. Qualitative research, on the other hand, is especially used to study what Ragin calls 'commonalities', that is common properties, within a relatively small number of cases of which many aspects are taken into account. 'Cases are examined intensively with techniques designed to facilitate the clarification of theoretical concepts and empirical categories.' But as I suggest throughout my book, a further distinction can be made within the qualitative category, as ethnomethodological studies can be distinguished in various ways from other kinds of qualitative research. I will, again for the sake of argument, put these 'other kinds' together in one class, provisionally labelled 'conventional qualitative research'.

The overall purpose of quantitative research is hereby more or less clear: the identification of general patterns of covariation within a set of chosen variables, often in the format that variations in a set of dependent variables are 'explained' in terms of variations in a set of independent variables. The choice of the variables to be considered can be based on experience, convention and/or theory. The favoured method of data gathering for this type of research is, of course, the large-scale survey using questionnaire-based, standardized interviews. The contrast of this kind of research with ethnomethodology is also quite clear. The data for a quantitative analysis are treated as approximations of objective 'social facts', while the ways in which these data are produced are treated as technical problems of survey design and interview technique, not as phenomena in their own right. For ethnomethodology, on the other hand, the interest is in these latter aspects, to treat the 'social facts' not as given but as accomplished. In Harold Garfinkel's recent book (2002), this interest is presented as a kind of exhumation of a neglected aspect of Durkheim's sociological perspective. A number of ethnomethodologists and conversation analysts have, in fact, investigated standardized interviewing as a methodical, locally organized interactive activity.[1]

It is much less easy to specify the purpose of 'conventional' qualitative research as there is no overall paradigm for this type of work. The goal of studying 'commonalities' may not be shared by all researchers, while 'intensive examination' does not specify the conceptual format of the investigation. The theoretical object of ethnography may be formulated as 'a particular form of life', sometimes 'a culture', sometimes 'an institution', or a part of it, or even 'a scene'. But the target of interview studies is often something like the 'perspective', 'viewpoint' or 'experience' of a particular category of people. These glosses do not cover all and possibly not even most projects in the 'conventional' qualitative category. On a more general level, however, the purpose of qualitative research can be formulated as 'getting close to the lives/perspectives of the people studied', that is: the researcher will want to be in a position to make extensive statements about the people studied that fit their actual activities and experiences. There is a large variation in the kinds of statements to be made: descriptive or also explanatory, particularized or more general. For ethnomethodology, as one kind of qualitative research, 'intensive examination' is certainly the way to proceed, but that examination has a clearly defined focus, which can be glossed as a 'procedural interest'.

The problem of 'generalities'

The goal of studying 'commonalities' is, for ethnomethodology, more problematic, as it is a more prominent objective in some branches than in others. Conversation analysis, for instance, is much more clearly oriented to formulating general properties than, say, recent ethnomethodological studies of specialized scientific work. I would suggest that the evident tension between the general and the specific is not a matter of arbitrary preference, 'taste' or 'ambition', but rather that it seems to be inherent in the ethnomethodological enterprise as such. Take some of the general expressions in Garfinkel's *Studies*, like 'the documentary method', or 'the etcetera provision' or even 'reflexivity' and 'indexical expressions' – these are indeed extremely general concepts and ideas. But at the same time they point to features of phenomena that are entirely specific and unique to their local production. Similarly in conversation analysis, there is a repertoire of analytic concepts which foreground extremely general features of local interactions, as in 'adjacency pair', 'turn construction unit', or more topically applied, 'a canonical model for telephone conversation openings' (Schegloff, 1986). But again whether two consecutive utterances have the character of an adjacency pair construction is a matter of local interactional achievement. And again, whether a piece of talk works as a 'turn construction unit' is the product of specifiable local design features (Schegloff, 1996a). Even the 'canonical model for telephone conversation openings' is not treated as actually descriptive of observed openings, but rather as an explication of members' orientations (cf. Hopper, 1992: 71–91). In fact, the paper in which that 'canonical model' was originally explicated, was entitled 'The routine as *achievement*' (Schegloff, 1986, italics added; cf. also various contributions to Luke & Pavlidou, 2002).

In a similar way, Stephen Hester and Peter Eglin (1997: 11–22) have commented on the ambiguity in Harvey Sacks' observations on 'membership categorization'. Some of his formulations suggest a 'decontextualized model' of membership categories and collections of categories as 'pre-existing' any occasion of use, while at other times he stresses the occasionality of any actual usage. Hester and Eglin stress that for ethnomethodology 'membership categorization is an *activity* carried out in particular local circumstances'. It should be seen as 'in situ achievements of members' practical actions and practical reasoning'.

> Categories are 'collected' with others in the course of their being used. . . . this means that the 'collection' to which a category belongs (for this occasion) is constituted through its use in a particular context; it is part and parcel of its use *in that way.* Its recognizability is part of the phenomenon itself. What 'collection' the category belongs to, and what the collection *is*, are constituted in and how it is used *this time.* (Hester & Eglin, 1997: 21–2 (italics in original))

In other words, when a researcher is dealing with materials in which particular categories and categorical systems are being used, he or she has a choice in how to analyse these data. On the one hand, one can take a 'culturalist' tack and talk about the availability in 'the culture' of particular categories and categorization devices, such as 'age' or 'sex' (gender). But, as Hester and Eglin suggest, a more purely ethnomethodological analysis would focus on the particularities of any occasioned use of the categories and categorization devices, *this time.*

In the 'methodological appendix' to *The spectacle of history: speech, text, and memory at the Iran-Contra hearings,* Michael Lynch and David Bogen (1996) write about their 'refusal to assign priority' to various abstract models and cultural schemes, including references to the 'context' of a text in terms of 'particular historical, ethnic, class, and gendered epistemologies and identities'. They link this refusal to the way in which Wittgenstein 'divorced his conception of philosophy from the prevailing "craving for generality" of his day', because philosophers, in line with their idea of the method of science, displayed what he called a "contemptuous attitude towards the particular case".

> Such a contemptuous attitude denigrates mere description for its failure to subordinate the concrete details of a case to a theoretically specified foundation, ideology, or generalized discourse. For Wittgenstein, descriptions of singular activities are valuable precisely because they cast into relief diverse, unexpected, yet intelligible organizations of language use. (Lynch & Bogen, 1996: 269–70)

What is resisted in ethnomethodology is the effect of invoking general schemes and models of reducing members to what Garfinkel (1967a:) has called 'cultural dopes':

> By 'cultural dope' I refer to the man-in-the sociologist's-society who produces the stable features of the society by acting in compliance with preestablished and legitimate alternatives of action that the common culture provides. (Garfinkel, 1967a: 68)

In other words, the use of such models may lead to a reduction of actors to rule-following machines, rather than active producers of intelligible actions, making their productive work invisible. Ethnomethodologists do not deny, of course, that 'linguistic and cultural codes and paradigms' do 'provide resources for producing and understanding conduct', but the actual usage made of these resources should be chosen *in situ* from a larger set of possibilities (cf. Lynch & Bogen, 1996: 271).

It can be argued, therefore, that the tension between the generality of codes, rules, etc. and the specificity of any actual case should be *preserved* rather than evaded. In working toward the achievement of a local social order, participants in a scene use a locally adapted version of generally shared methods and resources for accomplishing intelligibility. In studying this 'work', ethnomethodologists differ in how they balance their description and analysis towards the general or towards the particular features. Whether the balance-as-chosen is adequate to the occasion and/or the overall purpose of the inquiry can, of course, be disputed.

Ethnomethodological indifference?

For most if not all people who develop an interest in ethnomethodology, it is hard to 'place' it in the range of scientific, philosophical. epistemological and moral positions available. When you read characterizations, like the ones quoted or paraphrased in this book on the contrast between resource and topic, you might infer that ethnomethodology tends to be outright *critical* of established practices of social research, and that it claims a unique position *outside* those practices. This kind of inference has been stimulated by the early inclusion in the ethnomethodological corpus of Aaron Cicourel's work, which was indeed rather critical in this regard, as in his *Method and measurement in sociology* (1964) and *Theory and method in a study of Argentine fertility* (1974).

As I mentioned in Chapter 2 (p. 18), while he was affiliated with ethnomethodology in the early days, he later diverted to other pursuits.

In the late 1960s Harold Garfinkel made some rather sharp comments to distinguish ethnomethodology from such critical ambitions:

> Ethnomethodological studies are not directed to formulating or arguing correctives. They are useless when they are done as ironies. . . . They do not formulate a remedy for practical actions, as if it was being found about practical actions that they were better or worse than they are usually cracked up to be. Nor are they in search of humanistic arguments, nor do they engage in or encourage permissive discussions of theory. (Garfinkel, 1967a: viii)

And in their collaborative essay Harvey Sacks and he even coined a slogan for this position of judgmental abstention, when they formulated a 'procedural policy' which they called 'ethnomethodological indifference'. This would mean that when doing ethnomethodological studies one should be 'seeking to describe members' accounts of formal structures wherever and by whomever they are done, while abstaining from all judgments of their adequacy, value, importance, necessity, practicality, success, or consequentiality' (Garfinkel & Sacks, 1970: 345). And they add

> Our work does not stand . . . in any modifying, elaborating, contributing, detailing, subdividing, explicating, foundation-building relationship to professional sociological reasoning, nor is our 'indifference' to those orders of task. Rather, our 'indifference' is to the whole of practical sociological reasoning, and *that* reasoning involves for us, in whatever form of development, with whatever error or adequacy, in whatever forms, inseparably and unavoidably, the mastery of natural language. (Garfinkel & Sacks, 1970: 346)

The major function of this 'indifference' seems to be to clear the way for a reconsideration of practical phenomena in their local specifics, rather than in terms of any pre-given schema or rule-set. For instance, in the course in 'observation' which I discussed in the previous chapter, students quite often wrote down their observations in judgmental terms, like following the rules or deviating from the rules: crossing at the green light or at the red light. I did, however, encourage them to observe how the participants *used* the lights, for instance watching the traffic carefully when the lights were red, while crossing without attending to the traffic when they were green. In terms of later ethnomethodological concepts, the notion of rules, rule-following and deviation from rules should be *re-specified as members' practices*. In this way, 'ethnomethodological indifference' does not deny the rules, etc. to which it is indifferent, but holds them up for inspection as possible resources for members in actually lived situations. For instance, when a pedestrian tried to continue crossing during a red light period, a car driver used his horn, the crosser backtracked and made a gesture of excuse, and so confirmed the other's right and his own obligations.

To return for a moment to survey research and standardized interviewing, current ethnomethodology is not – like Cicourel earlier – in the business of criticizing those practices *per se*, although it may use survey research – just like 'constructive analysis' (Garfinkel & Sacks, 1970) or 'formal analysis' (Garfinkel, 2002) – as a contrast in order to define itself as different.

Maynard and Schaeffer write in the introduction to their co-edited volume of studies of survey interviewing:

> We do not conceive of the contributions in this volume as offering an *alternative* to the survey interview. Our attempt to capture *alternation*, by appreciating analytically the tacit work of skilful interviewing, is different from aspiring to change the form of the interview.
>
> . . .
>
> Accordingly, *analytic alternation*, in the context of the survey interview, means investigating practitioners' work. The work of interviewers . . . involves both adherence to formal inquiry – the use of rules, procedures, and instruments for conducting the interview – and the exercise of taken-for-granted, tacit skills. These skills are exhibited in the produced, orderly detail of everyday talk and embodied action that reflexively supports and helps achieve the accountability of the formal inquiry. *Accountability* means that the interview gets done in ways that are acceptably – for all practical purposes – standardized and scientific. (Maynard & Schaeffer, 2002: 12–13, italics in original)

They contrast their approach with the one evident in Cicourel's work by characterizing the latter as 'critical remediation'. Elsewhere (2000: 335), they have remarked that: 'the qualitative critique tells us more about what survey researchers do *not* do than what they actually do, whereas we are arguing that careful studies of interviewers' workaday world are in order'. And they remark:

> As opposed to the stance of critical remediation, (ethnomethodological) CA studies of the survey enterprise involve being familiar with that enterprise *from within* so as to understand its goals and issues. To don the methodology of analytic alternation, the strategy is that investigators pose problems that are relevant to the survey enterprise, performing analyses that are possibly informative to that enterprise. This does not mean that (ethnomethodological) CA takes on the agenda of (survey research) *except as an understanding of and orientation to that agenda is a topic of order to be investigated as part of the 'work' in which the interviewer and respondent are engaged.* (Maynard & Schaeffer, 2000: 338, italics in original)

It should be noted, then, that the relation of 'analytic alternation' between ethnomethodological studies and formal-analytic ones, like survey interviewing, is an *asymmetrical* one. That is, while ethnomethodology's approach can be used to study the practices of formal-analytic investigations, it is not possible for a formal-analytic inquiry to uncover the work and phenomena of ethnomethodology's studies (cf. Garfinkel & Wieder, 1992; Garfinkel, 2002: 117).

The upshot of such an asymmetry is that ethnomethodology's phenomena are, in a special way, *unavailable* to formal-analytic reasoning, and therefore to people who are somehow limited to that kind of reasoning. This conclusion is supported by some of the earlier reported 'resistances' to ethnomethodological findings, as in the cases of Goode (p. 162–3) and Whalen

& Vinkhuyzen (p. 169), which occurred especially among people whose involvement with the activities studied was one of abstract design or management at a distance, while people who were 'closer' were more easily convinced.

It should be stressed, therefore, that 'ethnomethodological indifference' does not, in my view, imply that an ethnomethodologist should avoid knowing about formal-analytic considerations which are implied in situated activities and their local accountability. It is rather that such considerations do not offer a purchase on what is specific about ethnomethodological phenomena as such. The critique that is discernible in many ethnomethodological writings concerning approaches like (or based on) 'artificial intelligence', for instance, can be read as a critique of AI's neglecting of practical *in situ* reasoning, or, more strongly stated, its 'blindness' to the level of phenomena that ethnomethodological studies exhume and in a way 'celebrate.'[2]

As Garfinkel notes in his recent book:

> Ethnomethodology is not critical of formal analytic investigations. But neither is it the case that EM . . . has no concern with a remedial expertise and has nothing to promise or deliver. Ethnomethodology *is* applied Ethnomethodology. However, its remedial transactions are distinctive to EM expertise. (Garfinkel, 2002: 114)

In other words, what ethnomethodology has to offer is not a *replacement* of formal-analytic knowledge and its application in various practical activities, but rather an addition, supplementation, or even 'completion'. Ethnomethodology can investigate and then demonstrate in which ways formal instructions (plans, schemes, forms, etc.) need practical supplements – what I have elsewhere (Ten Have, 1999a: 184–200) called 'local rationalities' (cf. also Heap, 1990) – in order to be (more) effective. In such a way, then, one could not only talk about 'ethnomethodological indifference', but equally, although in a different sense, about a certain 'ethnomethodological commitment'.

Such a commitment is already present in Garfinkel's rather sarcastic comments on sociology's treatment of people as 'cultural dopes' (1967a: 68), and can be further illustrated with a number of the previously discussed studies, which brought to light the tacit skills or actual competences used by persons who were considered to be 'incapable' in one or another way, ranging from the children studied by David Goode to the often low-ranked 'users' of various systems designed at a distance from the shop-floor on formal-analytic grounds. Celebrating such hidden possibilities – and also explicating the problems generated by their being ignored – could be called 'emancipatory'. 'Top-down' applications of 'knowledge', one could say, are essentially incomplete when 'bottom-up' knowledge is not taken into account.

To sum up: ethnomethodology is only selectively aloof, indifferent and at a distance from everyday life, as it is also committed to a particular immersion in, and explication of, the details of everyday life. Ethnomethodological discoveries are always discoveries 'from within' the society. Furthermore, practical orders are always and inevitably moral orders. And this, of course, also applies to ethnomethodological studies themselves.

Final reflections

What I have tried to do, in this book, is to present some ideas raised by an ethnomethodologically informed look at qualitative research methods as preached and practised in qualitative social research at large, as well as 'within' ethnomethodology. In their projects, qualitative researchers try to formulate some sensible expressions about people's lives. Some of these expressions will be largely descriptive, others may tend to be more or less analytic – conceptually organized conclusions of possibly wider relevance. Qualitative researchers differ as to the aspects of social life that they consider worthwhile to report on, and therefore they differ in their analytic preferences. And these analytic preferences may, in their turn, be related to preferences as regards concrete topics and kinds of empirical methods and materials. Ethnomethodologists do not have a primary interest in what seems most important to other qualitative researchers, for instance personal experiences and viewpoints, or group cultures. Their procedural interests, on the other hand, do not seem to be very attractive to most other qualitative researchers. In a way, then, writing this book can be seen as swimming upstream in both directions, trying to raise a mutual interest across the border. What I wanted to do is to invite qualitative researchers who are not committed to ethnomethodology to take another look at their own research practices, as well as the ones current in ethnomethodology. Explicating some of the half-hidden aspects of conventional methods and learning about the dilemmas that are topics of debate within ethnomethodology may be helpful, I hope, in stimulating a reconsideration of the inevitable choices that have to be made in any research project.

I have tried to avoid taking on a voice of authority or orthodoxy. I would encourage researchers to take into consideration a wide range of options in any project. But I would also want to say that choices made have to have good reasons: theoretically, methodologically and practically. And one should strive to attain a reasonable consistency in a project. The kinds of data collected should be compatible with one's theoretical objectives, and the analysis should fit both.

Many projects are based on just one type of data. Combining different sorts of research materials has often been recommended under the slogan of *triangulation* (cf. Bloor, 1997; Silverman, 2001 for critical discussions). I think this is the wrong metaphor. In combining different 'data', 'methods' or even 'theories' in qualitative research, one does something other than positioning an object by determining its direction from two known positions. For any 'method' one chooses, one should have good reasons to assess its informative value for the problems one is investigating. And furthermore, as we have seen in several cases considered above, one piece of data may function as an *instruction* to see the meaning of another, and sometimes vice versa. What I suggested was to search for a 'dialogical' solution to the dilemmas raised by combining data sources. Considerations that take off from closely examined recordings may stimulate questions for the ethnography, or for interviews, and vice versa (see pp. 127–8). Each time the value and usability of the data would have to be decided on their own terms, as well as in relation to issues raised by the others. Data do not 'speak for themselves'; they are materials to be assessed to decide their significance for the story that is being developed. Data that do not fit with that story should not be discarded, however, but taken up as a challenge as in 'deviant case analysis' – a major contribution from the tradition of 'analytic induction' (cf. Chapter 7, above, at p. 135).

In some ways, current qualitative research and ethnomethodology may convey similar messages, for instance stressing the discrepancies between, on the one hand, overall political and moral debates and policies, and, on the other, the actual practices to which they are said to refer. This is a clear message in the two ethnographic studies of euthanasia practices in Dutch hospitals by Robert Pool and Anne-Mei The, discussed in Chapter 6 (pp. 120–2). For them, it was as if those debates lost their relevance the moment they entered the hospitals. But then, of course, such outside relevancies can be imposed upon practitioners, if only in the sense of framing their accountability.

In other ways, ethnomethodology and other kinds of qualitative research may take completely different paths. This was, perhaps, clearest in Chapter 7, in my discussion of the 'scientism' discernible in the 'grounded theory' approach, which seems to be based on the 'craving for generality' which is denounced by Wittgenstein and many ethnomethodologists. But then, of course, there are other contrasts discussed here and there in my text, as in the explication/explanation contrast and the one between 'members' and 'persons'.

I started my overall discussion of social research methods with a reference to Charles Ragin's 'simple model of social research', suggesting that 'social research involves a dialogue between ideas and evidence' (pp. 1–3). I also noted some more or less obvious limitations of it, such as the suggestion that 'ideas' and 'evidence' would function as relatively stable 'givens' (p. 12). After all the preceding discussions, his model and its basic terms may now be discarded, as they have been useful starting points that are no longer needed. For instance, 'ideas' has turned out to be a rather mixed category, which includes both formal concepts and substantive elaborations. Furthermore, some concepts seem to belong to the analyst's toolbox, while others are part of the lived reality under study. For some traditions in qualitative research, the ideal end product of research is 'a theory' of greater or smaller scope, relatively independent of the 'data' from which it was 'generated'. For parts of ethnomethodology, some ideas, such as rationality, truth or morality, serve as topics to be re-specified *as* members' methods, and in the process seem to lose their abstractness as they are part and parcel of some concrete lived reality. For other ethnomethodologists and conversation analysts, some general features of situated practices may be formulated abstractly, in technical terms like TCU (turn-constructional unit) or MCD, as formulation of generic implications of those practices, which may never be formulated as such by the members who use them.

The notion of 'evidence', as provided by 'the data', also deserves a more subtle treatment than it often receives. As Michael Procter once suggested, the very idea of 'data', as 'givens', seems to hide their character as always and inevitably being *produced* in one way or another, and therefore they should be called 'capta', taken, what one has 'taken' from the stream of life in order to be used as evidence.[3] This issue resonates with the ideals of unobtrusive data, 'naturally occurring' events, etc., which we encountered before (p. 84 and note 14 to that paragraph). And what the reader ultimately encounters is a further 'work-up' of the 'kept' data, in selective quotations, more or less simplified transcripts, screen-shots, etc.[4] In other words, rather than treating 'data' as indisputable grounds for an argument, they might be considered as interesting arguments in themselves, constructed for a purpose. As such they are 'stand-ins' for the lives they represent, render accessible and point to.

Doing research of any kind is a serious job, but wanting to bring that seriousness across should not lead to undue reification. Or at least, one could be open to research being an artful achievement. I can only hope that my reflections, recorded and explicated in this book, help to stimulate your reflections on whatever you are doing as a researcher (or reader of research reports).

Notes

1 Cf. Houtkoop-Steenstra (2000) and a number of contributions to Maynard et al., eds (2002); the contrast is most explicitly made in the chapter by Michael Lynch (2002). See also Ten Have (1999a: 170–80, 187–9).

2 Cf. Suchman (1987), Coulter (1989), Button (1991), Button et al. (1995), among others..

3 '. . . to use the word 'data' is something of a misnomer. *Data* is the Latin word for "things given"; it is more appropriate to call it (it collectively, or them, if you are thinking about individual items of information) *capta*: "things taken", or indeed wrestled with a great deal of effort from a recalcitrant social world' (Procter, 1993: 255).

4 Cf. the discussion of 'rendition practices' in the previous chapter, p. 168–71, and the references given there.

Appendix: Transcription Conventions

The glossary of transcript symbols given below is meant to explain the major conventions for rendering details of the vocal production of utterances in talk-in-interaction as these are used in most current CA publications. Most if not all of these have been developed by Gail Jefferson but are now commonly used with minor individual variations. The glosses given below are based on, and simplified from, the descriptions provided in Jefferson (1989: 193–6), at times using those in Atkinson & Heritage (1984), Psathas & Anderson (1990), Psathas (1995), or Ten Have & Psathas (1995). I have restricted the set given below to the ones most commonly used, omitting some of the subtleties provided by Jefferson.

Sequencing

[A *single left bracket* indicates the point of overlap onset.
]   A *single right bracket* indicates the point at which an utterance or utterance-part terminates *vis-à-vis* another.
=   *Equal signs*, one at the end of one line and one at the beginning of the next, indicate no 'gap' between the two lines. This is often called *latching*.

Timed intervals

(0.0)   *Numbers in parentheses* indicate elapsed time in silence by tenth of second, i.e. (7.1) is a pause of 7 seconds and one tenth of a second.
(.)   *A dot in parentheses* indicates a tiny 'gap' within or between utterances.

Characteristics of speech production

word   *Underscoring* indicates some form of stress, via pitch and/or amplitude; an alternative method is to print the stressed part in *italic*.
::   *Colons* indicate prolongation of the immediately prior sound. Multiple colons indicate a more prolonged sound.
-    A *dash* indicates a cut-off.
.,??   *Punctuation marks* are used to indicate characteristics of speech

production, especially intonation; they are not referring to grammatical units.

. A *period* indicates a stopping fall in tone.

, A *comma* indicates a continuing intonation, as when you are reading items from a list.

? A *question mark* indicates a rising intonation

? The *combined question mark/comma* indicates stronger rise than a comma but weaker than a question mark.

The absence of an utterance-final marker indicates some sort of 'indeterminate' contour.

↑↓ *Arrows* indicate marked shifts into higher or lower pitch in the utterance part immediately following the arrow.

WORD *Upper case* indicates especially loud sounds relative to the surrounding talk.

° Utterances or utterance parts bracketed by *degree signs* are relatively quieter than the surrounding talk.

< > *Right/left carets* bracketing an utterance or utterance part indicate speeding up.

·hhh A *dot-prefixed row of* hs indicates an inbreath. Without the dot, the hs indicate an outbreath.

w(h)ord A parenthesized h, or a *row of* hs *within a word* indicates breathiness, as in laughter, crying, etc.

Transcriber's doubts and comments

( ) *Empty parentheses* indicate the transcriber's inability to hear what was said. The length of the parenthesized space indicates the length of the untranscribed talk. In the speaker designation column, the empty parentheses indicate inability to identify a speaker.

(word) *Parenthesized words* are especially dubious hearings or speaker identifications.

(( )) *Double parentheses* contain transcriber's descriptions rather than, or in addition to, transcriptions.

References

Alasuutari, Pertti (1995) *Researching culture: qualitative method and cultural studies*. London: Sage

Arminen, Ilkka (2001) 'Workplace studies: the practical sociology of technology in action', *Acta Sociologica*, 44: 183–9

Ashmore, Malcolm, Darran Reed (2000) 'Innocence and nostalgia in conversation analysis: the dynamic relations of tape and transcript', *Forum Qualitative Sozialforschung / Forum: Qualitative Social Research*, 1 (3). Available at: http://qualitative-research.net/fqs-texte/3–00/3–00ashmorereed-e.htm

Atkinson, J. Maxwell (1978) *Discovering suicide: studies in the social organization of sudden death*. London: Macmillan

Atkinson, J. Maxwell (1983) 'Two devices for generating audience approval: a comparative study of public discourse and texts'. In: Konrad Ehlich, Henk van Riemsdijk, eds. *Connectedness in sentence, discourse and text*. Tilburg: Katholieke Hogeschool Tilburg: 199–236

Atkinson, J. Maxwell, John Heritage, eds. (1984) *Structures of social action: studies in Conversation Analysis*. Cambridge: Cambridge University Press

Atkinson, Paul, David Silverman (1997) 'Kundera's *Immortality*: the interview society and the invention of the self', *Qualitative Inquiry*, 3: 304–25

Atkinson, Paul, Amanda Coffey, Sara Delamont, John Lofland, Lyn H. Lofland, eds. (2001) *Handbook of ethnography*. London, etc.: Sage

Baker, Carolyn (1997) 'Membership categorization and interview accounts'. In: David Silverman, ed. *Qualitative research: theory, method and practice*. London: Sage: 130–43

Ball, Michael (1998) 'Remarks on visual competence as an integral part of ethnographic fieldwork practice: the visual availability of culture'. In: Jon Prosser, ed. *Image-based research: a sourcebook for qualitative researchers*. London: Falmer: 131–47

Barter, Christine, Emma Renold (1999) 'The use of vignettes in qualitative research', *Social Research Update* 25 (University of Surrey)

Baruch, Geoffrey (1981) 'Moral tales: parents' stories of encounters with the health professions', *Sociology of Health and Illness*, 3: 275–95

Becker, Howard S. (1963) *Outsiders: studies in the sociology of deviance*. New York: Free Press

Becker, Howard S. (1998) *Tricks of the trade: how to think about your research while you're doing it*. Chicago: University of Chicago Press

Benson, Douglas, John Hughes (1991) 'Method: evidence and inference-evidence and inference for ethnomethodology'. In: Graham Button, ed., *Ethnomethodology and the human sciences*. Cambridge: Cambridge University Press: 109–36

Berg, Marc (1997) *Rationalizing medical work: decision support techniques and medical practices*. Cambridge, MA: MIT Press

Bergmann, Jörg (1981) 'Frage und Frageparaphrase: Aspekte der redezuginternen und sequenziellen Organisation eines Äusserungsformats' [Question and question paraphrase: aspects of utterance internal and sequential organization of an utterance format]. In: P. Winkler, Hg. *Methoden der Analyse von Face-to-Face-Situationen*. Stuttgart: Metzler: 128–42

Bjelic, Dusan, Michael Lynch (1992) 'The work of a (scientific) demonstration: respecifying Newton's and Goethe's theories of prismatic color'. In: Graham Watson, Robert M. Seiler, eds. *Text in context: contributions to ethnomethodology*. London: Sage: 52–78

Blomberg, Jeanette L. (1995) 'Ethnography: aligning field studies of work and system design'. In: Andrew Monk, Nigel Gilbert, eds. *Perspectives on HCI: diverse approaches.* New York: Academic Press: 175–97

Bloor, Michael (1997) 'Techniques of validation in qualitative research: a critical commentary'. In: Gale Miller, Robert Dingwall, eds. *Context and method in qualitative research.* London: Sage: 37–50

Blumer, Herbert (1969) *Symbolic interactionism: perspective and method.* Englewood-Cliffs, NJ: Prentice-Hall

Boden, Deirdre, Don H. Zimmerman, eds. (1991) *Talk and social structure: studies in ethnomethodology and conversation analysis.* Cambridge: Polity Press

Boelen, W.A. Marianne (1992) '*Street corner society*: Cornerville revisited', *Journal of Contemporary Ethnography* (special issue on '*Street corner society* revisited'), 21(1): 11–51

Bogen, David (1999) *Order without rules: critical theory and the logic of conversation.* New York: SUNY Press

Bunt, Henk. G. van de (1986) *Officieren van justitie: verslag van een participerend observatieonderzoek.* [Public prosecutors: report on a participant observation study]. Zwolle: Tjeenk Willink

Bunt, Henk.G. van de (1987) 'Public prosecutors in the Netherlands', *Netherlands' Journal of Sociology*, 23: 102–15

Button, Graham, ed. (1991) *Ethnomethodology and the human sciences.* Cambridge: Cambridge University Press

Button, Graham, ed. (1993) *Technology in working order: studies of work, interaction and technology.* London: Routledge

Button, Graham, Jeff Coulter, John R.E. Lee, Wes Sharrock (1995) *Computers, minds and conduct.* Cambridge: Polity Press

Carlin, Andrew (1999) 'The works of Edward Rose: a bibliography', *Ethnographic Studies* 4: 61–77

Charmaz, Kathy (2000) 'Grounded theory: objectivist and constructivist methods'. In: Norman K. Denzin, Yvonna S. Lincoln, eds. *Handbook of qualitative research*, 2nd edn. Thousand Oaks, CA: Sage: pp.509–35

Cicourel, Aaron V. (1964) *Method and measurement in sociology.* New York: The Free Press

Cicourel, Aaron V. (1968) *The social organization of juvenile justice.* New York: Wiley

Cicourel, Aaron V. (1974) *Theory and method in a study of Argentine fertility.* New York: Wiley

Clayman, Steven E., Douglas W. Maynard (1995) 'Ethnomethodology and conversation analysis'. In: Paul ten Have, George Psathas, eds. *Situated order: studies in the social organization of talk and embodied activities.* Washington, DC: University Press of America: 1–30

Coulter, Jeff (1989) *Mind in action.* Cambridge: Polity Press

Coulter, Jeff (1991) 'Cognition: cognition in an ethnomethodological mode'. In: Graham Button, ed., *Ethnomethodology and the human sciences.* Cambridge: Cambridge University Press. 176–95.

Daalen, Rineke van (1997) *Klaagbrieven en gemeentalijk ingrijpen: Amsterdam 1865–1920.* [Public complaints and government intervention: letters to the municipal authorities of Amsterdam 1865–1920] Amsterdam, Sociological Institute, University of Amsterdam

Davis, Fred (1991) *Passage through crisis: polio victims and their families.* New Brunswick: Transaction (first edition 1963)

Denzin, Norman K., Yvonna S. Lincoln, eds (1994) *Handbook of qualitative research.* Thousand Oaks, CA: Sage

Denzin, Norman K., Yvonna S. Lincoln, eds (2000) *Handbook of qualitative research: second edition.* Thousand Oaks, CA: Sage

Dey, Ian (1999) *Grounding grounded theory.* Orlando, FL: Academic Press

Douglas, Jack D. (1976) *Investigative social research: individual and team field research.* London: Sage

Drew, Paul, John Heritage, eds (1992) *Talk at work: interaction in institutional settings*. Cambridge: Cambridge University Press

Duranti, Alessandro (1997) *Linguistic anthropology*. Cambridge: Cambridge University Press

Durkheim, Émile (1897) *Le suicide: étude de sociologie*. Paris: Alcan [translated as *Suicide: a study in sociology*. Glencoe, IL: Free Press]

Elias, Norbert (1939) *Über den Prozess der Zivilisation: Soziogenetische und psychogenetische Untersuchungen* (2 Bd). Basel: Haus zum Falken

Elias, Norbert (1978) *The civilising process*. Oxford: Blackwell

Elteren-Jansen, Marianne (2003) '"Een beetje hangerig . . .". Alledaags handelen van Nederlandse, Nederlands-Indische en Surinaams-Hindoestaanse moeders bij alledaagse gezondheidsproblemen van hun kinderen' ['A bit listless' Everyday action of Dutch, Dutch–East Indies and Surinam-Hindustan mothers concerning health problems of their children]. PhD thesis, University of Amsterdam

Emerson, Robert M., Rachel I. Fretz, Linda L. Shaw (1995) *Writing ethnographic field notes*. Chicago: University of Chicago Press

Fielding, Nigel G., Raymond L. Lee (1998) *Computer analysis and qualitative research*. London, etc.: Sage

Fontana, Andrea, James H. Frey (2000) 'The interview: from structured questions to negotiated text'. In: Norman K. Denzin, Yvonna S. Lincoln, eds *Handbook of qualitative research: second edition*.Thousand Oaks, CA: Sage: 645–72

Garfinkel, Harold (1963) 'A conception of, and experiments with, "trust" as a condition of stable concerted actions'. In: O.J. Harvey, ed. *Motivation and social interaction: cognitive approaches*. New York: Ronald Press

Garfinkel, Harold (1964) 'Studies in the routine grounds of everyday activities', *Social Problems*, 11: 225–50 (reprinted in: David Sudnow, ed. *Studies in social interaction*. New York: Free Press, 1972)

Garfinkel, Harold (1967a) *Studies in ethnomethodology*. Englewood Cliffs, NJ: Prentice-Hall

Garfinkel, Harold (1967b) 'Practical sociological reasoning: some features in the work of the Los Angeles Suicide Prevention Center'. In: E.S. Shneidman, ed. *Essays in self-destruction*. New York: Science House: 171–287 (reprinted in: M. Travers, JohnF. Manzo, eds *Law in action: ethnomethodological & Conversation Analytic approaches to law*. Aldershot, UK: Dartmouth: 25–41)

Garfinkel, Harold (1974) 'The origins of the term "Ethnomethodology"'. In: Roy Turner, ed. *Ethnomethodology: selected readings*. Harmondsworth: Penguin: 15–18 [Excerpt from Hill, Crittenden, eds 1968]

Garfinkel, Harold (1991) 'Respecification: evidence for locally produced, naturally accountable phenomena of order*, logic, reason, meaning, method, etc. in and as of the essential haecceity of immortal ordinary society (I) an announcement of studies'. In: Graham Button, ed. *Ethnomethodology and the human sciences*. Cambridge: Cambridge University Press: 10–19

Garfinkel, Harold (1996) 'An overview of ethnomethodology's program', *Social Psychology Quarterly*, 59: 5–21

Garfinkel, Harold (2002) *Ethnomethodology's program: working out durkheim's aphorism*, edited and introduced by Anne Rawls. Lanham, MD: Rowman & Littlefield

Garfinkel, Harold, Michael Lynch, Eric Livingston (1981) 'The work of a discovering science construed with materials from the optically discovered pulsar', *Philosophy of the Social Sciences*, 11: 131–58

Garfinkel, Harold, Harvey Sacks, (1970) 'On formal structures of practical action'. In: John C. McKinney, Edward A. Tiryakian, eds *Theoretical sociology: perspectives and developments*. New York: Appleton-Century-Crofts: 338–66

Garfinkel, Harold, D. Lawrence Wieder (1992) 'Two incommensurable, asymmetrically alternate technologies of social analysis'. In: Graham Watson, Robert M. Seiler, eds *Text in context: studies in ethnomethodology*. Newbury Park, etc.: Sage: 175–206

Gibbs, Anita (1997) 'Focus groups', *Social Research Update*, 19 (University of Surrey)

Glaser, Barney G. (1978) *Theoretical sensitivity: advances in the methodology of grounded theory*. Mill Valley, CA: The Sociology Press

Glaser, Barney G. (1992) *Emergence vs. forcing: basics of grounded theory analysis*. Mill Valley, CA: The Sociology Press

Glaser, Barney G. (1998) *Doing grounded theory: issues and discussions*. Mill Valley, CA: The Sociology Press

Glaser, Barney G. (2002) 'Constructivist grounded theory?' [47 paragraphs]. *Forum Qualitative Sozialforschung / Forum: Qualitative Social Research* (on-line journal), 3(3). Available at: http://www.qualitative-research.net/fqs-texte/3–02/3–02glaser-e.htm

Glaser, Barney, Anselm L. Strauss (1965) *Awareness of dying*. Chicago: Aldine

Glaser, Barney G., Anselm L. Strauss (1967) *The discovery of grounded theory: strategies for qualitative research*. Chicago: Aldine

Glaser, Barney, Anselm L. Strauss (1968) *Time for dying*. Chicago: Aldine

Goffman, Erving (1961) *Asylums: essays on the social situation of mental patients and other inmates*. Garden City, NY: Doubleday

Goffman, Erving (1963) *Behavior in public places: notes on the social organization of gatherings*. New York: Free Press

Goffman, Erving (1967) 'On face-work: an analysis of ritual elements in social interaction'. In his *Interaction ritual: essays in face-to-face behavior*. Garden City: NY: Doubleday: 5–45 (first edition 1955)

Goffman, Erving (1972) *Relations in public: microstudies of the public order*. Harmondsworth: Penguin (first edition 1971)

Goffman, Erving (1974) *Frame analysis: an essay on the organization of experience*. New York: Harper & Row

Goffman, Erving (1989) 'On fieldwork', transcribed and edited by Lyn H. Lofland, *Journal of Contemporary Ethnography*, 18: 123–32

Goode, David (1994) *A word without words: the social construction of children born deaf and blind*. Philadelphia: Temple University Press

Goodwin, Charles (2000) 'Action and embodiment within situated human interaction', *Journal of Pragmatics*, 32: 1489–522

Goodwin, Charles (in press) 'Pointing as situated practice'. In: Sotaro Kita, ed. *Pointing: where language, culture and cognition meet*. Mahwah, NJ: Lawrence Erlbaum

Goodwin, Marjorie Harness (1996) 'Informings and announcements in their environment: prosody within a multi-activity work setting'. In: Elisabeth Couper-Kuhlen, Margeret Selting, eds *Prosody in conversation: interactional studies*. Cambridge: Cambridge University Press: 436–61

Greatbatch, David, Christian Heath, Paul Luff, Peter Campion (1995) 'Conversation analysis: human–computer interaction and the general practice consultation'. In: Andrew F. Monk, G. Nigel Gilbert, eds *Perspectives on HCI: diverse approaches*. New York: Academic Press: 199–222

Gubrium, Jaber F., James A. Holstein, eds (2002) *Handbook of interview research: context and method*. Thousand Oaks, CA: Sage

Hammersley, Martyn, Paul Atkinson (1983) *Ethnography: principles in practice*. London: Tavistock

Harper, Douglas (1994) 'On the authority of the image: visual methods at the crossroads'. In: Norman K. Denzin, Yvonna S. Lincoln, eds *Handbook of qualitative research*.Thousand Oaks, CA: Sage: 403–12

Harper, Douglas (2000) 'Reimagining visual methods: Galileo to *Neuromancer*'. In: Denzin, Norman K., Yvonna S. Lincoln, eds *Handbook of qualitative research: second edition*.Thousand Oaks, CA: Sage: 717–32

Have, Paul ten (1990) 'Methodological issues in conversation analysis', *Bulletin de Méthodologie Sociologique*, 27 (June): 23–51

Have, Paul ten (1999a) *Doing conversation analysis: a practical guide..* London, etc.: Sage

Have, Paul ten (1999b) 'Structuring writing for reading: hypertext and the reading body', *Human Studies*, 22: 273–98

Have, Paul ten (2000) 'Computer-mediated chat: ways of finding chat partners', *M/C – A Journal of Media and Culture* 4/3 http://www.media-culture.org.au/archive.html#chat

Have, Paul ten (2001a) 'Lay diagnosis in interaction', *Text*, 21: 251–60

Have, Paul ten (2001b) 'Revealing orders: ideas and evidence in the writing of ethnographic reports', paper read at the IIEMCA conference on 'Orders of Ordinary Action,' 9–11 July, Manchester, UK

Have, Paul ten (2002a) 'The notion of member is the heart of the matter: on the role of membership knowledge in ethnomethodological inquiry' [53 paragraphs]. *Forum Qualitative Sozialforschung / Forum: Qualitative Social Research* (on-line journal), 3(3). Available at: http://www.qualitative-research.net/fqs/fqs-eng.htm

Have, Paul ten (2002b) 'Conceptualization in "grounded theory" analysis: some critical observations'. In: Jörg Blasius, Joop Hox, Edith de Leeuw, Peter Schmidt, eds *Social Science Methodology in the New Millennium: Proceedings of the 5th International Conference on Logic and Methodology.* Leverkusen, Germany: Verlag Leske & Budrich (CD-ROM)

Have, Paul ten (2003) 'Teaching students observational methods: visual studies and visual analysis', *Visual Studies*, 18: 29–35.

Have, Paul ten (forthcoming) 'Reflections on transcription', *Cahiers de Praxématique* (Université Paul Valéry, Montpellier III, France)

Have, Paul ten, George Psathas, eds (1995) *Situated order: studies in the social organization of talk and embodied activities.* Washington DC: University Press of America.

Heap, James L. (1990) 'Applied ethnomethodology: looking for the local rationality of reading activities', *Human Studies*, 13: 39–72

Heath, Christian (1981) 'The opening sequence in doctor–patient interaction'. In: Paul Atkinson, Christian Heath, eds *Medical Work: Realities and Routines.* Farnborough: Gower: 71–90

Heath, Christian (1982) 'Preserving the consultation: medical record cards and professional conduct', *Journal of the Sociology of Health and Illness*, 4: 56–74

Heath, Christian (1986) *Body Movement and Speech in Medical Interaction.* Cambridge: Cambridge University Press

Heath, Christian (1997) 'The analysis of activities in face to face interaction using video'. In: David Silverman, ed. *Qualitative research: theory, method and practice.* London: Sage: 183–200

Heath, Christian, Hubert Knoblauch, Paul Luff (2000) 'Technology and social interaction: the emergence of "workplace studies".' *British Journal of Sociology*, 51: 299–320

Heath, Christian, Paul Luff (2000) *Technology in action.* Cambridge: Cambridge University Press

Heritage, John (1984a) *Garfinkel and ethnomethodology.* Cambridge: Polity Press

Heritage, John (1984b) 'A change-of-state token and aspects of its sequential placement'. In: J. Maxwell Atkinson, John Heritage, eds *Structures of social action: studies in conversation analysis.* Cambridge: Cambridge University Press: 299–345

Heritage, John (1985) 'Analyzing news interviews: aspects of the production of talk for an overhearing audience'. In: Teun A. van Dijk, ed. *Handbook of discourse analysis*, Vol. 3. London: Academic Press: 95–117

Heritage, John, J. Maxwell Atkinson (1984) 'Introduction'. In: J. Maxwell Atkinson, John Heritage, eds *Structures of social action: studies in conversation analysis.* Cambridge: Cambridge University Press: 1–15

Heritage, John, Marja-Leena Sorjonen (1994) 'Constituting and maintaining activities across sequences: *and*-prefacing as a feature of questioning design', *Language in Society*, 23: 1–29

Heritage, John C., D. Rodney Watson (1979) 'Formulations as conversational objects'. In: George Psathas, ed. *Everyday language: studies in ethnomethodology*. New York: Irvington: 123–62

Hester, Stephen, Peter Eglin, eds (1997) *Culture in action: studies in membership categorization analysis*. Washington, DC: University Press of America

Hindmarsh, Jon, Christian Heath (2000) 'Sharing the tools of the trade: the interactional constitution of workplace objects', *Journal of Contemporary Ethnography*, 29: 517–56

Holstein, James A., Jaber F. Gubrium (1995) *The active interview*. Thousand Oaks, CA: Sage (Qualitative Research Methods, vol. 37)

Holstein, James A., Jaber F. Gubrium (1997) 'Active interviewing'. In: David Silverman, ed. *Qualitative research: theory, method and practice*. London: Sage: 113–29

Hopper, Robert (1992) *Telephone conversation*. Bloomington: Indiana University Press

Houtkoop-Steenstra, Hanneke (1995) 'Meeting both ends: standardization and recipient design in telephone survey interviews'. In: Paul ten Have, George Psathas, eds. *Situated order: Studies in the social organization of talk and embodied activities*. Washington, DC: University Press of America: 91–106

Houtkoop-Steenstra, Hanneke (2000) *Interaction and the standardized interview. The living questionnaire*. Cambridge: Cambridge University Press

Houtkoop, Hanneke, Harrie Mazeland (1985) 'Turns and discourse units in everyday conversation', *Journal of Pragmatics*, 9: 595–619

Hutchby, Ian, Robin Wooffitt (1998) *Conversation analysis: principles, practices and applications*. Cambridge: Polity Press

Jayyusi, Lena (1984) *Categorization and the moral order*. Boston, etc.: Routledge & Kegan Paul

Jefferson, Gail (1985) 'An exercise in the transcription and analysis of laughter'. In: Teun A. van Dijk, ed. *Handbook of discourse analysis*, Vol. 3. London: Academic Press: 25–34

Jefferson, Gail (1989) 'Preliminary notes on a possible metric which provides for a "standard maximum" silence of approximately one second in conversation'. In: Roger, D., Peter Bull, eds. *Conversation: an interdisciplinary perspective*. Clevedon: Multilingual Matters: 166–96

Jefferson, Gail (1990) 'List-construction as a task and a resource'. In: George Psathas, ed. *Interaction competence*. Washington, DC: University Press of America: 63–92

Johnson, John M. (1975) *Doing field research*. New York: Free Press

Knorr-Cetina, Karin (1981) 'Introduction: the micro-sociological challenge of macro-sociology: towards a reconstruction of social theory and methodology'. In: Karin Knorr-Cetina, Aaron V. Cicourel, eds *Advances in social theory and methodology: toward an integration of micro- and macro-sociologies*. London: Routledge & Kegan Paul: 1–47

Knorr-Cetina, Karin (1988) 'The micro-social order: towards a reconception'. In: Nigel G. Fielding, ed. *Actions and structure: research methods and social theory*. London: Sage: 21–53

Labov, William, David Fanshel (1977) *Therapeutic discourse: psychotherapy as conversation*. New York: Academic Press

Landow, G. P. (1992) *Hypertext: the convergence of contemporary critical theory and technology*. Baltimore: Johns Hopkins University Press. [cited in McHoul, Roe, 1996]

Latour, Bruno (1987) *Science in action: how to follow scientists and engineers through society*. Cambridge, MA: Harvard University Press

Law, John, Michael Lynch (1988) 'Lists, field guides, and the descriptive organization of seeing: Birdwatching as an exemplary observational activity', *Human Studies*, 11:271–304

Livingston, Eric (1986) *The ethnomethodological foundations of mathematics*. London: Routledge & Kegan Paul

Livingston, Eric (1987) *Making sense of ethnomethodology*. London: Routledge & Kegan Paul

Livingston, Eric (1999) 'Cultures of proving', *Social Studies of Science*, 29: 867–88

Locker, David (1981) *Symptoms and illness: the cognitive organization of disorder*. London: Tavistock

Lofland, John, Lyn H. Lofland (1984) *Analyzing social settings: a guide to qualitative observation and analysis*, 2nd edn. Belmont, CA: Wadsworth

Lonkila, Marrku (1995) 'Grounded theory as an emergent paradigm for computer-assisted qualitative data analysis'. In: Udo Kelle, ed. *Computer-aided qualitative data analysis: theory, methods and practice*. London: Sage: 41–51

Luff, Paul, Jon Hindmarsh, Christian Heath, eds (2000) *Workplace Studies: Recovering Work Practice and Informing Systems Design*. Cambridge: Cambridge University Press

Luke, Kang Kwong, Theodossia-Soula Pavlidou, eds (2002) *Telephone calls: unity and diversity in conversational structure across languages and cultures*. Amsterdam: John Benjamins (Pragmatics & Beyond New Series 101).

Lynch, Michael (1985) *Art and artifact in laboratory science: a study of shop work and shop talk*. London: Routledge & Kegan Paul

Lynch, Michael (1993) *Scientific practice and ordinary action: ethnomethodology and social studies of science*. New York: Cambridge University Press

Lynch, Michael (2000) 'Against reflexivity as an academic virtue and source of privileged knowledge', *Theory, Culture & Society*, 17: 27–53

Lynch, Michael (2002) 'The living text: written instructions and situated actions in telephone surveys'. In: Douglas W. Maynard, Hanneke Houtkoop-Steenstra, Nora C. Schaeffer, Johannes van der Zouwen, eds *Standardization and tacit knowledge. Interaction and practice in the survey interview*. New York: John Wiley: 125–51

Lynch, Michael, David Bogen (1994) 'Harvey Sacks' primitive natural science', *Theory, Culture & Society*, 11: 65–104

Lynch, Michael, David Bogen (1996) *The spectacle of history: speech, text, and memory at the Iran-Contra hearings*. Durham, NC: Duke University Press

Lynch, Michael, Eric Livingston, Harold Garfinkel (1983) 'Temporal order in laboratory life'. In: Karin D. Knorr-Cetina, Michael Mulkay, eds *Science observed: perspectives on the social study of science*. London: Sage: 205–38

Macbeth, Douglas (2001) 'On "reflexivity" in qualitative research: two readings, and a third', *Qualitative Inquiry*, 7: 35–68

McCall, George J., J.L. Simmons (1969) *Issues in participant observation: a text and reader*. Reading, MA: Addison-Wesley

McHoul, Alec W. (1982) *Telling how texts talk: essays on reading and ethnomethodology*. London: Routledge & Kegan Paul

McHoul, Alec, P. Roe (1996) 'Hypertext and reading cognition'. In: B. Gorayska, J.L. Mey, eds *Cognitive technology: in search of a humane interface*. Elsevier: 347–59 (also available at: http://kali.murdoch.edu.au/~cntuum/VID/cognition.html)

Madriz, Esther (2000) 'Focus groups in feminist research'. In: Norman K. Denzin, Yvonna S. Lincoln, eds *Handbook of qualitative research: second edition*.Thousand Oaks, CA: Sage: 835–50

Markham, Annette N. (1998) *Life online: researching real experience in virtual space*. Walnut Creek/London/New Delhi: AltaMira Press

Maso, Ilja (1984) *Verklaren in het dagelijks leven: een inleiding in etnomethodologisch onderzoek* [Explaining in everyday life: an introduction to ethnomethodological research]. Groningen: Wolters-Noordhoff

Maynard, Douglas W. (1984) *Inside plea bargaining: the language of negotiation*. New York: Plenum

Maynard. Douglas W. (1996) 'From paradigm to prototype and back again: interactive aspects of "cognitive processing" in standardized survey interviews'. In: N. Schwarz, S. Sudman, eds *Answering questions: methodology for determining cognitive and communicating processes in survey research*. San Francisco: Jossey-Bass

Maynard, Douglas W., Nora C. Schaeffer (1997) 'Keeping the gate: declinations of the request to participate in a telephone survey interview', *Sociological Methods & Research*, 26: 34–79

Maynard, Douglas W., Nora C. Schaeffer (2000) 'Toward a sociology of social scientific knowledge: survey research and ethnomethodology's asymmetric alternates', *Social Studies of Science*, 30: 323–70

Maynard, Douglas W., Nora Cate Schaeffer (2002) 'Standardization and its discontents'. In: Douglas W. Maynard, Hanneke Houtkoop-Steenstra, Nora C. Schaeffer, Johannes van der Zouwen, eds *Standardization and tacit knowledge. interaction and practice in the survey interview*. New York: John Wiley: 3–47

Maynard, Douglas W., Hanneke Houtkoop-Steenstra, Nora C. Schaeffer, Johannes van der Zouwen, eds (2002) *Standardization and tacit knowledge. Interaction and practice in the survey interview*. New York: John Wiley

Mazeland, Harrie (1992) *Vraag/antwoord sequenties* [Question/answer sequences]. Amsterdam: Stichting Neerlandistiek VU

Mazeland, Harrie, Paul ten Have (1996) 'Essential tensions in (semi)open research interviews'. In: Ilja Maso, Fred Wester, eds *The deliberate dialogue: qualitative perspectives on the interview*. Brussels: VUB University Press: 87–113

Mazeland, Harrie, Mike Huiskes (2001) 'Dutch "but" as a sequential conjunction. Its use as a resumption marker.' In: Margaret Selting, Elisabeth Couper-Kuhlen, eds *Studies in interactional linguistics*. Amsterdam/Philadelphia: Benjamins: 141–69

Mehan, Hugh, Houston Wood (1975) *The reality of ethnomethodology*. New York: Wiley

Mennell, Stephen (1992) *Norbert Elias: an introduction*. Oxford: Blackwell

Miller, Jody, Barry Glassner (1997) 'The "inside" and the "outside": finding realities in interviews'. In: David Silverman, ed., *Qualitative research: theory, method and practice*. London: Sage: 99–112

Mullarney, Killian, Lars Svensson, Dan Zetterström, Peter J. Grant (2000) *ANWB Vogelgids van Europa*. [ANWB Birdguide of Europe]. Den Haag: ANWB [Dutch edition of Swedish original]

Pels, Dick (2001) 'Wetenschap als onthaasting: En onthaasting van de wetenschap' [Science as unhastening: and unhastening of science], *Krisis: Tijdschrift voor empirische filosofie*, 2/3: 6–25

Peräkylä, Anssi (1997) 'Reliability and validity in research based on tapes and transcripts'. In: David Silverman, ed., *Qualitative research: theory, method and practice*. London: Sage: 201–20

Peterson, R.T,, G. Mountfort, P.A.D. Hollom (1984) *Petersons vogelgids van alle Europese vogels*. [Peterson's bird guide of all European birds] Amsterdam: Elsevier [Dutch 17th edition of British original]

Pike, Kenneth (1967) *Language in relation to a unified theory of the structure of human behavior*. The Hague: Mouton

Pollner, Melvin (1974) 'Sociological and commonsense models of the labelling process'. In: Roy Turner, ed. *Ethnomethodology: selected readings*. Harmondsworth: Penguin: 27–40

Pollner, Melvin, Robert M. Emerson (2001) 'Ethnomethodology and ethnography'. In: Paul Atkinson, Amanda Coffey, Sara Delamont, John Lofland, Lyn H. Lofland, eds *Handbook of ethnography*. London, etc. Sage:118–35

Pomerantz, Anita (1988) 'Offering a candidate answer: an information seeking strategy', *Communication Monographs*, 55: 360–73.

Pool, Robert (1996) *Vragen om te sterven: euthanasie in een Nederlands ziekenhuis*. [Requesting to die: euthanasia in a Dutch hospital]. Rotterdam: WYT-Uitgeefgroep

Pool, Robert (2000) *Negotiating a good death: euthanasia in the Netherlands*. New York: Haworth Press

Procter, Michael (1993) 'Analysing other researchers' data'. In Nigel Gilbert, *Researching social life*. London: Sage: 255–69

Psathas, George (1995) *Conversation analysis: the study of Talk-in-Interaction.*Thousand Oaks, CA: Sage (Qualitative Research Methods 35)

Psathas, George, Tim Anderson (1990) 'The "practices" of transcription in conversation analysis', *Semiotica*, 78: 75–99

Ragin, Charles C. (1987) *The comparative method: moving beyond qualitative and quantitative strategies.* Berkeley: University of California Press

Ragin, Charles C. (1992) '"Casing" and the process of social inquiry'. In: Charles C. Ragin, Howard S. Becker, eds *What is a case? Exploring the foundations of social inquiry.* Cambridge: Cambridge University Press: 217–26

Ragin, Charles C. (1994) *Constructing social research: the unity and diversity of method.* Thousand Oaks, CA: Pine Forge Press

Rawls, Anne Warfield (2002) 'Editor's introduction'. In: Harold Garfinkel, *Ethnomethodology's program: working out Durkheim's aphorism.* Lanham, MD: Rowman & Littlefield: 1–64

Regt, Ali de (1984) *Arbeidersgezinnen en beschavingsarbeid: ontwikkelingen in Nederland 1870–1940; een historisch-sociologische studie* [Working-class families and the civilization of workers: developments in the Netherlands 1870–1940; a historical sociological study]. Amsterdam: Boom

Robillard, Albert B. (1999) *Meaning of a disability: the lived experience of paralysis.* Philadelphia: Temple University Press

Ryave, A. Lincoln., James N. Schenkein (1974) 'Notes on the art of walking'. In: Roy Turner, ed. *Ethnomethodology.* Harmondsworth: Penguin: 265–74

Sacks, Harvey (1967) 'The search for help: no one to turn to'. In: E.S. Shneidman, ed. *Essays in self destruction.* New York: Science House: 203–23

Sacks, Harvey (1972a) 'An initial investigation of the usability of conversational data for doing sociology'. In: David Sudnow, ed. *Studies in social interaction.* New York: Free Press: 31–74

Sacks, Harvey (1972b) 'On the analyzability of stories by children'. In: John J. Gumperz, Dell Hymes, eds *Directions in sociolinguistics: the ethnography of communication.* New York: Rinehart & Winston: 325–45

Sacks, Harvey (1984a) 'Notes on methodology'. In: J. Maxwell Atkinson, John Heritage, eds *Structures of social action: studies in conversation analysis.* Cambridge: Cambridge University Press: 2–27

Sacks, Harvey (1984b) 'On doing "being ordinary"'. In: J. Maxwell Atkinson, John Heritage, eds *Structures of social action: studies in conversation analysis.* Cambridge: Cambridge University Press: 413–29

Sacks, Harvey (1992) *Lectures on conversation,* 2 vols. Edited by Gail Jefferson with introductions by Emanuel A. Schegloff. Oxford: Basil Blackwell

Sacks, Harvey, Emanuel A. Schegloff (1979) 'Two preferences in the organization of reference to persons in conversation and their interaction'. In: George Psathas, ed., *Everyday language: studies in ethnomethodology.* New York: Irvington: 15–21

Sacks, Harvey, Emanuel A. Schegloff, Gail Jefferson (1978) 'A simple systematics for the organization of turn taking for conversation'. In: Jim Schenkein, ed., *Studies in the organization of conversational interaction.* New York: Academic Press: 7–55 (first edition 1974)

Schaap, Frank (2002) *The words that took us there: ethnography in a virtual reality.* Amsterdam: Aksant

Schatzman, Leonard, Anselm L. Strauss (1973) *Field research: strategies for a natural sociology.* Englewood Cliffs, NJ: Prentice-Hall

Schegloff, Emanuel A. (1986) 'The routine as achievement', *Human Studies*, 9: 111–52

Schegloff, Emanuel A. (1991) 'Reflections on talk and social structure'. In: Deirdre Boden, Don H. Zimmerman, eds *Talk and social structure: studies in ethnomethodology and conversation analysis.* Cambridge: Polity Press: 44–71

Schegloff, Emanuel A. (1996a) 'Turn organization: one intersection of grammar and interaction'. In: Elinor Ochs, Emanuel A. Schegloff, Sandra A. Thompson, eds., *Interaction and grammar*. Cambridge: Cambridge University Press: 52–133

Schegloff, Emanuel A. (1996b) 'Some practices for referring to persons in talk-in-interaction. A partial sketch of a systematics.' In: B. Fox, ed. *Studies in anaphora*. Amsterdam/Philadelphia: Benjamins: 437–85

Schegloff, Emanuel A. (1997) 'Whose text? Whose context?', *Discourse & Society*, 8: 165–87

Schegloff, Emanuel A., Harvey Sacks (1973) 'Opening up closings', *Semiotica*, 8: 289–327

Schenkein, James N. (1979) 'The radio raiders story'. In: George Psathas, ed. *Everyday language: studies in ethnomethodology*. New York: Irvington: 187–202

Schutz, Alfred (1962) *Collected papers I: the problem of social reality*. The Hague: Nijhoff

Schutz, Alfred (1972) *The phenomenology of the social world*. London: Heinemann (translation of Schütz, 1974/1932) (1967)

Schütz, Alfred (1974) *Der sinnhafte Aufbau der sozialen Welt: eine Einleitung in die verstehende Soziologie*. [The meaningful construction of the social world: an introduction to interpretative sociology]. Frankfurt: Suhrkamp (first edition 1932)

Schwartz, Howard, Jerry Jacobs (1979) *Qualitative sociology: a method to the madness*. New York: Free Press

Scott, John (1990) *A matter of record: documentary sources in social research*. Cambridge: Polity Press

Seale, Clive (1998) 'Qualitative interviewing'. In: Clive Seale, ed. *Researching society and culture*. London: Sage: 202–16

Seale, Clive, David Silverman, Jay Gubrium, Giampietro Gobo, eds (forthcoming) *Inside qualitative research: craft, practice, context*. London: Sage

Sharrock, Wes, Bob Anderson (1986) *The ethnomethodologists*. Chichester: Ellis Horwood

Silverman, David (1985) *Qualitative methodology and sociology: describing the social world*. Aldershot: Gower

Silverman, David (1993) *Interpreting qualitative data: methods for analysing talk, text and interaction*. London: Sage

Silverman, David, ed. (1997) *Qualitative research: theory, method and practice*. London: Sage

Silverman, David (1998) *Harvey Sacks: social science and conversation analysis*. Oxford: Policy Press

Silverman, David (2001) *Interpreting qualitative data: methods for analysing Talk, Text and Interaction*. 2nd edn. London: Sage

Slack, Roger S. (2000) 'The ethno-inquiries of Edward Rose', *Ethnographic Studies*, 5: 1–26

Smith, Dorothy E. (1978) '"K is mentally ill": the anatomy of a factual account', *Sociology*, 12: 23–53

Smith, Dorothy E. (1987) *The everyday world as problematic: a feminist sociology*. Toronto: University of Toronto Press

Speer, Susan (2002) '"Natural" and "contrived" data: a sustainable distinction?', *Discourse Studies*, 4: 511–25

Strauss, Anselm L. (1987) *Qualitative analysis for social scientists*. Cambridge: Cambridge University Press

Strauss, Anselm, Juliet Corbin (1990) *Basics of qualitative research: grounded theory procedures and techniques*. London: Sage

Strauss, Anselm, Juliet Corbin (1994) 'Grounded theory methodology: an overview'. In: Norman K. Denzin, Yvonna S. Lincoln, eds. *Handbook of qualitative research*. Thousand Oaks, CA: Sage: 273–85

Strauss, Anselm, Juliet Corbin (1998) *Basics of qualitative research: techniques and procedures for developing grounded theory*, 2nd edn. London: Sage

Suchman, Lucy (1987) *Plans and situated action: the problem of human-machine communication*. Cambridge: Cambridge University Press

Suchman, Lucy, Brigitte Jordan (1990) 'Interactional troubles in face-to-face survey interviews', *Journal of the American Statistical Association*, 85: 232–41

Sudnow, David (1967) *Passing on: the social organization of dying.* Englewood Cliffs, NJ: Prentice-Hall

Sudnow, David (1978) *Ways of the hand: the organization of improvised conduct.* London: Routledge & Kegan Paul

Sudnow, David (2001) *Ways of the hand: a rewritten account.* Cambridge, Mass. MIT Press

The, Anne-Mei (1997) *'Vanavond om 8 uur...' Verpleegkundige dilemma's bij euthanasie en andere beslissingen rond het levenseinde* ['This evening at 8 o'clock'. Nursing dilemmas concerning euthanasia and other decisions around the end of life]. Houten: Bohn Stafleu Van Loghum

Turner, Roy (1971) 'Words, utterances, activities'. In: Jack D. Douglas, ed. *Understanding everyday life: towards a reconstruction of sociological knowledge.* London: Routledge & Kegan Paul: 169–87 (first edition 1970)

Turner, Roy, ed. (1974) *Ethnomethodology: selected readings.* Harmondsworth: Penguin

Vallis, Rhyll (2001a) 'Applying membership categorization analysis to chat-room talk'. In: Alec McHoul, Mark Rapley, eds *How to analyse talk in institutional settings: a casebook of methods.* London: Continuum: 86–99

Vallis, Rhyll (2001b) 'Sense and sensibility in chat rooms.' PhD thesis, University of Queensland, Brisbane, Australia

Van Maanen, John, ed. (1995) *Representation in ethnography.* Thousand Oaks, CA: Sage

Voysey, Margaret (1975) *A constant burden: the reconstitution of family life.* London: Routledge & Kegan Paul

Walsh, David (1998) 'Doing ethnography'. In: Clive Seale, ed. *Researching society and culture.* London: Sage: 217–32

Watson, Rod (1997a) 'Ethnomethodology and textual analysis'. In: David Silverman, ed. *Qualitative research: theory, method and practice.* London: Sage: 80–98

Watson, Rod (1997b) 'Some general reflections on "categorization" and "sequence" in the analysis of conversation'. In: Stephen Hester, Peter Eglin, eds. *Culture in action: studies in membership categorization analysis.* Washington, DC: University Press of America: 49–76

Whalen, Jack (1995a) 'A technology of order production: computer-aided dispatch in public safety communication'. In: Paul ten Have, George Psathas, eds *Situated order: studies in the social organization of talk and embodied activities.* Washington, DC: University Press of America: 187–230

Whalen, Jack (1995b) 'Expert systems versus systems for experts: computer-aided dispatch as a support system in realworld environments'. In: Peter J. Thomas, ed. *The Social and interactional dimensions of human-computer Interfaces.* Cambridge: Cambridge University Press: 161–83

Whalen, Jack, Eric Vinkhuyzen (2000) 'Expert systems in (inter)action: diagnosing document machine problems over the telephone'. In Paul Luff, Jon Hindmarsh, Christian Heath, eds *Workplace studies: recovering work practice and informing systems design.* Cambridge: Cambridge University Press: 92–140

Whalen, Jack, Don H. Zimmerman, Marilyn R. Whalen (1988) 'When words fail: a single case analysis', *Social Problems*, 35: 333–62

Whyte, William, F. (1955) *Street corner society: the social structure of an Italian slum*, 2nd edn. Chicago: University of Chicago Press (first edition 1943)

Whyte, William, F. (1992) 'In defense of *Street corner society*', *Journal of Contemporary Ethnography* (special issue on *'Street corner society* revisited') 21(1): 52–68

Wieder, D. Lawrence (1974a) *Language and social reality: the case of telling the convict code.* The Hague: Mouton

Wieder, D. Lawrence (1974b) 'Telling the code'. In: Roy Turner, ed. *Ethnomethodology: selected readings.* Harmondsworth: Penguin: 144–72

Zimmerman, Don H. (1969) 'Record-keeping and the intake process in a public welfare agency'. In: Stanton Wheeler, ed. *On record: files and dossiers in American life*. New York: Russell Sage: 319–45

Zimmerman, Don H., Melvin Pollner (1971) 'The everyday world as a phenomenon'. In: Jack D. Douglas, ed. *Understanding everyday life: towards a reconstruction of sociological knowledge*. London: Routledge & Kegan Paul: 80–103 (first edition 1970)

Zimmerman, Don H., D. Lawrence Wieder (1977a) 'You can't help but get stoned: notes on the social organization of marijuana smoking', *Social Problems*, 25: 198–207

Zimmerman, Don H., D. Lawrence Wieder (1977b) 'The diary – diary-interview method', *Urban Life: a Journal of Ethnographic Research*, 5: 479–98

Index